Law's Political Foundations

ELGAR STUDIES IN LEGAL THEORY

Series Editor: Wojciech Sadurski, *Sydney Law School, University of Sydney, Australia*
Elgar Studies in Legal Theory is a new series designed to cultivate and promote high quality works of scholarship on all aspects of legal theory. The focus of the series is on the development of original thinking in legal theory, with topics ranging from law and language, logic and legal reasoning, morality and the law, critical legal studies, and transnational law. Innovative work is encouraged from both established authors and the new generation of scholars.

Titles in this series include:

Understanding the Nature of Law
A Case for Constructive Conceptual Explanation
Michael Giudice

Comparative Law as Critique
Günter Frankenberg

Law's Political Foundations
Rivers, Rifles, Rice, and Religion
John O. Haley

Law's Political Foundations

Rivers, Rifles, Rice, and Religion

John O. Haley

William R. Orthwein Distinguished Professor of Law Emeritus, Washington University in St. Louis, USA

ELGAR STUDIES IN LEGAL THEORY

Edward Elgar
PUBLISHING

Cheltenham, UK • Northampton, MA, USA

Published by
Edward Elgar Publishing Limited
The Lypiatts
15 Lansdown Road
Cheltenham
Glos GL50 2JA
UK

Edward Elgar Publishing, Inc.
William Pratt House
9 Dewey Court
Northampton
Massachusetts 01060
USA

A catalogue record for this book
is available from the British Library

Library of Congress Control Number: 2016931785

This book is available electronically in the **Elgar**online
Law subject collection
DOI 10.4337/9781785368509

MIX
Paper from
responsible sources
FSC
www.fsc.org
FSC® C013056

ISBN 978 1 78536 849 3 (cased)
ISBN 978 1 78536 850 9 (eBook)

Typeset by Columns Design XML Ltd, Reading
Printed and bound in Great Britain by TJ International Ltd, Padstow

In Memory of

Jack Dull

A wise and gentle
teacher, scholar, administrator, and friend

Contents

Introduction viii

1. Defining law's political foundations 1
2. Rivers, rifles, rice, and religion: paradigms and trajectories of legal change 37
3. Rivers, rifles, and rice: foundations of public law and private ordering in China 61
4. Rice and rifles: foundations of private law and private ordering in Japan 98
5. Rivers, rifles, and religion: the primacy of private law in Western Europe 128
6. Rifles and religion: the transformation and transplantation of Western law in Hispanic America 164

Epilogue: beyond Magellan's world 200

References 202
Index 217

Introduction

This book began as an effort to explain a fundamental divergence in the legal regimes of the world's two most highly developed and influential legal traditions—the centrality of public law in Imperial China and the contrasting primacy of private law in Western Europe. It soon became an even more daunting venture. By all accounts, systems of private and public law developed historically within the context of the diverse configurations of multiple political regimes. The political foundations of these two basic systems of law—indeed even more broadly of law itself—became increasingly apparent. Consequently, to answer the question of how and why private and public law regimes (as defined here) develop, one must first understand how the political systems in which they first appeared evolved. In the process, a second theme emerged: how and why patterns of extralegal ordering within legal orders persist or are transformed into legal rules.

From inception my inquiry related primarily to China not only as one of the earliest but also the most enduring public law order and to Western Europe as the source of what became the private law structures of legal systems worldwide. Japan is also an essential central focus. For over a millennium Japan had adapted Chinese political and legal institutions. Yet Japan also developed an embryonic private law system through adjudication that paralleled European developments. Moreover, Japan was the first and most successful independent nation to transplant Western-sourced political and legal institutions. Its experience is also singular as the world's only major polity that for nearly two millennia did not experience either conquest or even significant migration from abroad. Along with China Japan was among a mere handful of contemporary nation-states that at the turn of the twentieth century had remained independent in a world ruled by Western European powers, the Russian czars, and the Ottoman Turks. They included only Korea (until 1910), Iran (Persia), Thailand (Siam), and Ethiopia, as well as Afghanistan and a cluster of Himalayan kingdoms. The political and legal systems of these few at least nominally independent states were thus of their own making. None compare to either China or Japan in terms of institutional continuity or enduring economic and political influence.

My principal arguments and conclusions are explained in Chapters 1 and 2 in the context of defining law, its elements, aims, paradigms, and trajectories. They rest on two simple propositions. The first is that rulers past and present share above all else a need and deeply rooted desire for resources and control. Acquisition of wealth and its allocation for structures of governance by those who rule past and present are thus keystones of the argument. The second is the positivist proposition that legal institutions and processes—even the definition of law itself—ultimately are products of the systems of governance within which they function.

Inasmuch as law reflects the authority as well as the power (also as defined for our purposes in Chapter 1) of those who govern, in all societies across time and cultures, political institutions determine processes for both the recognition and enforcement of legal rules. Those who govern define the content of legal rules and also create the means for their enforcement. In so doing, they profoundly influence perceptions of law itself. The means of law enforcement are critical. Herein lies the basic distinction between private and public legal orders as well as the differentiation of private ordering from both. All legal orders require authority—that is, the legitimacy of those who rule. Private legal orders, however, do not involve the same manner of law enforcement as public legal orders. A cadre of adjudicating judges suffices for the former but an array of law-enforcing officials who police and prosecute is necessary for the latter. Rather, private law enforcement enables judges and the parties to define the focal issues and aims of legal rules that are made in the process. Public law orders require more resources and some sort of command-and-control mechanisms—salaried officials, for example—to be effective and enduring. Private ordering in turn substitutes for both. By definition, within private orders those who rule neither determine the applicable rules nor participate, even in the "shadows," in their enforcement.

The institutions and processes of law thus necessarily vary with the patterns of governance or, simply put, the capacity of those who govern to enforce legal rules. To the extent that those who rule are able to maintain order and to implement policies by means of an effective regulatory system, as exemplified by virtually all industrial democracies today, private law becomes at best a residual, less preferred means of governance. Civil suits are left to minor matters of relatively little concern of the state. If, however, those who rule for lack of resources or other cause lack the means of coercion—defined here as "power"—either they must rely on private law or private ordering. To the extent that rulers seek a degree of control over the legal rules, they will, I argue, favor private law. From the perspective of those who govern, private ordering is thus the least desirable means of maintaining order.

The development of political institutions is a complex and, as demonstrated here, a varied story. Basic features of political regimes, their authority or legitimacy as well as their power or ability to coerce, have historically been greatly influenced if not determined in turn by geography, the manner and means of producing wealth, and the capacity of rulers to appropriate wealth and to muster and control human resources, and, most importantly, new technologies. As detailed in the chapters that follow, geography and early agriculture played instrumental roles. Legal regimes like their political foundations develop along trajectories that are shaped by the past. Shared beliefs also play a significant role in shaping the formation and development of both political and legal structures. In combination all of these factors contribute in determining the paths that such formation and development take. Path dependency is thus as fundamental to the narratives of how legal systems develop as it is to the trajectories of political and economic change.

Multiple stories can be told of the development of political systems and legal institutions. Both have evolved historically in varying ways. Yet all share certain common threads. The political foundations of law, its origins, aims and development, and especially the modes of its enforcement in China, Japan, and Western Europe, three dominant legal orders bridging both past and present, involve diverse yet related narratives, capsulated here as stories of rivers, rifles, rice, and religion.[1]

Many persons gave generously of their time in making this book possible. I am especially indebted to the many colleagues and friends who long listened patiently to the ideas—some incorporated, some discarded—raised in various settings.

Former colleagues at the University of Washington, Dan Fenno Henderson, Dan Foote, Donald Clarke, and especially Susan Handley and Kozo Yamamura, channeled many of my initial ideas. In the final months of this project, I received invaluable suggestions and ideas from

---

[1] For earlier versions of the argument, see John O. Haley, "Rivers and Rice: What Lawyers and Legal Historians Should Know about Medieval Japan," *Journal of Japanese Studies*, vol. 36(2) (2010), pp. 313–349 and John O. Haley, "The Evolution of Law: Political Foundations of Private Law in Medieval Europe and Japan," in Debin Ma, J.L. van Zanden and Jan Luiten (eds), *Law and Long-term Economic Change: A Eurasian Perspective* (Stanford Economics and Finance, 2011), pp. 19–45.

Dongsheng Zang, Clark Lombardi, R. Kent Guy, Richard Zerbe, Hugh Spizer, and other colleagues who read and commented on final drafts.

I should thank many former colleagues at Washington University in St. Louis, Saint Louis University, and the University of Missouri, St. Louis: Gwen Bennett, William Bubelis, Mark A. Burkholder, Gerrit DeGeest, Neil Hackett, Robert Hegel, David Konig, Warren Treadgold, and Richard Walter. Jill Harris, Andrea McDowell, and Matthew Mirow also took the time and effort to review early versions of individual chapters and offer singularly helpful comments and suggestions.

Colleagues at two law schools where I taught and lectured in the summer of 2014 contributed especially useful suggestions. They notably include Mark Levin and Williamson Chang at the University of Hawaii and Dan Puchniak, Michael Dowdle, and Weitseng Chen at the National University of Singapore.

I owe special thanks also to John Henry Merryman and David S. Clark, who kindly invited me to join them in compiling the first edition of their comparative casebook, published in 1994 under the title *The Civil Law Tradition: Europe, Latin America, and East Asia*. The principal ideas for this book germinated in that effort and the decades that followed as I regularly taught a course with an historical focus on the global development of the Civil Law Tradition. Needless to say, the several hundred students who studied this material with me also contributed significantly to the development of these ideas.

Above all I must acknowledge Jack Dull, to whom this book is dedicated, who was among the first colleagues to suggest I should examine similarities and differences among ancient civilizations and the first empires. Over our long friendship he consistently invited questions, stimulated new ideas, and always encouraged my efforts.

Special thanks also are extended to my assistant, Nancy C. Cummings, Keiko Yokota-Carter of the Far East Library, and Robert Britt of the Comparative Law Library at the University of Washington in Seattle, Azusa Tanaka of the East Asian Library (currently at the University of Washington), Kathie Molynieux of the Law Library of Washington University in St. Louis, and, finally, my research assistant, Rodrigo Gonzalez of Washington University in St. Louis, and Comparative Law Librarian Catherine Deane at the Vanderbilt Law School. Each provided professional help that made this project possible and for which I am deeply grateful. I am equally beholden to many others as well—those who took the time and effort to review drafts of individual chapters and correct my many omissions and errors. I owe Robert Hegel and Roger Des Forges particular thanks for their painstaking review of the chapter on China in its final phase. I am equally grateful to librarians Azusa

Tanaka at the University of Washington, Catherine Deane at Vanderbilt, and Wei Luo at Washington University in St. Louis for last minute help with citations. Finally but not least, I am indebted to Diane Wardle for her remarkably able efforts in ferreting out omissions and errors in the final manuscript. All that remain are mine alone.

1. Defining law's political foundations

We begin in this chapter with a set of basic propositions defining for our purposes here what is meant by law, its elements, processes, aims, and development. They are essential to an understanding of the political foundations of law and underpin the argument and analysis in the chapters that follow on the formation of structures of government and law in Imperial China, Japan, and Western Europe. The critical factors were, as argued here, the capacity of early rulers during these formative periods to control material wealth and human resources, and their ability to allocate both for purposes of governance in light of more urgent demands for territorial acquisition and defense. This capacity was in turn significantly influenced by the manner and means of producing such wealth, as well as prevailing institutional and ideological systems of belief and values. All of these factors in combination—in short, the role and importance of rivers, rifles, rice, and religion—were, we argue, determinative in the formation of the two historically greatest legal traditions—the public law order of Imperial China and the private law order of Western Europe.

WHAT IS LAW?

This book is first and foremost about law. Hence, what I mean here by "law" and more particularly "private" and "public" law orders should be clarified at the outset. We need first to keep in mind that law is no more or no less than a matter of words. Law does not exist except in words. Every legal tradition has a special vocabulary, terms with special meanings, its particular "grammar," to borrow Mirjan Damaška's term.[1] English, for example, is a common law language but, except for Louisiana, only a common law language. Thus English is the legal

[1] Mirjan Damaška, "A Continental Lawyer in an American Law School: Trials and Tribulations of Adjustment," *University of Pennsylvania Law Review*, vol. 116 (1968), pp. 1363–1378. Also available in Faculty Scholarship Series. Paper 1592. http://digitalcommons.law.yale.edu/fss_papers/1592. Last visited January 26, 2016.

language in all or virtually all common law systems around the world, from Australia to Zimbabwe.

The legal language—the "law words"—used in continental Europe and in all countries whose legal systems derive from those of continental Europe—i.e., virtually all countries outside of England and the former British colonies—generally have common origins in Roman law Latin and thus can usually be translated accurately in every language but English. No English law word exists for such basic terms as "real" or "thing" rights, although this is a basic concept in nearly all languages except English (e.g., *droits réels*, *diritto reale*, *derechos reales*, *direitos reais*, *Sachenrecht*, and 物権). The common law term "property" comes close in meaning but the most accurate equivalent requires Latin—*in rem* rights. Even the word "law" in English does not have a perfect equivalent in any other language, including those within the now universal Western legal tradition. How, for example, does one translate into English the Latin *ius* or *lex* or the German *Recht* or *Gezetz* or Japanese "*hō*" (法) or "*hōritsu*" (法律)? The meanings differ.

Added to the complexity of legal terminology even within a shared legal tradition is the use of different words that have the equivalent meanings within particular national legal systems as, for example, the term "natural justice" in English commonwealth countries and "due process" in the United States. Both include the right to a fair hearing with an unbiased adjudicator.

Remarkably, what we mean by the word "law" even within our own legal system is rarely defined. Most books and articles on or about law implicitly treat its meaning as self-evident. Even schools of law seldom if ever attempt to define with any precision what the members of their faculties teach as their common focus. The reason is simple. Law has no generally accepted or agreed definition. Within all national legal systems today a cluster of what H.L.A. Hart called "rules of recognition" determine which rules or standards are accorded the status of law as the "primary rules" of the particular legal system.[2]

Working or studying within a single national legal system, such rules and standards are largely learned interstitially and simply taken for granted. Lawyers and law students tend implicitly to accept the applicability of Hart's secondary rules of recognition. Most seem silently to assume that the rules and standards they treat as law are indeed what they purport to be—what a teacher of logic might refer to as one of the

---

2 H.L.A. Hart, *The Concept of Law* (Oxford: Clarendon Press, 1961), pp. 79, 97–107.

principal *enthymemes* of legal scholarship. The primary premise—the basic *lemma*—is left unstated. However, for any of the words we use in law actually to become law, including both Hart's rules of recognition and primary rules, something else is required. As explained below, that "something" is their recognition as binding *legal* rules by those with governmental authority to do so. In this sense, all law, as defined here, has political foundations.

For those concerned with more than one national legal system, with international law, or even comparative law, the lack of an agreed definition of law itself poses difficulties but not insurmountable problems—at least as long as they limit their focus to contemporary or relatively contemporary comparison and analysis. For the most part, the absence of universally shared definitions of law is not problematic. The rules of recognition may not be the same but they are sufficiently similar to allow comparative analysis. We seem to get along quite well so long as common understandings and conceptions are used within highly developed national or regional legal systems or even multiple legal systems or orders that share a common legal tradition. Few find it difficult to learn that the word "law" in English has several meanings that may be expressed in separate words in other languages. Hence "law" is best translated into German as *Recht* or in Japanese as *hō*, unless in context what is meant is a statute or legislation, for which *Gesetz* or *hōritsu* is the appropriate word. Conversely, the words *Gesetz* and *hōritsu* are best not translated as "law" in cases where they are used with the more narrow meaning of "legislation."[3] That still leaves room for doubt. Is *ius* to be understood in English as "law" or "rights"? Does *lex* necessarily mean statutes or legislation?

The problems of law as language are mitigated today in that, as noted, legal systems around the globe at least share a common heritage. Virtually all national legal systems as well as the basic understandings

[3] One example of the negative effects of such mistranslation is the universal translation in English of the word *hōritsu* as "law" in provisions on the "Rights of Subjects" in the 1889 Constitution of the Empire of Japan (the Meiji Constitution) that expressly allowed abridgment of some enumerated rights only by statute. The mistranslation had led many—including some in the Allied Occupation involved in the drafting of the postwar Constitution—to characterize the Meiji Constitution "authoritarian" or "absolutist" for lack of meaningful protection of basic human rights. In fact, however, like British subjects under a constitutional regime that guaranteed parliamentary supremacy—the paramount liberal democracy of nineteenth century Europe—Japanese citizens enjoyed basic civil rights that could only be limited by legislation.

and institutions of transnational law have European, Roman law moorings. By imposition, choice, or a combination of both, the structures and institutions of law of virtually all countries today are founded on Western law and the Western legal tradition. From Chile to China, India to Indonesia, Malaysia to Malawi, national law worldwide originates in institutions that initially evolved from Roman private law, either on the continent of Western Europe or in England. In turn, private law institutions and structures have determined many of the most basic features of our contemporary public law regimes. At base our notion of "rights" is an institution of private law expanded and applied in "public law" spheres. As a result, Eurocentric conceptions and assumptions generally work reasonably well.

Before making the effort to determine what rules are "legal" in a given system, we might well ask why we should care. What difference does it make? If two rules are identical in content and function, why should we care whether we characterize either or both as "law"? If the effects or consequences are the same, isn't whether a library rule is called a legal rule or not simply a semantic problem? The answer depends, of course, on whether or not the effects or consequences of the two rules are in fact the same despite identical content and function. Context also matters. An anthropologist might well treat a contemporary Navajo tribal norm as a legal rule, but a lawyer might with equal justification reject such characterization in a case in which a tribal law that does not recognize the norm applies. We have to take care what we call law.

The lack of universally accepted definitions poses special problems, however, for comparative law especially in historical contexts. Once we begin to consider the meaning of law in diverse cultures over time, the problem of definition becomes acute. Without common points of reference, meaningful comparison of legal systems in different, particularly non-Western, cultural and institutional contexts becomes difficult, if not impossible. Most comprehensive comparative law efforts suffer from the failure to offer an analytically useful conception of law. For a comparative venture such as this, to articulate some definition as a common basis for comparison seems essential.

To resolve this definitional conundrum, the recurring approach is to focus again on the function of law. Yet, we might ask whether all norms —expressed as rules or standards—that have or appear to have similar if not identical functions are to be defined as law? We might, for example, equate "customary" rules of the Japanese village with similar, if not identical, rules that are generally conceded to be law in classical Athens and Rome. If so, how then are we to differentiate rules or standards with identical functions that are unquestionably not law—at least for the lawyer—in contemporary societies? To these and similar questions, social scientists, historians, and lawyers offer varied and at times conflicting answers.

The problems of words and their meanings are not limited to law words alone. We face equally difficult issues in translating into contemporary languages what appear to us at least today to be law-related words used in very different cultural and historical contexts. Take the example of the word "justice." As defined in my well-worn copy of the Fifth Edition of *Webster's Intercollegiate Dictionary*, "justice" means:

> 1. The maintenance or administration of that which is just; also, merited reward or punishment. 2. A person duly commissioned to hold courts, or to try and decide controversies and administer justice; a judge or magistrate. 3. Administration of law, according to the rules of law or equity. 4. The principle of rectitude and just dealing of men with each other;—also, conformity to it; integrity; rectitude. 5. Rightfulness; as *the justice of a cause.* 6. *Obs.* A court of justice, or its jurisdiction.

"Justice" is above all a law-related word, connoting the inseparability of normative values and law. The standard Greek translation (or derivative) is δικαιοσύνη (*dikaiosune*). Hence *The New English Bible* translates the Greek into English as such (e.g., Matthew 6:33). Yet, as used by Matthew and especially Paul (e.g., Romans 3:5)—interestingly writing to Christian adherents in Rome in Greek—the word is better translated in my view as "righteousness." But the Greek term as well as both of the English translations can be understood as law-related terms that conflate law with moral behavior and outcomes. Take, however, the compound of ideographs 正義 used in Chinese and Japanese as well as Korean. The standard English translation of the compound today in all three languages is indeed "justice." However, it too may be more accurately translated as "righteousness." As used historically it was not a law-related word in any sense. Instead, it reflected Imperial China's profoundly positivist legal tradition and the utter separation of law (法律) and morality (道德). Here we should note that law and morality were inseparably joined in both language and practice in all territories that had been or continued to be subject to rule by a Western European power as well as throughout the Russian and Ottoman empires. Understandings of law influenced by Judaism, Christianity, or Islam prevailed in each. Within each, admonitions of God were understood as predominant legal commands. By 1900 such conceptions of law and the joinder of legal and moral obligation thus held sway throughout the world outside of only four countries: China, Japan, Korea, and possibly Siam.

Suggested here to resolve these problems is a particular approach. Not all social scientists or lawyers will necessarily find it helpful or appropriate. Hopefully, however, it suffices for the purposes of the comparative historical analyses offered here. An attempt to compare law and legal institutions across time and cultures forces us to confront questions that go beyond definition—namely, whether regardless of content and function rules deemed to be law have attributes that distinguish them from rules that are not. Moreover, attempts to do so in static terms flounder. We must also ask whether ascribed attributes are shared by legal rules across systems, traditions, and cultures in both time and space. At least initially, therefore, I would put aside any emphasis on functional equivalents and, at the threshold of comparative inquiry, ask instead whether we can ascertain elements, features, and attributes of law in contemporary legal systems that also pertain, at least propositionally, in more culturally or temporally remote societies. In other words, can we identify basic elements and processes, as well as attributes common to law in multiple societies at all stages of development? To be sure, with contemporary legal systems as the definitional point of departure, this approach necessarily takes on a Eurocentric cast. Moreover, without perfect knowledge, no definitive answers to these questions are possible. At best we can modestly posit a few possibilities and test them in relation to at least a few representative legal systems.

LAW'S ELEMENTS

In contemporary contexts at least, the conception of "law" encompasses two separate but interrelated core elements—*norms* and *sanctions*—and the related institutions and processes for making and enforcing both. At first glance the initial cluster—norms and law-making institutions—would seem to require little explanation. In all contemporary societies, substantive norms expressed as rules or standards of law are as familiar as the institutions and processes of their making. We readily recognize as law, for example, rules directly or indirectly proscribing undesirable conduct—armed robbery, for instance—or mandating desired actions—such as paying taxes—enacted by legislatures, administrative agencies, courts, or analogous governmental organs as well as the procedures distinctive to each for making and enforcing such rules. Less apparent but no less significant are the constitutive relationships between legal norms and the formal processes and institutions through which they are recognized, articulated, changed, and ultimately enforced.

Within all developed political orders, certain institutions and processes are endowed or entrusted with "law making" competence or authority. Among my favored examples are rules for use of the Marian Gould Gallagher Law Library at the University of Washington in Seattle and identical rules for use of the law library at Washington University in St. Louis. The University of Washington is a public university and thus a state agency. As such, its library rules are legally enforceable administrative rules. They must be made through a statutorily prescribed process for administrative rulemaking. They are published in the state's administrative law code. Moreover, the law library rules are justiciable as law in the courts. They are unquestionably legal rules—law. In contrast, identical rules for use of the law library at Washington University, a private university, are not subject to any statutorily prescribed procedures. They can be made, modified, or abandoned according to whatever procedures the university or the law school or perhaps even the law librarian might choose. They are not published in any state code. No one, except those who might credibly claim a "contractual" duty owed to them by the university (or conversely a "right" they hold against the university[4]), thereby endowing the rule with the attributes of law as a contract, has any justiciable claim to their enforcement in the courts. In other words, although identical to the library rules of the University of Washington, the Washington University rules are not legal rules.

Even more relevant to our inquiry here is the question whether the so-called *lex mercatoria* was initially "law" as a corpus of customary and legislated rules of commerce recognized and enforced within the merchant community. Only later were these commercial rules recognized by adjudication in England or both cases and code in continental Europe. What if similar rules tended to pertain in commercial dealings and trade globally and across time? For example, what if without any codification similar rules were recognized in commercial dealings by both Chinese and Spanish merchants? Should we deem them to be legal rules prior to their governmental recognition? Would we say that the sales of Chinese gold for Spanish silver in Manila during the seventeenth century were subject to Chinese or Spanish sales *law*? My answer is "no." Such rules did not become legal rules, at least as defined here, until recognized by those with law-making authority. We revisit this issue below in the discussion of extralegal or "private" ordering as well as in subsequent

---

[4] On the now classic correlation of "rights" and "duties" in Western private law, *see* Wesley Newcomb Hohfeld, *Fundamental Legal Conceptions as Applied in Judicial Reasoning and Other Legal Essays* (New Haven, CT: Yale University Press, 1919).

chapters in the context of customary commercial ordering in China and the embryonic development of a private law regime in Japan as well as the extensive commercial interactions between Chinese and Spanish merchants in Manila in the seventeenth century.

Just as only the rules or standards recognized by institutions with law-making authority can be considered to be law, similarly only those sanctions recognized and imposed through accepted processes by law-enforcing institutions with the requisite competence can be considered "legal" sanctions. Moreover, because only rules deemed to be "legal" are enforceable through these processes by virtue, as explained below, of the attribute of "justiciability," law enforcement necessarily involves the formal recognition of a rule or standard as a rule or standard of law. Hence law-enforcing processes have a law-making function as well. This is not to say, I should emphasize, that all legal rules are justiciable. Some by their terms, as described below, are not. Nonetheless, only legal rules are justiciable, thereby giving adjudicatory and other law-enforcing governmental agencies the intrinsic capacity to recognize rules as law and thereby "make" law. I have more to say about this below.

The determination of which rules or standards are law begins, as noted, by delineating the specific institutions and processes that have the competence or authority to make or to enforce them. In other words, legal systems must internally define which norms and sanctions are accorded the status of law by designating which institutional processes make and enforce legal as opposed to non-legal rules. All legal orders must therefore have at least implicitly two separate categories of rules. The first encompasses those norms regarded as the law in that system. The second, however, includes those rules that define which norms are to be included in the first category. The selection of norms and rules defined, to return to H.L.A. Hart, as the "primary" legal rules of the law in a particular legal system,[5] is determined by "secondary" rules of recognition.

As indicated, such "secondary" rules are not universal. They are the product of developed political orders and are most often particular to individual legal systems. To repeat what has been stated before, not all rules and sanctions recognized and applied by those who exercise political authority are deemed to be law. Legal comparativists who focus on contemporary legal systems may be able to rely on the prevalence of shared rules of recognition. However, contemporary rules of recognition are of little help for comparison of legal traditions or systems in separate

[5] Hart, *Concept of Law*, pp. 77–96.

cultures in different historical periods. A more useful starting point is to identify attributes that seem to be common to all.

Implicit from what has been said, legal rules share a fundamental attribute. In all instances, by definition, they depend on recognition by those with *political authority*. Political authority, I posit, is the foundational feature of law in all contemporary societies. As noted above, within our conceptually Eurocentric legal world, lawyers today look to legislatures, administrative agencies, courts, or analogous governmental organs to determine what rules or standards have legal effect and can be considered to be law. All communities and organizations today have rules and standards of conduct, norms that are enforced in various ways by various means. Some, as we shall see, may be purely customary; others are adopted through some formal processes as what I shall refer to as nongovernmental or private institutional rules or standards. As in the case of the law library rules of Washington University in St. Louis or medieval European merchant guilds, such rules may even be identical in all respects to the rules or standards made by a similar governmental organ, such as a public university or a governmental regulatory agency, but they are not accorded the status of law unless and until recognized as such—for example, as a contract right—by some governmental organ with law-making or law-enforcing authority. Hence, by my definition, legal rules and standards require recognition by some sort of governmental or political authority.

As used here, the terms authority and legitimacy are nearly synonymous. Both denote widespread societal recognition and acceptance of an entitlement to deference and respect, leadership and command. In normative terms, those who request or demand obedience within the scope of their authority should be obeyed. In descriptive terms those who exercise authority in fact receive deference and respect and thereby possess the capacity to influence what others do and how they behave. A community's sense of legitimate authority is grounded in culture and custom. Shared religious symbols, social myths, and "folk ways" sanctified by habit and expectation are among the common sources. Like custom simply by longevity rulers tend to acquire a mantle of acceptance over time. Political legitimacy thus may be simply a function of time or "habitual legitimacy," to use Rodney Barker's phrase.[6] The factors that contribute to political legitimacy ultimately also determine legal legitimacy.

---

[6] Rodney Barker, *Political Legitimacy and the State* (Oxford: Clarendon Press, 1990), pp. 29–33.

Legal norms acquire legitimacy from two entirely separate sources. They are considered legitimate first because of the legitimacy of the norm itself. Thus norms may be accepted as legitimate because they are sourced in widely shared religious or ethical beliefs. A provision in a criminal code proscribing with more severe penalties the killing of a parent, for example, may be considered legitimate because of Mosaic Law within societies influenced by Judeo-Christian–Islamic beliefs or by virtue of other prevailing moral precepts as in Confucian-influenced cultures. Yet rules unrelated to any cultural norms may also be deemed as legitimate solely by virtue of the legitimacy or authority of the political authority that promulgates or enforces them as law.[7] Smoking bans are a prime example.[8] In other words, rules articulated in a statute, judicial decision, or administrative regulations are legitimate as law ultimately as a result of the legitimacy of those processes themselves. This is what I refer to as the "derivative legitimacy" of legal rules. Conversely, if either the actors or the processes they use for promulgating a rule as law are deemed illegitimate, the rules they create also risk being considered illegitimate. If, however, the institutions for law making are themselves viewed as legitimate, they tend to legitimate the rules they create. Judicial decisions on highly controversial issues, for example, may themselves foster consensus to the extent that the courts have a special degree of legitimacy.[9] Potentially at least, law has therefore a consensus-creating capacity.

LAW'S ENFORCEMENT

The forms that legal rules take differ, however, depending on the nature of the political regime, particularly the extent and scope of its authority and its capacity to ensure compliance of those who rule—i.e., its power. The manner and means of law's enforcement are of special significance.

---

[7] *See* Max Weber, *Economy and Society: An Outline of Interpretive Sociology* (G. Roth and C. Wittich, eds., Berkeley, CA: University of California Press, 1978), pp. 212–215.

[8] From my personal experience, smoking first in classrooms and ultimately on entire campuses ended abruptly with the introduction of such bans. Discussed below is the role of community disapproval as the primary if not sole sanction.

[9] *See*, e.g., James W. Stoutenborough, Donald P. Haider-Markel, and Mahalley D. Allen, "Reassessing the Impact of Supreme Court Decisions on Public Opinion: Gay Civil Rights Cases," *Political Research Quarterly*, vol. 59(3) (September 2006), pp. 419–433.

Law enforcing differs from law making with respect to the underlying conditions for its effectiveness. Law making, as noted, depends upon the political legitimacy or authority of those who make the rules, the legitimacy of the rule itself, or better yet, both. Add legal sanctions and law enforcement to the mix and another, separate aspect of law becomes apparent—power. The terms authority and power in English as well as most Romance languages, such as French (*autorité* and *pouvoir*), and Spanish (*autoridad* and *poder*), are generally used interchangeably. For example, the French term *les pouvoirs publique* is quite accurately translated into English as "the public authorities." For our analysis here, the terms *Authorität* and *Macht* in German more accurately reflect the applicable differences of meaning. As used herein, power means simply the *capacity* to coerce.

The distinction between authority and power with respect to coercion is particularly significant. Coercion can of course be defined to include various modes and degrees of persuasion. In relation to political rule or governance comprising political actors and institutions, certain political offices or actors may enjoy so substantial authority that, as a consequence solely of which, their commands may be obeyed despite their lack of any capacity to compel compliance by force. The Roman Catholic Church in medieval Europe, as described in Chapter 5, is exemplary of a "political" entity that could command compliance by means of its extraordinary legitimating authority without coercive power.

As a distinctive feature of legal rules, I have previously labeled their potential influence as consensus-creating capacity. Similarly, however, some commands are obeyed despite the lack of any claim to authority or political legitimacy of those who issue them solely because they have proven capacity to coerce compliance. Few if any of such regimes endure. Their ruins litter landscapes around the globe. To be sure, seldom do those with authority have no capacity at all to coerce or those with power make no claim to sources that entitle them to authority. One might well conceive of both positioned along a spectrum with authority without power and power without authority at the extremes. Conflating authority and power may also have utility as a rhetorical device.[10] Ultimately, however, coercion requires more than bargaining leverage or dominant influence. At its core lies the capacity to compel compliance by the credible threat of the use of force. Not to differentiate coercion from

---

10 *See*, e.g., Michel Foucault, *The History of Sexuality: Volume 1: An Introduction* (New York: Vantage Books, 1990), on the "sovereign power" over life and death, pp. 135–145.

forms of persuasion that do not involve force or its threat inhibits clarity and rigorous analysis.

Authority with or without power and power with or without authority are of course possible. Authority and power become mutually necessary only with respect to effective law enforcement by those who govern. Authority is all that may be required to govern quite effectively. We can imagine, for example, a relatively elementary political order based on kinship ruled by a small group of household heads who by custom and convention are eldest sons who are in turn led by the eldest household head. By definition, therefore, an authoritative, legitimate basis exists for governance and succession. To the extent the group wishes to change the customary or conventional rules regarding succession to the household headship or the designation of the eldest as leader, they face problems of authority and power. First, the ruling household heads must have sufficient political authority to create a new norm—i.e., for the community to accept the new norm as legitimate, the community must have also accepted the law-making authority of those who made it. Such community consensus eliminates the need for any mechanism for enforcing the new rule. By definition community acceptance of its legitimacy produces compliance—in other words, the derivative legitimacy of the rule.[11] The viability rule will thus depend like any customary rule upon community acceptance and conformity. If the legitimacy of the new rule is effectively challenged, however, its formal enforcement becomes necessary. To the extent that the rulers can coerce compliance, they may be able to effect the change. But unless and until the community accepts the legitimacy of the new rule (and rulers), those who seek to govern will continue to need the capacity to coerce compliance. In such event our hypothetical simple polity risks transformation from one of authority without power to one of power without authority. By definition, the former remains a stable legal regime. The latter does not. With little if any claim to legitimacy, the regime is likely to be subject to competing claims to rule and remain unstable.

By treating law making and law enforcing as separate components of the legal process, we are able to explain both the fundamental dynamics of legal rules and factors that determine the role and limits of law in a given society. The resources devoted to the enforcement of particular legal rules also tell us much about law's aims, i.e., the priorities of the law makers. Many studies of law tend to focus on legal rules and the

---

[11] *See* John Owen Haley, *Authority without Power: Law and the Japanese Paradox* (Oxford and New York: Oxford University Press, 1991), p. 6.

processes for their recognition or creation and overlook the mechanisms for their enforcement. The consequence is to neglect a pivotal feature of all legal orders and the determinative role that law enforcement plays. Our analysis of this role begins with two propositions.

The first is that enforcement frees the viability of a legal norm from community consent and consensus. This can perhaps best be stated negatively: *unless a legal rule is enforced its viability depends like custom directly on the community's collective acceptance of the rule and its collective willingness to ensure that members comply*. This pertains with respect to the legitimacy of the content of the particular norm itself or the legitimacy of the norm as law or both. As illustrated once again by a taboo against smoking, the effectiveness of a statute prohibiting use or possession of tobacco without any penalty depends upon voluntary compliance—i.e., individual consent—or social sanctions for noncompliance. In both instances, the effectiveness of the rule depends on community acceptance. In other words, the rule largely functions as a customary norm. In my own experience, smoking bans have been overwhelmingly effective without any formal enforcement. Social disapproval—when someone might light up, polite nods toward the "no smoking" sign—has been sufficient. However, the value of having a legal rule rather than simply customary convention or a "private" institutionalized rule (e.g., a company rule) is its indirect or derivative legitimacy and thus its consensus-creating capacity. The "legalization" of a rule helps to foster or at least buttress consensus.

The second proposition follows from the first. If enforcement determines whether legal rules are viable independently from community acceptance, then, to this extent, those who control the enforcement process control or at least influence the viability of the legal rule. Prosecutorial discretion, broadly defined to include control over all forms of law enforcement, thus becomes or should become the central focus of any inquiry as to the role and efficacy of law in any community. The answer to the question of who exercises such discretion tells us much about who governs.

Control over the law enforcement process in most legal systems can be divided into two basic categories. In what I shall call regulatory or *public law regimes*, control over enforcement is entrusted to those with the political authority to govern, such as officials in law-enforcing bureaucracies. They may include prosecutors or police, magistrates or judges, or administrative officials of all sorts. Whatever the label, government officials in such regimes monopolize control over the coercive mechanisms for law enforcement. Although in some instances private parties may initiate enforcement by complaint or petition, the prosecution of the case and control over its ultimate resolution, whether by settlement or the application of sanctions, rest with those who exercise political authority. Prosecutors, for example, exercise that discretion in most contemporary criminal justice systems with the notable exception of Germany and other countries that have adopted a system of mandatory prosecution influenced by the German legality principle.[12]

In *private law regimes*, in contrast, discretion or control over the means of formal law enforcement or legitimization of self-help is controlled by private parties, whose authority to exercise such "prosecutorial" powers is delineated in a variety of forms, such as standing, capacity, or indeed, the concept of *legal rights*. A private law regime requires some mechanism to allocate the authority to control the application of remedies and sanctions, to determine who could bring what action against whom and for what remedy. The concepts of "rights" and "duties" provide such means insofar as these notions serve to delineate persons with the legally recognized capacity to control the processes of enforcing prescribed substantive legal rules, whether made by legislative, judicial, or administrative organs or, as in the case of contracts, private citizens with rule-making capacity. Consequently, all private law regimes require some conception of legal "rights" and "duties" or their equivalent. The enforcement of the Athenian *eisphora* by citizen-initiated enforcement actions in the law courts[13] exemplifies "private law" enforcement of what we would consider today to be a public law duty.

---

[12] The German principle of mandatory prosecution required under the legality principle (*Legalitätsprinzip*) was not coincidentally influenced by Friedrich Carl von Savigny (1779–1861), Germany's preeminent nineteenth century private law scholar. *See Promemoria der Justizminister Savigny und []Uhden über die Einführung der Staats-Anwaltschaft* [Memorial of Justice Minister Savigny and Uden on the establishment of state prosecution in criminal procedure] in Werner Schubert and Jürgen Regge, eds., *Preussische Gesetzrevision*, 1825–1848 [Prussian legislative reforms, 1825–1848], vol. 11 (Vaduz, Liechtenstein: Topos, 1981), p. 1284. By restricting prosecutorial discretion, German criminal law enforcement paralleled private law enforcement in that it ensured what were in effect legally enforceable claims—in effect "rights" to enforcement —by crime victims.

[13] *See* Matthew R. Christ, "Liturgy Avoidance and *Antidosis* in Classical Athens," *Transactions of the American Philological Association*, 120 (1990), pp. 147–169; also Carl Hampus Lyttkens, "Institutions, Taxation, and Market Relationships in Ancient Athens," Working Paper, Department of Economics, Lund University, Sweden. http://ideas.repec.org/p/hhs/lunewp/2008_009.html. Last visited January 26, 2016.

Private law as process is central to the Western legal tradition. Roman private law—the *ius civilis*—was primarily a system of rights defined as the claims of individuals either to protection by specific procedures and remedies or to legitimate resort to self-help. Latin and other Western European languages do not distinguish between "law" and "right." The words *ius*, *Recht*, *droit*, *derecho* denote both. In this sense, the *ius civilis* is by definition a system of rights. Stripped to essentials, the notion of a legal right or rights in Western law expresses the capacity of the individual to activate and control the process of enforcing legal norms. Although today the term in English is used more broadly—for instance, to define property—other terms such as interest, estates, entitlements, or simply the Latin *dominium* are more appropriate. The notion of a legal right is most meaningful, therefore, only when it entitles the holder to legal protection upon demand. The maxim *ubi ius ibi remedium* ("where there is a right, there is a remedy") is more than an aphorism. It expresses the crux of private law.

A concept of rights is not necessary, of course, for the enforcement of legal rules in public law orders. Duties alone suffice. We rarely if ever speak of the government's "right" to tax or the rights of either the public or, for that matter except in a very narrow sense, victims in criminal law. Similarly, law in Imperial China did not require a concept of rights for enforcement. The compound of ideographs 法律 (*falǚ*) that we translate as "law" meant regulatory penal rules. Codes and statutes were administrative and criminal. Legal rules were uniformly proscriptive. There were no rights, only duties. Although "civil" or private law rules as defined in substantive terms today can be identified in traditional East and South Asian law[14]—i.e., rules governing family, contracts, property, commercial transactions, and other private matters—they were generally expressed either as "minor matters" or more accurately minor crimes that could be compromised in the interests of resolving the dispute or, if significant to those who ruled as commands, violation of which was subject to some prescribed penalty or to what is best described as administrative enforcement by an essentially regulatory state. Viewed from this perspective, courts are above all else law-enforcing institutions. From a litigant's perspective, at least, the primary function of litigation is to enforce legal rules, not to resolve disputes. The essential difference between private

14 *See*, e.g., Laws of Manu, Chapter VIII, Sections 3–7 (trans. Buhler), *Indian History Sourcebook*, www.fordham.edu/halsall/india/manu-full.html. Last visited January 26, 2016.

lawsuits and criminal or administrative proceedings is that private parties rather than state officials control the process of enforcement.

Do the distinctions among public, private, and customary processes for law enforcement really matter? After all, identical rules can be enforced in either or both processes. Legislators may proscribe dumping toxic waste in rivers as either a regulation subject to administrative fines or criminal sanctions or they may treat such dumping as a tort or civil delict to be enforced through litigation as a private law action with compensation to those harmed as the remedy. To increase preventive deterrence, class actions and treble damages may also be added to increase the incentives for such private law enforcement. What matters is not the "public" or "private" law category of the rules but control over the process of their enforcement.

As defined the mechanisms for law enforcement differ essentially in who manages and controls them. Control over the enforcement of the legal rules considered significant by those who govern is entrusted nearly always to one or more official, public agencies. In all public law regimes by definition those who rule control the enforcement processes. They choose whether and which legal rules to enforce. Those who rule and their agents thus have the discretion to enforce the law and in exercising that discretion not only what legal norms will be enforced but also what norms are legal. In the most elemental political orders, the rulers themselves may exercise this discretion; in the most complex, agents of the state, administrative officials, police, and prosecutors have this choice. The appropriateness of the choices they make may become issues of control between the governing principals and their prosecutorial agents but their subjects, those who are governed, do not get to choose. Private parties—the victims of a crime or of some other infraction—may file complaints and may thereby have some voice in initiating the enforcement process, but their voice diminishes once the process of enforcement is initiated. They may petition or plead, but they do not determine whether to proceed or to stop. Only in a few legal systems in rare instances—such as rape[15]—can they end the process by withdrawing their complaint or reaching a settlement with the offender. In most contemporary systems, the bargains reached with those accused of violating the applicable rules are negotiated between public officials and the miscreant, not the victims—those affected most by the infraction of the legal norm. Justified in terms of "public interest"—the rhetorical

---

[15] *See*, e.g., the *querela* in Italian criminal law: Italian Penal Code of 1996, Art. 609.

rubric for the policy preferences of those who rule or seek influence—public law enforcement by definition lodges prosecutorial discretion and control in the hands of those who exercise political authority and power.

At this point some readers may ask, "what about the victims of administrative infractions? Don't these involve lawsuits against officials and state agencies that the complainants control? Yet don't we classify these as 'public law' rather than 'private law' actions?" The answer is of course "yes." Some jurisdictions do denote suits against the state and state agencies for violations of "rights" as public law actions. The notion that we have "rights" of redress against the state as a matter of "public law" is, however, simply an extension of conceptions derived from private law and the mechanisms of private law enforcement into the public law arena. No notable differences exist between such suits adjudicated by the regular courts under German private law and those adjudicated by French administrative courts as a matter of "public law."[16] In either case a party asserts a "right" to compensation against the state for breach of a "duty" owed the claimant. Such "public law" rights in fact reflect the primacy of private law in the Western legal tradition and serve as a prime example of the continuing legacy of that primacy in the age of the regulatory state.

As defined here, private law enforcement also involves formal, ruler-sponsored mechanisms but, in contrast to public law enforcement, private law enforcement is subject to the control of private parties—in other words, the subjects of political authority. I argue here private law regimes, exemplified by their earliest development in Athens and Rome, are generally those in which by choice or necessity or a combination of both, those who ruled lacked the means or the desire for a public law system and relied instead on a system in which "citizens" had "rights" to have claims adjudicated and to control, manage, and themselves pay the costs of enforcement.

Private law enforcement thus usually represents either a willingness by rulers to give up control or, more commonly, recognition of their inability to control at least fully the enforcing process. Public law systems require dependent agents. Unless administrators, police, prosecutors are salaried and thereby made dependent on rulers as their principals, they are at least potentially capable of developing independent sources of wealth and thereby independent power and ultimately authority. Such dependency,

---

[16] Duncan Fairgrieve, *State Liability in Tort: A Comparative Study* (London and New York: Oxford University Press, 2003).

however, requires revenue. Unless rulers are able to control and accumulate resources for redistribution as official salaries, they cannot create, expand, or sustain public law regimes. For public law orders those who rule have to be able to appropriate sufficient wealth to allocate resources for law enforcement. Other needs may take priority—such as warfare. If the resources at the disposal of the rulers are not sufficient, other, less costly means for enforcing law and maintaining order become necessary. Needless to say, this is a pivotal notion in any analysis of the development of political institutions. As detailed in subsequent chapters, our stories of rivers and rifles encompass such concerns.

The adjudication of private law rules is not necessarily distinct from the adjudication of public law rules. As legal systems develop, in transitions from meditation, to adjudication, to the prosecutorial and administrative enforcement of regulatory law, the basic distinctions drawn here are rarely ever clearly delineated. As, for example, the adjudication of claims for compensation based on wrongful injury moved toward criminal prosecution with non-compensatory sanctions, at least in Western Europe, the adjudicative procedures and control over prosecution changed only gradually. Even today, those convicted of crimes may be required to pay compensation. Well into the contemporary era, private prosecution of crimes remained a prominent feature in many European legal systems. Only with increasing revenues and the further development of governmental structures did public prosecutors become the norm.

Conceptualizations of law and the legal rules also matter. How, for example, do rulers justify collection of revenues? Is law or legal authority necessary? Historically for most rulers, legal justification was irrelevant. Aside from *corvée* labor and booty by conquest, tax collection was generally intrinsic to their legitimacy or authority. (Whether rulers were actually able to collect is a separate issue related to their coercive capacity.) For instance, the authority of those who ruled Imperial China required no legal basis or formulation. Law conceived as a set of regulatory rules enforced through penal sanctions was not relevant as a source or justification of such authority. Non-payment of taxes was not included as one of the ten abominations of Imperial Chinese law. Nor did classical Roman law provide much assistance. Importantly, Roman rulers, like their Imperial Chinese counterparts, could legally justify collection of tribute and revenue and all manner of booty gained simply by coercive power under the unlimited legal authority they exercised as holders of *imperium*. Otherwise, legal concepts related to public authority remained embryonic at best. In both Japan and Western Europe, however, legal concepts were decisive not only in justifying but also enforcing their appropriations of wealth from producers. As described subsequently in

Chapters 4 and 5, the development and use of concepts such as *shiki* in Japan and acquisition of royal estates and fiefs in Western Europe gave rulers proprietary interests to the produce of specific wealth-producing communities or land with "rents" rather than "taxes" as a principal source of revenue. As a result, law-enforcing processes with overlords as the ultimate adjudicators developed as the primary legal means for enforcing such proprietary claims by warrior retainers. Such adjudicatory processes were instrumental in the creation of an embryonic private law order in Japan and, conceptually as well as institutionally, an increasingly highly developed one in Western Europe.

The processes of both public and private law enforcement are, to repeat, formal and official. They involve resort to established state institutions and state actors. The difference is who exercises prosecutorial discretion and control. To focus on the norm or rule subject to enforcement as public or private law and to ignore the processes for their enforcement deflect attention from the pivotal difference in who controls. Those who rule and their agents do not control the process. Private law enforcement thus reflects constraints on the powers of those who rule and in effect limits at least the scope and reach of their authority. Even adjudicating judges in purely private law enforcement do not initiate or determine whether to proceed or whether to terminate the process. They may determine and permit the sanction but for the most part do not participate in its actual application. That aspect of the process is again left to the parties and the aid of law-enforcing authorities.

Law enforcement processes inexorably serve dual purposes. To the extent that law enforcement or its threat affects behavior, those who control enforcement control the efficacy of the legal rule. In other words, because enforcement ultimately determines the efficacy of the legal rules, those who control the public or private enforcement control the recognition and the continued viability of the norms.

The legal enforcement of norms whatever their source involves formal and official recognition and thus an independent phase in their "making" as law. For example, a customary rule subject to formal law enforcement becomes viable as a legal rule and indeed, as described below, inevitably acquires the attributes of the legal rule. For this reason, whether intended or not, through the articulation and enforcement of particular norms as either rules or standards, adjudicatory or "judicial" processes by those who rule are, or necessarily become, law-making processes in which judges have a decisive voice. With these insights we can begin to appreciate the central role of the magistrate in the public law system of Imperial China (Chapter 3) as well as the Castilian *audiencia* in the first transformative era of Western law in Hispanic America (Chapter 6)—and perhaps even the contemporary "politicalization" of judiciaries world-wide.

We also speak of private law making by contract. However, it is not the adoption of rules by private consent in an agreement but the enforcement of that agreement as "contract" that transforms the rules of the agreement into rules of law. Were, for whatever reason, the agreement to be deemed legally invalid, then the rules set out by the parties would have neither the force nor the legitimacy of law; rather they would remain formally or legally unenforceable despite the fact that they might well be readily enforceable through marketplace or other extralegal sanctions. As suggested above, to the extent that the rules of commerce and trade are made (or recognized) and enforced through extralegal means—both the marketplace as well as extra-governmental institutions such as guilds—by definition such rules are not "legal" rules. In this sense, there can be private ordering, as detailed below, but not private law making.

Not all legal rules are ever formally or "legally" enforced. One can at least imagine a political order in which all legal rules are left to informal means of enforcement. In such systems of private ordering, legal rules as well as customary norms may indeed be enforced. Whatever the norms or their source, however, their viability or efficacy will depend on those who control such enforcement—perhaps the community at large or leaders of the gang. Such is the crux of private ordering.

Public international law exemplifies many aspects of our analysis. The actors are juridically recognized states—like, as it were, the citizens of Athens or Rome. A variety of recognized international law-making as well as law-enforcing organizations and processes exist. The United Nations, the World Trade Organization, and other supranational organizations have recognized competence to make internationally binding legal rules. States may individually agree to be bound by mutual agreement to rules in treaties and conventions that function like contracts as sources of legal rights and duties. Other rules may be "customary" in that they are accepted by state practice and general consensus (*opinio juris*) as a rule of law, but until otherwise recognized through some competent, formal law-making process, such as their "ratification," or are actually enforced, by our definition, they lack status as legal rules. As a consequence, international law becomes a subtopic of comparative national law.

One example should suffice. Until recently, all but one state (the United States) have long refrained from taxing income derived from sources outside of the state's territory by non-resident citizens (including those with dual nationality). Thus we might have concluded that a customary international norm existed disallowing such practice—with allowances for the United States as the most powerful "citizen" in the community. Whether such norm constitutes a binding "legal" norm as a matter of public international law, however, would additionally require some authoritative statement to such effect. Inasmuch as such practice was tolerated and its disallowance not recognized as a legally binding rule through any competent law-making or law-enforcing process, the practice did not violate a "legal" norm. The United States Supreme Court rejected such claim in 1924[17] and all tax treaties with the United States rest on the assumption that the US will otherwise legally tax the worldwide income of its non-resident citizens. And like all custom, advantageous non-conformity with a customary norm invites imitation. (Here I am reminded of an episode involving a chain-smoking university provost—who incidentally died in his late 60s of lung cancer. At a meeting I attended with him, despite a prominent no-smoking sign, he pulled out his package of cigarettes and lit up. No one, I first thought, even dared to object. Then one by one others pulled out cigarettes and began to smoke.)

International courts also exist. The International Court of Justice (ICJ) is an adjudicative body empowered to adjudicate the respective rights and duties of states pursuant to these and other international law rules. Insofar as the ICJ can only act at the initiative and continuing request of claimants, it functions like an adjudicative body in a private law regime. In contrast, the International Criminal Court and other international criminal tribunals with independent prosecutors are akin to criminal courts in public law regimes.

No international organization today, however, has the capacity to compel compliance with international law rules by force or its threat. Hence the efficacy of the rules of international law, even those recognized and "enforced" by international criminal tribunals, depends ultimately on state actors who do have the capacity to coerce and agree to assist. In other words, the rules of public and private international law, like the norms of customary orders and of gangs, depend upon consent and consensus by those who exercise power—the "gang" of world powers—in other words, those with more or better rifles.

---

17 Tait v. Cook, 265 U.S. 47 (1924).

LAW'S AIMS

As a tool or expression of political authority and power, the basic aims of law are easily perceived. If, by definition, legal rules depend on recognition by those with political authority, if they are made by those who exercise such authority, legal rules will necessarily reflect the aims and ambitions of those who rule. We can thus anticipate that similar rules or rules with similar purposes will exist in most if not all established political regimes.

Political regimes, it needs to be said, are generally not created by law but are protected and ordered by law. Those who draft constitutions may not have functioning political authority, as those in the late eighteenth century who drafted the constitutions in what became the United States and the First Republic in France. Yet they generally aspire, as presumably did John Adams, Thomas Jefferson, James Madison, as well as Maximilien de Robespierre and his Montagnard followers, to having a future role in the governing institutions they propose. Nonetheless, those who validate such proposals as law must already have sufficient authority as well as power to ensure that the effort can be realized. The aim of the constitution makers is to create a framework within which the political order that they envision can be established and long maintained. Adams, Jefferson, and Madison succeeded; Robespierre failed.

A principal purpose of law in all legal systems is thus to maintain an existing or an envisioned political order. Constitutional and subsequent legal rules vary, but the highest priority comprise rules designed to protect those who have already begun to rule and to preserve the system of governance in which they participate. Treason, sedition, threats to the security of existing political orders, for example, have been treated universally across time as the most serious criminal offenses. The first three of the ten abominations of all of Imperial Chinese dynastic codes were plotting rebellion, sedition, and treason against the imperial dynasty in place. They were the only "abominations" subject to a mandatory death penalty. Few readers need to be reminded of the priority of laws for national security in the United States.

By the same token rules designed to ensure that those who rule have and retain access to wealth and to its appropriation are also universally evident. To the extent that rulers seek to acquire the resources they need or want from landholding, we can expect that land ownership will receive a significant degree of legal recognition and protection. If instead a ruler's revenues depend on commercial activities, we can similarly anticipate the imposition of various regulatory rules such as required licensing with fees or of direct taxation of business profits.

The maintenance of community peace and stability is a third discernible aim of legal rules across time and cultures. Few if any polities have not had legal rules (with sanctions) for murder, theft, and other behaviors considered by rulers and the communities they rule to threaten the social order.

The content of legal rules thus always reflects the priorities of rulers. To the extent that rulers depend on the consent of the governed, rulers will make and enforce rules that they believe those they govern want or need. Some rules reflect community values that are shared or at least recognized by those who rule. To take the life of a lineal ascendant was also one of the "ten abominations" of Imperial Chinese law and is still treated as a more severe criminal offense in South Korea. Sodomy was a crime in much of the United States, and adultery by a wife remains a crime in parts of the Islamic world. Values change and many of these are no longer proscribed offenses—more often than not as a result of judicial decisions and the changing values of the judges. Those who govern, including judges, control. Whatever the motive, the law's aims are ultimately rulers' aims.

LAW'S DEVELOPMENT

The trajectory of law's political development has more than one path. Nor does advancement necessarily mean praiseworthy progress. Between the developmental extremes are varied forms of social organization and governance. This social and political complexity should be kept in mind. Even the most rudimentary political system will have developed some means to command and control the resources needed to sustain it. All political systems thus have as noted some means for securing revenue. Nor does any politically developed nation or state reflect a single homogeneous, cohesive community governed by a single set of informal or formal institutional arrangements.

In all societies exist lesser communities of neighborhoods, towns, and villages, of families and firms, of voluntary associations, occupational organizations, and other social organizations and subcultures. Within each, customary as well as both formal and informal processes for making and enforcing rules operate. Thus multiple forms of customary or private ordering exist. That complexity allows us to distinguish two primary modes of social ordering: customary and institutionalized. For our purposes, within both modes, two additional patterns stand out. The first comprises purely customary orders or institutionalized private ordering in which the rules are both recognized and enforced without reference to law. Arguably at least, similar rules and practices were recognized and enforced because they made sense within the commercial and trading communities in Imperial China, Tokugawa Japan and medieval Europe. At that point and in that sense they exemplified the first pattern of private ordering. The second pattern includes a variety of mixed types in which either the rules are sourced or are at least enforceable through formal legal processes *but not both.* To the extent that the rules are legally enforceable, they become in effect legal rules. Thus in both Tokugawa Japan and Western Europe, as such commercially sensible rules and practices were recognized by adjudication or by codification, they became legal rules. If not enforced, however, in effect formally recognized legal rules become customary. Their efficacy, as with the purely customary commercial rules, depends on community disapproval of infractions or other extralegal means of enforcement. The first option takes us back to customary orders, the simplest and earliest form of social organization and private ordering.

Customary Orders

In purely customary orders, rules—or more general norms of behavior—are sourced in custom and customary norms and enforced by means of consensus and habitual community responses. Similarly the capacity for coercion depends on collective, community action. Enforcement is generally left to various expressions of community disapproval of inappropriate conduct—"shaming" to use John Braithwaite's term.[18] We might be hard pressed to identify a purely customary social order—for by definition no hierarchy of authority exists in such a society and thus equality of voice among all members (however defined) would be required. Customary orders of one kind or another exist, however, in all societies. Norms of behavior may even be imposed as legal rules by those who govern from the outside, but if their enforcement—and thus their continued viability—is left to some form of social disapproval, in terms of efficacy and change, such legal rules do not differ from purely customary rules.

Commercial private ordering under certain conditions provides a prime example of customary ordering. Sustainable commerce across cultures

---

[18] John Braithwaite, *Crime, Shame and Reintegration* (Cambridge and New York: Cambridge University Press, 1989), p. 100.

and legal systems requires trust. Trade requires that the parties will adhere to basic rules and practices. Legal rules may matter. Infractions of the terms of agreements or shared practices may have legal consequences —such as breach of contract lawsuits. However, if such ordering operates fully outside of law's enforcing domain—as most do—or if the parties are not bargaining within law's "shadow" or the like, then such transactions can be understood as reflecting patterns of customary private ordering in which reputation for trustworthiness is essential. Any conduct that diminishes such trust risks expulsion from the commercial community. As described in Chapter 3, commerce in Imperial China operated in such a customary order in which the parties adhered to commercial rules and practices because they either shared belief that they were necessary or at least made commercial sense—coupled perhaps with concern that noncompliance would result in refusals to deal or some other form of unwanted commercial community disapproval, or a bit of both. Trust that all parties to the transaction would comply with the rules that they have agreed or are otherwise expected to honor was the essential glue that made such ordering feasible.

Anthropologists and archeologists commonly consider the development of sustainable political institutions and structures to have commenced within the earliest hunting and gathering societies. We think of them defined by kinship, lineage, mutual dependency, and the need for cooperative endeavor. Political and moral authority tended to be undifferentiated. Political organization was rudimentary and rare. Family hierarchy and accepted reference to what is "sacred" are common sources of authority. Despite inequalities, particularly in terms of status and wealth, such societies were largely equalitarian. Custom and customary processes prevailed. Distinctions between public and private spheres had little meaning. Everyday life was socially interactive within familial and communal structures. The norms and customary rules that provided order and channeled behavior related primarily to the responsibilities of each person to others and the community in general. Predominant were those related to marriage, kinship, and residence. They were transmitted and internalized through ritual, language, and legend.[19]

Compliance was generally also customary—the product of habit, attachment, and self-interest. As Bronislaw Malinowski put it: "The force of habit, the awe of traditional command and a sentimental attachment …

[19] Alasdair MacIntyre, *After Virtue* (Notre Dame, IN: University of Notre Dame Press, 2nd ed., 1984), p. 122.

the desire to satisfy public opinion—all combine to make custom obeyed for its own sake."[20] He appropriately adds reciprocity.[21]

When sanctions were considered necessary, expressions of community disapproval from ridicule to ostracism and other forms of out-casting were the principal means for maintaining and enforcing the norms that maintain the social order. Even in the simplest hunting and gathering societies without organized government, Robert Lowie notes, there are leaders whose opinions "carry weight," but without means of coercion enforcement of community standards depends on community disapproval.[22] The sanctions applied to persons who repeatedly offend community norms range from various forms of out-casting to threats of extreme physical injury.[23] For example, in the taro-producing communities of Hawai'i, persons who "shirked" in their task of maintaining irrigation canals, which were critical to the well-being of the entire community, could be put to death and left in their assigned canal as an example to others.[24]

Such sanctions—putting aside homicide or its threat—persist across time and cultures in all societies, including those with the most highly developed political systems. The English word *ostracism* derives from the ancient Athenian practice (*ostrakophoria*) of exiling citizens who threatened the stability of the political order. In Japanese villages the extreme form of community ostracism was called *murahachibu*—cutting recalcitrant offenders from nearly all community contact and cooperative support.[25] Exotic examples aside, whatever the label—shunning, being "sent to Coventry," and the like—social out-casting has been and remains a formidable penalty employed by communities through collective action and consensus to maintain adherence to customary norms. The more

---

[20] Bronislaw Malinowski, *Crime and Custom in Savage Society* (New York: The Humanities Press; London: Routledge & Kegan Paul, 1951), p. 52.

[21] *Id.*, pp. 22–27.

[22] *See*, e.g., Robert H. Lowie, *The Origin of the State* (New York: Harcourt, Brace & Company, 1927), pp. 5–6, citing A.R. Radcliffe-Brown, *The Andaman Islanders* (1922), pp. 13, 22–87. *See also* David Tait, "The Territorial Pattern on Lineage System of Konkomba," in John Middleton and David Trait, eds., *Tribes Without Rulers* (London: Routledge & Kegan Paul, 1958), pp. 167, 189.

[23] For a vivid example, *see* J.P. Gillin, "Crime and Punishment Among the Barama River Carib," *American Anthropologist*, vol. 36, pp. 331, 343, quoted in E. Adamson Hoebel, *The Law of Primitive Man* (Cambridge, MA: Harvard University Press, 1954), p. 300.

[24] Williamson Chang at the Richardson School of Law (University of Hawai'i) informed me of this practice in July 2014.

[25] See Richard K. Beardsley, John W. Hall and Robert E. Ward, *Village Japan* (Chicago and London: University of Chicago Press, 1959), pp. 257–258.

mutually interdependent the community in terms of their collective well-being, as in the example of taro-producing Hawai'ians and rice-producing Japanese, the more effective community-imposed customary sanctions become.

All communities also develop processes for determining whether a violation of customary norms has occurred and whether persons accused are actually responsible. In most, if not all, of these societies reconciliation is also sought. The process is not always orderly. Even in societies lacking political organization, mediators appear. In some societies these persons may be identified as "the lawgiver" whose "primary function," as construed by Paul Vinogradoff, is "to *find the law* and give expression to the sense of the community."[26] Adamson Hoebel provides a telling example among the Ifugao, a mountain tribe in the Philippine island of Luzon, without chieftains or tribal or village councils. As disputes arise that cannot be resolved within a kinship group, a go-between becomes necessary. The Ifugao turn to a *monkalun*, an "admonishing mediator of limited authority but of usually persuasive effectiveness" to facilitate a settlement. In Hoebel's words:

> The *monkalun* is always a member of the *kadangyang* class and ordinarily a man of reputation as a head hunter. This means that he enjoys general influence emanating from his personal prestige, but more than this he is in a position to marshal effective support from his own kinsmen in a pinch.[27]

From such persons of authority—or "charisma" in Weberian terms[28]—and potential power, chiefs emerge. Like all other aspects in the evolution of political institutions, their emergence is not linear. As subsequent chapters detail, organizational changes in governance occur within all societies. They reflect continuously changing internal as well as external conditions. Pressures from both within and without compel reorientation and various modes of organizational change. Governance in few if any societies is static. Nor are the consequences of change inexorable. Some societies organizationally move backwards to earlier stages in the trajectory; some more rapidly toward more developed forms. Patterns are difficult to discern, at least with certainty. Yet the common threads of the trajectory remain. We can identify factors and consequences that appear so repeatedly that we can at least surmise some causality.

---

[26] Paul Vinogradoff, *Historical Jurisprudence*, vol. 1 (London: Oxford University Press, 1920), p. 361.

[27] Hoebel, *The Law of Primitive Man*, p. 114.

[28] *See* Max Weber, *Economy and Society*, esp. pp. 241–244.

All societies even today contain a variety of constituent customary orders and variations of private ordering, however marginal or insignificant they may appear. In such contexts, both norms, as customary rules and standards, and sanctions exist, but both require community consensus to remain viable. Take, for example, a highly interdependent community at an early stage of development or a contemporary community in which shirking is unacceptable, a taboo, if you will, as in the taro-producing communities of Hawai'i. We can observe both the norm as taboo as well as the sanction by simple observation of what occurs when anyone fails to perform an assigned task. We would note that anyone who did shirk would be subjected to some sort of social disapproval or "shaming" that can take various forms from ridicule to physical injury. To the extent that the community begins to condone shirking, the norm has changed. The taboo no longer exists. As indicated subsequently, historically the best known and most influential private law regimes originated in customary orders as political authority emerged but was diffused among those entitled to govern in the early Athenian and Roman citizen-ruled republics.

Since custom to be custom depends upon mutual conformity, a norm that ceases to be recognized or obeyed by the community as a legitimate or binding guide for conduct ceases by definition to be a customary rule. Similarly, only the sanctions a community can and will apply against non-conforming conduct remain viable. We can thus identify customary rules of conduct by conforming conduct as well as the imposition of sanctions for non-conformity. Take a taboo against use of a particular word as an example; if conduct changes and an increasing number of members of the community or subculture begin to use the word without incurring some form of social disapproval, the rule is thereby altered. If, however, the community consensus holds—i.e., few if any use the word and anyone who does becomes subject to community sanctions and hardly anyone either continues to use it or even considers using it—the taboo is preserved. However, should others in increasing numbers imitate the non-conforming conduct and start themselves to speak the taboo word, we may correctly conclude that the norm is changing. The taboo is breaking down. Use of the word is becoming less unacceptable. The opposite is also true. Words once widely accepted and used can become taboo words.

Shirking and word taboos are only examples. Even taxation may be customary. The reliance in classical Athens on *liturgies*—contributions by the most prosperous citizens to be used for public purposes—is a case in point. Liturgies at some early stage are thought to have been purely voluntary and a mark of status for which the donor gained social prestige.

They eventually became a social duty, infractions of which were met by various forms of social disapproval. Ultimately, the liturgy atrophied, to be replaced by new forms of legal taxation of wealth. One, the *eisphora*, was enforced—albeit not very successfully—in the Athenian law courts as an essentially private law duty.[29] "There is" with custom, Roberto Unger notes, "a point at which deviations from the rule remake the rule itself. Thus, every act leads a double life: it constitutes conformity or disobedience to custom at the same time that it becomes part of the social process by which custom is defined."[30]

Once political authority and institutions for governance develop, custom may still be a source of legal rules but it ceases to function as law. Within politically organized societies, customary rules are not legal rules as defined at least for purposes of this study unless they are at least incidentally recognized and applied by those with recognized political authority. For those who govern either to codify or otherwise to identify a customary norm as an enforceable rule, as Unger also notes, transforms the norm from custom into law. Other legal rules may be understood to originate in a transcendental moral order or even deistic command, but only in fully theocratic states in which by definition religious and political authority combine can such commands or principles be considered law. Otherwise it is left to those who exercise political authority as rulers to determine whether and what moral or religious norms are deemed to be "law" or perhaps which religious actors and institutions are recognized to have law-making or -enforcing authority. The result, however, is to free what had been a customary rule from dependence upon habit and consent. Instead, as law the otherwise customary norm becomes dependent like all other legal norms on institutional processes for definition, change, and their continued legitimacy. In a sense two sets of norms or rules exist, one legal and as such dependent on institutional processes; the other customary, supported by persisting habit. In ancient Athens and Rome, custom became law as those entitled to rule as "citizens" began to make and enforce rules. In Japan, however, as we will see, within the ambit of Imperial Chinese conceptions of law and governance, the rules of the village, albeit functionally equivalent to legal rules in the Athenian *polis* and the Roman *civitas*, remained customary as made and enforced through private ordering by virtue of community consensus and collective action. Similarly commercial rules and trade

---

29 *See* Christ, "Liturgy Avoidance."

30 Roberto Unger, *Law in Modern Society* (New York: The Free Press, 1976), p. 49.

practices remained customary among the Mediterranean traders at least prior to and after the *Pax Romana* as well as Japan until recognized through adjudication or codes in Western Europe and adjudication in England and Japan, whereupon constituted a corpus of commercial law rules and thereby at least embryonic private law regimes. In contrast, without such recognition they remained customary in Imperial China. The distinction remains obscure and functionally insignificant until one or the other changes and conflict between law and custom ensues.

Only a tiny fraction of all the norms and sanctions that order social life in any community are actually defined as law. In most societies, for example, to keep one's word or promise and to honor one's parents are widely accepted social norms. The first is commonly recognized in codes, statutes, and decisional law as a moral basis for the law of contract. But in no legal system does any legal rule obligate a person to keep all promises made. The legal rules reflect a selection of which promises the law makers have determined should be legally enforced. Similarly, a duty to honor one's parents as a clearly recognized legal norm is rare in legal systems within the Western European tradition even though perhaps incidentally reflected in certain legal rules. Yet violations of the duty of filial piety were subject to criminal sanctions in all of Imperial China's dynastic codes. It was also the basis for provisions in the criminal codes of both Japan and South Korea that impose heavier penalties for crimes against lineal ascendants than other persons. (These provisions in the Japanese Code were repealed in 1995.[31])

Institutional Ordering—Private and Public (Legal)

As social and political structures become more complex, private ordering also becomes institutionalized. The consequence is an additional set of rules and means of enforcement. In the process, we begin to be able to discern and to distinguish rules and sanctions recognized and enforced within collective associations and other institutionalized private communities from those made and enforced by those who rule even though they may be functionally equivalent. The commercial rules developed and enforced within the merchant communities of the Mediterranean and trade guilds of medieval Europe were thus not "law" until incorporated into the *ius commune* by judicial decision and codes. Within Western

---

[31] *See* Criminal Code (*Keihō*) [Law No.47, 1907 as amended], Articles 200 and 205(2). Repealed by Law No. 91 (1995). Over two decades earlier, in Aizawa v. Japan, 27 Keishū 265 (Sup. Ct., G.B.) (1973), the Japanese Supreme Court had held the former, Article 200, to be unconstitutional.

Europe they also developed within a legal culture in which law was increasingly understood in terms of a coherent system of private law rights and duties. As the *ius commune* expanded through official recognition, notions of law and accepted rules for commercial conduct also developed. In this regard, Paul Vinogradoff's description of the "ancient lawgiver," quoted above,[32] seems especially apt. As the authority of the ruler-as-law maker becomes increasingly accepted, new rules can be promulgated by the rulers as positive law. At this point the authority of law-making rulers becomes increasingly critical. The greater the distance from custom, the more innovative become the rules themselves and the more necessary the authority of the ruler.

Moreover, in this process, hierarchies of control evolve and processes for rule making and enforcement also emerge that may be identical in every respect to legal or public ordering except the rules created or recognized and enforced are by definition not legal rules. As noted previously, only certain institutions in any society have authority to legislate or authority and capacity to enforce legal norms. These and only these constitute the institutions and processes of the legal system. The difference between institutionalized private and legal ordering is not limited to rules. As noted, the manner and means of enforcement too can be private (nongovernmental) or public (governmental). Take, for instance, the Tribunal of Water of Valencia, Spain. Established initially by Muslim peasant farmers prior to the conquest of Valencia by James I of Aragon,[33] it continues today to function as a water court within the agricultural communities of the *huerta* surrounding the city of Valencia to resolve disputes and enforce rules established for water flows and timing for those who depend on irrigation for their livelihood.[34] Since the thirteenth century, the Tribunal has been an integral component of the irrigation system formally recognized by law and integrated into the legal structure. The Tuna Court described by Eric Feldman for the contemporary Tokyo fish market[35] functions in a similar manner as a private ordering system. Functionally, it might seem, there is no difference. If,

---

32 Vinogradoff, *Historical Jurisprudence*, p. 361.

33 *See* Thomas F. Glick, *Irrigation and Society in Medieval Valencia* (Cambridge, MA: Harvard University Press, 1970). The origins of the Valencia Tribunal of Water are described in greater detail in Chapter 5.

34 Elinor Ostrom, *Governing the Commons: The Development of Institutions for Collective Action* (Cambridge and New York: Cambridge University Press, 1990), pp. 69–74.

35 Eric Feldman, "The Tuna Court: Law and Norms in the World's Premier Fish Market," *California Law Review*, vol. 94 (2006), pp. 313–369.

however, changes to the system or those who manage it are desired or even when decisions are challenged, the distinction between institutionalized private and public adjudicatory organs becomes significant. For private systems, decisions made within the community by its prescribed rule-making procedures with all variations are determinative. For public, legal systems, those who govern—those who make the law—decide.

However otherwise law may be defined, the institutions that make and enforce law are instrumentalities of those who rule. So long as consensus and consent remained critical for both the recognition of norms of behavior as well as the means for their enforcement, the role of chiefs and others who exercised political authority remained circumscribed. Mediation, as Elman Service explains, is the predominant manner of resolving disputes in equalitarian societies.[36] They will tend like the Ifugao *monkalun* to mediate disputes brought to them and act as facilitators, if necessary, for collective community enforcement. Mediation in this form depends, as before, on community assent and consensus with respect to both the applicable norms as well as the sanctions that can be legitimately applied. Mediators in this role are essentially facilitators for collective action, a conduit through which the community speaks. Their function may also be prophylactic. They may direct community wrath away from persons accused of violating community norms or away from sanctions that, upon reflection, the community would consider inappropriate, at least with respect to the committed offense. Mediators may ideally be neutral facilitators of amicable settlement, but even as "go-betweens" mediators with even a vestige of authority are able to influence outcomes. Mediators in nearly all instances are able to select norms and sanctions that they perceive to be appropriate. To be sure, in customary orders their selection is circumscribed by community acceptance, but as both their authority and power increase they are able to choose among customarily acceptable norms and sanctions and to persuade the parties to accept solutions that seem fair to the mediator. Thus intrinsic even to mediation is a process of rule making and rule enforcing. Even this form of mediation, however, requires consent.

Such systems remain customary orders in that they are dependent on community-wide acceptance of both the rules being enforced as well as the sanctions to be applied. Mediators may act as catalysts for change by persuasion, but they cannot fully alter either norms or sanctions without

---

[36] Elman R. Service, *Origins of the State and Civilization: The Process of Cultural Evolution* (New York: W.W. Norton & Co., 1975), pp. 56–60.

community acceptance and approval. Only when the third party has the recognized authority to determine the outcome, when he or she is able to impose a decision based on personal authority, is mediation transformed by definition into private arbitration or adjudication.

Adjudication as a means of law enforcement does not necessitate power. As in early Athenian and Roman law, it may suffice to stigmatize wrongdoers socially or to legitimate resort to various forms of self-help. The result, of course, is to empower further those who have the capacity to coerce without the aid of those who govern. Adjudication does, however, require authority. As the ruler's capacity to coerce increases, however, the remedial features of adjudication become more concentrated as ruler prerogatives. Ruler-imposed sanctions thus tend to replace permissive self-help as decisions by adjudicators become enforceable orders. As a primary means of law enforcement, as detailed previously, adjudication, like mediation, is subject to constraints of both authority and power. With both modes the ruler acts reactively as a third party arbiter of voluntarily proffered claims. The claimant takes the initiative and retains with the option of withdrawal at least partial control.

Along with social and political stratification and hierarchy an even more significant change occurs. Those who rule are increasingly able to issue direct regulatory commands backed by sanctions they alone are legitimately entitled to impose. The effectiveness of such rule may be enhanced by the sense of legitimacy of the ruler and the rules themselves, but the threat of effective sanctions inevitably lurks behind compliance. Moreover, at this point on the trajectory, rulers begin to acquire the resources and manpower to permit oversight and policing to ensure the commands are obeyed. We can now distinguish between those who govern and those who are governed. Almost invariably commencing with tribute and other means for accumulating revenue, political regimes begin to introduce the fundamental features of public law regimes.

The capacity to coerce requires a particular sort of follower, persons willing to use violence against those who reject either the authority of the ruler in general or more specifically as maker of a particular rule. How such followers are recruited and maintained tells us much about the developmental maturity of any regime. Warrior bands recruited and held together by the promise of plunder or bonds of kinship or community identity are perhaps the most common. Whatever the origins, as rulers gain greater capacity to wage war with organized armies, they also acquire greater capacity to make and to enforce rules. With such capacity also come new modes of policing and regulatory enforcement.

Each of the three principal modes of law making and enforcing—mediation, adjudication, and regulation—thus corresponds to power, dependency, and subordination: the greater the power of the ruler and the dependency of those governed, the greater their subordination; the greater the control over sources of wealth, and thus the greater the capacity of the ruler to issue new laws and to enforce them through direct means of coercion.

Even the most elemental of known societies were all historically to some degree socially stratified. As they evolved and became more complex and rulers emerged, such stratification became even greater. Chiefs with followers, to whom wealth produced by those they governed was redistributed, constituted by all accounts the prevailing pattern. Law and the modes of law enforcement reflected such stratification. Thus chiefs mediated and relied on customary norms in disputes among or with those who occupied the highest strata but directly commanded and coerced those at the lowest. Resort to mediation, adjudication, or regulatory policing thus marked the extent and identity of the castes of social stratification and subordination, direct oversight, and control.

Increased social and political stratification produced profound legal change in terms of both authority and power. David Webster emphasizes the dilemma that warfare renders "ineffective" preexisting constraints on institutional change while creating a need for internal stability.[37] Rulers resolved the problem through law. As chiefs began to gain more authority and power they were able to begin to do more than confirm what was customary. As the authority of individual or closely knit groups to rule became secure, a characteristic consequence was the introduction of the first set of non-customary rules related to succession and stratification. New rules were promulgated—first and foremost, in Service's words, for "the creation and perpetuation of the office of Chief"[38] and secondarily to demarcate the hierarchical stratification of the society. They were generally followed closely by a second set of rules against acts and threats against the ruler and ruling elites. Rules designed to control force—the first in the trend toward Weber's monopoly of the legitimate use of violence[39]—soon appear, typically in the form of prohibitions against private revenge. Along with each set come rules designed to extend

---

[37] David Webster, "Warfare and the Evolution of the State: A Reconsideration," *American Antiquity*, vol. 40(4), (1975), pp. 464–470, at p. 467.

[38] Service, *Origins of the State and Civilization*, p. 146.

[39] *See* Max Weber, *Politik als Beruf* (Munich and Leipzig: Duncker & Humblot, 1919), reprinted in *Max Weber Gesamt Ausgabe*, vol. 1/17 (W.J. Mommsen and W. Schluchter, eds., Tubingen: J.C.B. Mohr [Paul Siebeck], 1992), pp. 158–159.

ruler control over resources—including the resources of neighboring communities.

Whatever the catalyst, few today disagree that warfare—i.e., rifles—is, as Robert Carneiro puts it, "a prime mover" in the process of change.[40] The effect of the combination of each of these factors operating together is to transform otherwise equalitarian communal orders into increasingly stratified societies.

As chiefs and their successors established order and provided security, they also enhanced their authority and the stability of their rule. And, once established, centralized governance tended to endure so long as unthreatened by external forces. With enduring legitimacy rulers were able to expand control over resources—an opportunity that they rarely if ever declined. Social order and stable governance in turn enabled increases in wealth-generating activities that would otherwise have been diverted for protection. Along with expanding ruler control over resources was a concomitant expansion of the apparatus of governance, including regulatory legal controls, which in turn enabled further expansion of the territorial reach of their authority and power through the recruitment of new agents. Such expansion continued until various conditions precluded further growth. Among the primary constraints was scarcity of resources resulting from geographic factors, internal conflicts, and external forces. Once expansion ended, whatever the cause, a state of equilibrium was reached that was only disrupted by either internal conflict or external force. How the interplay of the diverse factors influenced the development of individual political systems historically around the globe is well beyond the scope of this study, much less its author. Posited here is simply the incapacity of political regimes to develop public law regimes absent that equilibrium. Until rulers established sufficient control over resources to withstand both internal and external threats, they lacked both the authority and power necessary for their regimes to endure.

Longevity also required some means to assure orderly succession. This basic political necessity helps to explain the universal tendency to pass on rule and control to biological offspring. In the context of political succession, deeply embedded and universally shared kinship claims seem best understood as a primal source of customary legitimacy. Resort to kinship is a particularly predicable outcome in political systems in which the legitimacy of rulers is based on personal qualities. Such societies, by

---

[40] Robert L. Carneiro, "A Theory of the Origin of the State," *Science*, vol. 169(3947) (1970), pp. 733–738, at p. 734.

definition, lack the institutional maturity required for any other form of legitimate succession. The alternative to hereditary rule is some rule-based system that requires a relatively well-developed legal order. Heritable succession is of course no guarantee of internal political stability. Inexorably over time, intra-familial conflicts and contests over authority and power portend regime instability and further institutional change.

The intervention by those who govern may regularly take the form of mediation or adjudication depending upon the extent of their power to impose their preferences, but not until relatively advanced stages of political development are rulers generally able both to legislate and to enforce their preferred proscriptions. Centralized political authority governing through an increasingly complex variety of organized specialized agents with both effective authority and the capacity to coerce are common features of such orders. And as political institutions evolve so do understandings about the nature and conceptions of law.

Law operates within the dynamics of this framework. Rules are made and unmade, enforced and left to atrophy. Some are customary, others institutional. Some may be considered law; all impose a kind of order. The nature of the order depends only in part on the institutional arrangements for both law making and law enforcing—the traditional concern of lawyers and political scientists. Equally relevant are "cultural" factors: the habits that constitute custom and the values that both shape and sustain consensus and legitimacy. But culture too is dynamic. What I have described here as a "legal" process is in reality a process of social change. Habit and values are not exempt. They, too, change. What distinguishes one legal order from another, therefore, is less the role or rule of law, but who makes and enforces law by whatever means, and thus whose consensus and whose values control. In short, who enforces, governs. Ultimately, law's development is political.

2. Rivers, rifles, rice, and religion: paradigms and trajectories of legal change

Comparative law requires more than merely the identification of the elements and attributes of law, its enforcement, aims, and development. We cannot adequately overcome the hurdles of comparative analysis of law in diverse cultures and moments in time without an understanding of the historical foundations of law and the dynamics of legal change. How law develops historically should thus be the central concern of any comparative effort. Recall, however, that both the recognition of legal norms (law making) and their enforcement (law enforcing) involve an exercise of political authority, which, as described in the previous chapter, equates with legitimacy. Historically, therefore, law by definition first emerges in any society at the initial stages of the development of political institutions along with sources of political legitimacy. Similarly, in the first regimes in which, with or without political legitimacy, rulers developed the capacity to coerce, legal rules grounded on power also could be imposed.

Thus from an historical perspective, we cannot adequately appreciate much less compare legal systems without some understanding of their relative degrees of political institutional development. Assuming, moreover, that the same or similar factors help to explain institutional features they share, the development of political institutions in any single society is apt to be shared by other societies with common institutional experience. These propositions lead to a core proposition of this book that legal institutions rest on political institutions that in turn develop in relation to the sources and uses of wealth. In other words, legal institutions develop in conjunction with the capacity of rulers to appropriate wealth and acquire revenue, and the demands or needs they confront for the allocation of the material resources they control. Their capacity to govern also depends on their control over human resources—both as agents and subjects.

Traced historically the trajectories of political and legal development, it is argued, commenced with the emergence of social and political organization in the earliest societies. Custom and consent prevailed as sources of social norms or, to use a contemporary expression, "civility," with social disapproval and collective community sanctions the primary means for their enforcement. Ties of kinship defined these communities. Degrees of mutual dependency and the need for cooperative endeavor held them together but also produced a need for coercion to ensure that essential community interests prevailed over self-regarding conduct of its members. These dual demands proved to be particularly the case in the early sedentary agricultural communities of Southeast Asia, South China, Korea, and Japan that relied on networks of small irrigation systems for the cultivation of wet paddy rice. In these early sedentary communities, political and social authority initially tended to be undifferentiated, rudimentary, and relatively weak. In non-sedentary communities such conditions tended to persist as political authority remained weak or non-existent.[1] Family hierarchy and accepted claims to religious authority were common sources. Such were the earliest customary orders. As communities formed and society organized in sedentary communities, forms of political authority emerged. In the process communal norms and sanctions began to yield to rules and principles recognized and enforced by those with political authority and, with the advent of warrior rulers from within or without, the capacity to coerce. From these beginnings emerged what we recognize today as law.

At the other end of the developmental spectrum are the most politically advanced societies. They are characterized by complex organizational features and ordering arrangements for governance. All have well-established hierarchical systems with centralized agencies of governance. Specialized actors function as accountable agents of the state in offices and organizations for making and enforcing legal rules.[2] The legitimacy of the authority and the capacity to coerce of those who rule may differ, but they are able to make and enforce new rules of law. The legal rules they make tend to be proscriptive—generally expressed as regulatory rules with penal sanctions for noncompliance.

For all regimes, first and foremost are the regulatory rules for revenue —from tribute and rents to taxes. Rulers in all ages past and present enforce such rules through one or more institutional processes, including

---

1 For a seminal study of customary ordering without law focused on the upland regions of Southeast Asia, *see* James C. Scott, *The Art of Not Being Governed: An Anarchist History of Upland Southeast Asia* (New Haven, CT: Yale University Press, 2009).

2 *See*, e.g., S.N. Eisenstadt, *The Political Systems of Empires* (London and New York: Free Press of Glencoe, 1963), pp. 15–17.

criminal sanctions, subject to their direct or indirect control. The "law" related to rulers' appropriation of wealth differs depending on the sources and the rulers' capacity for control. As explained in greater detail in subsequent chapters, in the early polities of northern China and Western Europe in which production of gain and husbandry were the major sources of wealth, rulers relied on rents based on their control of land. Hence "ownership" and legal entitlements to landed property became core concerns. In contrast, ownership of land was less of a concern for the early rulers of Japan. They instead sought control over the wealth-creating communities and thus developed a conceptual proprietary claim as exemplified by the transformation of *shiki* from designated office to transferable proceeds—i.e., the rice itself.

We would err to presume, however, that today's industrial democracies represent historically the most advanced stage of this political and legal developmental trajectory. Nearly all of the features described as attributes of the most advanced political and legal orders had been fully satisfied in northern China by the beginning of the Common Era. Argued here is the proposition that China was the first and most enduring regime to achieve the status of an institutionally advanced public law order. No industrial state has even today fully replicated China's achievement.

The development of law has not been uniform or linear. Paralleling the developments of political institutions and structures and the vicissitudes of authority and power, law's domain has waxed and waned. The trajectories of change have varied and with each incremental change new conceptions and new processes for making and enforcing law have emerged. Some endure. Others vanish. Ultimately, however, the trajectories have led to expanded authority and power and the concomitant extension of the domain of law. Those trajectories have also varied as institutional developments of the past have influenced if not defined present and future parameters and the available paths of continuing institutional change.

Any extension of political authority and power by rulers over the activities and conduct of their subjects is by definition an extension of law's domain. Law's domain thus expands within public law regimes any time those who rule impose new administrative rules to regulate activities previously left to various forms of customary or private ordering. A similar but more pervasive extension occurs in private law regimes through the recognition of legally enforceable rights and duties. Unlike public law orders, in which the legal rules reflect the aims and policies of those who govern and enforce the law with private ordering otherwise left outside even the shadow of unmade rules, in private law orders the parties to litigation and lawsuits and the judges who adjudicate their disputes create law in the identification of relevant norms and their application. Hence when common law judges in England first determined that a particular form of commercial instrument was enforceable as a contractual right or recognized commercial practices more broadly as judicially enforceable, what occurred was the extension of the ambit of law's reach to include forms and practices that had been left theretofore to the private ordering within the relevant merchant community. A similar process arguably occurred in Tokugawa Japan as "money suits" were recognized and new precedents established through such adjudication in an analogous process of law making. The law-making role of adjudication inexorably ensured the expansive breadth of law's domain.

RIVERS

Basic geographical conditions influenced the foundational features as well as the pace and paths of the developmental journeys of all political regimes. For the earliest polities climate, terrain, and, above all else, rivers were preeminently determinative. Well before the modern era in a world in which agriculture was the primary source of wealth and of human resources, control of rivers and their rich productive valleys shaped the forms of governance that emerged and, in the process, law's foundational development. Law and "civilization" emerged first along rivers. The capacity of those who ruled—mostly the warriors who conquered and then established control over the earliest sedentary agricultural settlements—depended on their access to the wealth of these settlements and those who inhabited them. Rivers and their surrounding basins provided fixed sources of the wealth rulers could appropriate. Their military control of these basins and their inhabitants over time enabled them to expand both their territorial reach and the manner and means of governance.

Over past centuries empires have formed and reformed along the world's great rivers. Our first civilizations formed in the rich valleys of the Euphrates, the Tigris, the Indus and the Ganges, the Nile, the Yellow and the Yangzi—the great rivers of Mesopotamia, South Asia, North Africa, and China. Here by alliance and conquest, sedentary agricultural settlements were absorbed into the world's first and most highly developed political and legal orders. Rivers nurtured the principal sources of wealth. Control over these communities and their agricultural production provided a fixed source of revenue for all early political rulers. Their surrounding terrain and sources of wealth influenced the prevailing forms of social organization and the capacity of rulers to control and coerce human resources. Their geography also determined the nature of the polities that developed in their productive basins. In the case of the Nile, natural protections against outside invasion made possible effective, long-term control by rulers over the material and human resources of its valley, allowing accumulation and the redistribution of wealth and the growth of increasingly complex institutions of governance. Law too developed. Changing configurations of authority and power transformed the structures of law. In tandem with the various trajectories of political development, law's domain grew and the patterns of making and enforcing law altered. Customary orders were subsumed within institutionalized regimes.

None of the earliest empires that developed along the Tigris and Euphrates in Mesopotamia had lasting control over the rivers. Like Greece and Rome in later centuries, they relied heavily on tribute from the otherwise self-governing polities they conquered. All soon succumbed to more powerful neighbors. The first major polity, Sumer, comprised an alliance of city-states that reached its apogee as the Third Dynasty of Ur (c. 2212–2204 BCE) during which the Code of Ur-Nammu, the oldest known law text, was promulgated. The subsequent Akkadian Empire (2334–2154 BCE), which we generally refer to as Babylonia, was perhaps the most successful, with a brief territorial reach from the Mediterranean shore on the West to Shatt al-Arab, formed by the confluence of the Euphrates and the Tigris, at the apex of the Persian Gulf. It notably failed to resist conquest by warriors from the Zagros Mountains in the north. Nor were any polities that may have emerged in the Indus–Ganges river valleys any more successful.

Although a "Bronze Age" civilization (3300–1300 BCE) developed in the fertile Indus plain, apparently no evidence of a significant or enduring polity has yet been discovered. Pharaonic Egypt differed. For centuries its rulers enjoyed nearly complete control over the Nile valley without meaningful threat from neighbors. With full control over the human resources that produced the principal source of wealth—grain—Egypt rapidly developed into perhaps history's first unified polity ruled through a centralized bureaucratic system with salaried albeit hereditary officials that extended to all levels of the society. In this sense it was the first centralized bureaucratic empire. It was also one of the most enduring.

Most of the early empires and civilizations, however, ultimately collapsed and were left in ruins. The lack of natural barriers invited outside rivals and led repeatedly to armed contests for control of productive valleys. Their rivers served as logistical highways that enabled military conquest. Unable fully to control the rivers that provided their wealth and protection, rulers had to divert accumulated wealth and negotiate for additional sources of revenue. In the process, their power dissipated.

Rivers also provided avenues for communication and trade by linking otherwise isolated interior regions and ultimately expanding access to the sea. Commerce by river and sea in turn generated new, expanding, and, unlike agriculture, highly mobile means of creating wealth that few rulers could fully capture or control. The consequence was to disperse wealth and led, again, to a dissipation of power. Not coincidentally, the small, merchant-dominated polities of northern Europe developed at the mouths of the Rhine, the Elbe, and the Oder, major transcontinental rivers with tributaries that penetrated deep into the heartland, which no single or even collective alliance of rulers even today has ever been able completely to control. Sustained control of major rivers and their productive valleys within more compact territories—in England: the Severn and the Thames; in Portugal: the Lima, Cávado, Mondego, Sorraia, Sado, Mira, Douro, and above all the Tagus (or Tejo); in France: the Garonne, the Loire, the Seine, and the Somme—also enabled rulers to create smaller but more enduring kingdoms.

So too have rivers together with climate determined the prevailing forms of agriculture that in turn have profoundly influenced the patterns of social organization and the capacity of rulers to mobilize and control subject communities. Those engaged in upland pasturage or the dry-field cereal farms, as in Western Europe and northern China, could be replaced and controlled. Those who labored to produce millet or raise animals could be required to provide at least seasonal service to those who ruled. Corvée labor, David Burg tells us, was the "earliest and most widespread form of taxation."[3] Those engaged in the more labor-intensive, wet-paddy cultivation of rice, as in southern China, Japan, and even medieval Valencia, were not so easily displaced or fully controlled without disrupting the production of the wealth the rulers sought to acquire.

From the beginning of history, control of rivers and their wealth-producing basins has thus determined the capacity of rulers to garner sedentary wealth and command human resources and to withstand challenges from within and without. Sustained control of the wealth produced in fertile river valleys has in turn allowed rulers regardless of time and place to create political structures for more effective centralized administration of their domains. Failure to capture such wealth in turn led

---

[3] David F. Burg, *A World History of Tax Rebellions* (New York: Routledge, 2004), p. xi.

rulers along different paths. Some, vanquished by more powerful neighbors, simply vanished. Others developed more enduring structures for participatory or collective governance. Still others too poor or too well protected simply reached an equilibrium that retarded if not totally precluded further institutional and structural change. In elite citizen-governed polities, as in Athens and Rome, private law regimes appeared. With increased revenue and greater power, those who governed incorporated into their legal order previous forms of customary and private ordering. Ultimately in the wealthiest and most institutionally developed polities, centralized bureaucratic systems of governance emerged. They were the first public law orders. Perhaps the earliest was that of Pharaonic Egypt.

The Advent of the Public Law Order

Compared with the other early civilizations, a similar but considerably speedier progression from sedentary agricultural communities to a single, dominant dynastic kingdom occurred in Egypt. As in Mesopotamia the rulers claimed legitimacy through the invocation of a deity, although in Egypt the rulers soon claimed *personal* deistic status. Around each too developed a priestly governing elite. Egypt also developed one of the earliest forms of writing and the advent of an elite group of scribes. However, in Egypt no written collections of legal rules comparable to those in Mesopotamia has yet been discovered, although some scholars believe with "certainty" that they existed.[4] Also unlike Mesopotamia, Egypt rapidly developed into a unified polity ruled through a centralized bureaucratic system with salaried albeit hereditary officials that extended to all levels of the society. In this sense it was the first centralized bureaucratic empire. It was also one of the most enduring.

Pharaonic Egypt epitomizes a regulatory, public law regime. By conventional dating from about 3000 BCE from the royal residence at White Wall (*Ineb-hedj*) on the west bank of the Nile in the Memphis region south of modern Cairo, Egyptian rulers had subjugated all previously autonomous villages and households along a thousand kilometer stretch of the Nile valley from the delta to the first cataract at Aswan. By the end of the Early Dynastic Period (2686 BCE) as god-kings, they had reorganized the polity into an integrated dynastic kingdom with a salaried officialdom under their control. The central administration was

[4] David Lorton, "The Treatment of Criminals in Ancient Egypt: Through the New Kingdom," *Journal of the Economic and Social History of the Orient*, vol. 20 (1977), pp. 2–64, at p. 5.

organized into units with administrative oversight over the treasury, agriculture, granaries, public works, the army, and the armory. The kingdom was further divided into territorial administrative units (provinces in English or *nomes* in Greek), each with king-appointed governors (*nomarchs*) who governed the entire area, including large cities. Each province had tax assessors and collectors responsible to the central as well as local officials with both policing and judicial functions. Each also replicated the administrative structure of the central government. Initially a single vizier appointed by the Pharaoh headed the entire administrative structure. During the New Kingdom (c.1539–1075 BCE) two viziers were established, administratively dividing upper and lower Egypt.[5] All officials were subject to ruler direction. Although most significant posts tended to become hereditary, as commissioned, salaried officials they were dependent on those under whom they served. Nobles, scribes, and priests—some claim a mere 5 percent of the population, by the highest estimates[6] equivalent to percentage of those who were literate—constituted a "tiny" elite[7] that, as noted, remained remarkably constant.[8] The ruling class held claim to the most productive source of wealth—agriculture. During the Ramesside Period (1295–1069 BCE), temples—in other words, priests—constituted an estimated 90 percent of all landholders, controlling 15 percent of all productive land.[9] Most of the remaining 95 percent of the population were dependent and subordinated, their production and labor subject to extraction.

The principal function of this elaborate apparatus was to maintain order and security, and, above all, to acquire as much of the surplus agricultural wealth and labor as possible. How effective the rulers were in fully achieving their goals may be contested.[10] As might be expected, palace intrigue over succession was endemic. In fact, challenges from the

---

5 William F. Edgerton, "The Government and the Governed in the Egyptian Empire," *Journal of Near Eastern Studies*, vol. 6(3) (1947), pp. 152–160, at p. 155

6 *See* John Baines, "Literacy and Ancient Egyptian Society," *Man* (New series), vol. 18 (1983), pp. 572–599, at 586, estimated the literacy rate at 1 percent of the population.

7 *Id.*

8 *See* Samuel E. Finer, *The History of Government from the Earliest Times*, vol. 1, *Ancient Monarchies and Empires* (Oxford and New York: Oxford University Press, 1999), p. 133.

9 Russ VerSteeg, *Law in Ancient Egypt* (Durham, NC: Carolina Academic Press, 2002), p. 106, citing Sally L.D. Katary, *Land Tenure in the Ramesside Period* (London: Kegan Paul International, 1989), p. 63.

10 *See* VerSteeg, *Law in Ancient Egypt*, p. 191.

periphery as local governors gained personal control over resources and established independent bases of power were sufficiently successful to disrupt the continuity of central rule during the First Intermediate Period (2160–2055 BCE).[11] Their ultimate "redistributive" aims seem hardly to be in doubt.

Control over the principal sources of wealth—the Nile river valley—including monopoly grants to traders, enabled Pharaonic rulers to intensify further their capacity to coerce and their control. Protected by desert expanses from outside invasion, for nearly two and a half millennia they effectively maintained this system of centralized control and order. Only once during this period was centralized rule interrupted—what is today referred to as the First Intermediate Period, a relatively brief interval of internal upheaval and divided government. Thereafter Egypt was subject to divided rule only twice—during the Second (1650–1550 BCE) and Third Intermediate Periods (1069–664 BCE), when first Hyksos settlers ruled the north and later ethnic Libyans gained control of all but Thebes. Not until the Persian invasion in the sixth century BCE, however, did the Egyptian rulers succumb to outside invaders and external control. Even then and thereafter under Alexander, the Ptolemies, the Romans, and the Arabs, the internal structures of centralized rule remained largely intact. Theirs was in fact the only fully centralized bureaucratic empire ever to develop on Mediterranean shores.

The archeological findings related to law and, above all, law enforcement for ancient Egypt are remarkably sparse. As noted, no collection or even extensive record of legal rules before 700 BCE has been discovered. What we know of ancient Egyptian law is based largely on obscure references, guess-work, and analytical surmise. The first known written evidence of law is a small papyrus fragment from the city of Hermopolis in about 700 BCE known rather grandly as the "Hermopolis Legal Code."[12] The most complete set of documentary materials is the collection of writings from the community of workmen families at Deir el-Medina established under the reign of Tuthmosis (c. 1504–1492 BCE)

---

[11] Stephan Seidlmayer, "The First Intermediate Period," in Ian Shaw, ed., *The Oxford History of Ancient Egypt* (Oxford and New York: Oxford University Press, 2000), p. 121. Finer, *History of Government*, vol. 1, pp. 148–151, describing the conflict between the ruling authorities at the center and officials with control over local resources at the periphery as a continual constraint on royal power.

[12] *See* Girgis Mattha, *The Demotic Code of Hermopolis West* (Paris: Bibliothèque d' Étude [Institut Français d'Archéologie Orientale du Caire], George R. Hughes, trans., 1975).

during the 18th Dynasty on the west bank of the ancient city of Thebes south of the Valley of the Kings.

The Deir el-Medina texts—written on papyri, potsherds, and small flakes of limestone—are instructive. Thanks to a uniquely trained Egyptologist and law professor, Andrea McDowell, we have a carefully constructed analysis of legal enforcement and jurisdiction within the community.[13] Deir el-Medina was hardly an autonomous self-governing or even semi-autonomous community. It was a purposefully isolated, residential community of highly skilled laborers and their families, who were either commissioned or, more likely, commanded to build and decorate royal tombs for over four centuries. Their literacy—although never exceeding 40 percent of the community by one estimate[14]—attests to their status as privileged. Officials provided all foodstuffs and other needs, including laundry services. Officials also restricted access to the community. McDowell uses the metaphor of the "company town" but the closest contemporary analogues are the high security, government "towns" for rocket and nuclear scientists at Peenemunde, Los Alamos, and Zheleznogorsk. From the fragmentary evidence of law and law enforcement in Deir el-Medina even over the course of several centuries, no one can make reasonably accurate generalizations for all of Egypt. The patterns and processes of law enforcement do allow us, however, to discern something about the governing capacity of those who ruled Egypt and the modes of law enforcement available to them and the contexts in which they were used.[15]

The procedures for dealing with disputes and conduct within Deir el-Medina that touched on royal interests are indicative of a highly developed public law order. Although the Egyptians did not have an abstract conception of "law" and "legal" institutions as such; nonetheless, the subject matter of the disputes—marriage, divorce, succession, property, commercial transactions (based on barter), and above all various wrongs to persons and property—has led scholars to discern a wide variety of private law rules and principles.[16] More instructive are the processes and procedures. The community had a local "court" (*ḳnbt*)—

---

[13] A.G. McDowell, *Jurisdiction in the Workmen's Community of Deir el-Medina* (Leiden: Nederlands Institut voor het Nabia Oosten, 1990). *See also* A.G. McDowell, *Village Life in Ancient Egypt: Laundry Lists and Love Songs* (Oxford and New York: Oxford University Press, 1999).

[14] McDowell, *Village Life*, p. 4.

[15] *See* S. Allam, "Egyptian Law Courts in Pharaonic and Hellenistic Times," *Journal of Egyptian Archaeology*, vol. 77 (1991), pp. 109–127.

[16] VerSteeg, *Law in Ancient Egypt*, pp. 99–207.

described by Allam as a "sort of municipal council"[17]—whose members varied but, by most accounts, included the most influential members of the community along with local officials. Depending on the importance of the dispute to the administrators, the local members could be joined by one or two scribes attached to the office of the vizier, who reported to their superior on matters of interest in the village and in the Valley of the Kings. Proceedings were initiated by a charge or "report" (*smi*) but the petitioner did not control the process. Thereafter officials, particularly the scribes, took charge, referring disputes involving serious infractions—those that concerned the interests of the rulers—to the vizier for disposition by the central or provincial authorities. From the available documents, the majority of the disputes handled by the *ḳnbt* as a local court were brought by workmen against others of equivalent status involving economic transactions. Scribes are believed to have ordinarily recorded only those cases considered significant to the authorities.[18] Thus the Deir el-Medina texts describing the *ḳnbt* cases may be, as some believe, private documents kept for purpose of proof. For the most part they were minor disputes that did not end even after adjudication. Compensatory relief, other than restitution of property, appears to be rare. Such disputes may in fact have ultimately ended with compromise, but the role of the *ḳnbt* appears to have been almost exclusively to determine whether the claimant had a valid claim. In this sense, a principal function of the *ḳnbt* was adjudicatory—at least for disputes between members of the community of equivalent social and political status or rank. If the *ḳnbt* affirmed a claim, the case generally ended with an oath by the defendant to satisfy it. Rarely if ever, however, were sanctions applied for failure to comply. The documents reveal few examples of officials enforcing their decisions. The procedures were also fluid and imprecise without fixed rules or requirements.

Several basic aims and functions can be identified. The process was designed to maintain order by facilitating resolution of disputes among members of the community that did not affect the interests of those who governed. The formal process was adjudicatory in that officials acted at the request of claimants to determine the validity of their claims and at least attempted to ensure compliance with their decisions by requiring promises under oath to comply. These were in effect considered to be minor matters best left to the local community leaders and officials and households to handle if informal means of resolution failed. Whether or

---

17 Allam, "Egyptian Law Courts," p. 77.
18 McDowell, *Jurisdiction*, p. 189.

not one chooses to characterize whatever substantive principles seem to have been consistently applied in these cases as "private law rules," the process seems to have been intended to resolve the dispute—not to enforce or to recognize legal rules. In contrast, infractions that touched on royal interests, from tomb robberies to failure to report serious infractions, were accordingly treated in what we can appropriately describe as criminal enforcement processes. Local *ḳnbt* apparently did not handle such cases. Nor did their jurisdiction extend the cases involving land. Such matters were instead subject to direct vizier control and enforcement. Essentially punitive, the applicable sanctions—death, servitude, banishment, loss of civil identity, corporeal punishment, confiscation of goods or real property—varied with the perceived seriousness of infraction.

With respect to law enforcement, Deir el-Medina thus conforms to the shared patterns of nearly all highly developed public law orders. The community itself evidences a centralized bureaucratic polity with the capacity to mobilize, direct, and coerce its subject inhabitants to a degree that may not have been replicated in the West until the mid twentieth century. The law reflected ruler interests, and law enforcement tended similarly to be fully controlled by those in authority. The Deir el-Medina materials do evidence an adjudicatory system in which a person could initiate a process for enforcing claims against others. What is most notable, to anticipate subsequent discussion, about such a judicial process is that it appears to have been limited in effect to claimants of equal social and political status.

Private Law and the *Polis*

About 700 years before the Common Era an apparently unparalleled series of events occurred, we are told, in the Attic kingdom of Athens. At the end of the seventh century BCE the nobles of the city are said to have effectively abolished its hereditary kingship, reducing it to an *office* (*archon basileus*) whose designated occupant would govern along with six holders of the office of "law givers" (*thesmothetai*) to articulate the customary law. They were assisted by two other persons selected to be the chief civil authority (*archon eponymous*) and corresponding chief military authority (*polemarch*). All were to be selected annually by a council of nobles (*areopagus*) representing citizens (*politai*) of the city (*polis*), which included the urban center (*astu*) and the Athenian countryside (*khōra*). The reforms made as *citizens* the free male inhabitants of Athens and their male descendants full participants in governance. In some respects—particularly the adherence to community consent, customary norms, and collective community sanctions—these events might be viewed as a return to an earlier pattern of social and political organization. Yet, without common bonds of kinship and lineage, this development proved to be transformational.

Athens is credited as the first major polity based on an association of persons who shared elite status in terms of wealth and social position—i.e., their control over slaves and other subordinates. Their identity as members of a territorial political community was defined by citizenship rather than kinship or subordination. The glue that held these elite Athenians together was this shared identity as participatory members of a self-governing territorial community. Elemental features of structurally simple kinship-based polities were reshaped and adapted to a complex society. It was also the first known polity of institutional rather than personal rule and in this sense, at least in embryonic form, the first true state. Athens satisfied two prerequisites for both of these features. The number of Athenian citizens—those who were entitled to participate in governance with shared access to the available instruments of coercion—was too large for a purely customary order—despite elements of informal, customary enforcement—but small enough to allow the diffusion of authority and power that sustained Athens as a self-defined association of citizens. Not coincidentally, argued here, Athens also produced for its citizens an archetypal private law regime. We need to keep in mind, however, that the number of slaves, subordinated persons, and other non-citizens vastly outnumbered the number of citizens. Athens was never, in the contemporary sense, a fully democratic regime. How this came about and what were the consequences deserve attention.

Geography, as usual, explains a lot. Ancient Greece was a land of isolated villages and small farms located in the rugged hills and valleys of a mountainous peninsula thrusting into the Mediterranean and over 3000 adjacent islands in the Aegean and Ionian seas. Most of the inhabitants on the Greek mainland and the islands lived lives of subsistence based on agriculture, fishing, and herding. With limited surplus agricultural production and natural obstacles to control, few rulers could amass the wealth and power necessary for political consolidation or expansion. Relative to the Mesopotamian, Anatolian (Hittite), and Egyptian empires, even the early "palace" kingdoms of Minoan Crete and Mycenae seem poor and weak. The natural and man-made upheavals of the late thirteenth and twelfth centuries that ushered in what is today generally referred to as the "Dark Age" (c. 1200–800 BCE) destroyed many of these city-kingdoms, their buildings and their institutions, leaving some abandoned altogether and others smaller and poorer than before. Aided by dominance over the largest of the three Attic plains, Athens survived. Growing larger with migrants, it began to take on its paradigmatic social and institutional features as *polis*.

As the Archaic Age (800–500 BCE) commenced, the Greek peninsula and adjacent islands were characterized by predominantly small pastoral and agricultural households organized into discrete independent settlements, each with its own cult and shrines. Within these communities and their more urban centers, chieftains (*basileus*) had emerged and along with an aristocratic class of wealthier landholders had begun to consolidate power and political authority aided by innovations in metal armor as well as the use of horses and increasing landholding, especially in the most favorable locations. A growing population added other pressures—propelling, some argue,[19] the spread of Greek settlements, each a "colony" with ties to particular cities, in all directions along the Mediterranean shores. By the middle of the seventh century BCE another military innovation forever altered the growing conflict—the *stasis*—of social classes. The organization of well-armed infantrymen in close formation or phalanx gave the Greeks a formidable military advantage in war but also meant a shift of influence from warrior-aristocrats in favor of those "commoners" who could afford their own equipment. Now affluent commoners not only had a critical military function but also could demand a share in governance.

Except for colonization, Athens shared nearly all of the patterns and pressures of eighth and seventh century BCE Greece. By all accounts the pivotal event for Athens was the election of Solon as the sole "law giving" *archon* at the beginning of the sixth century BCE. Solon refused appeals to become "tyrant" and his first official act was allegedly to issue the *seiachtheia* ("shaking off of burdens") canceling all existing debts secured by land, permanently eliminating debt-bondage, and prohibiting outright the enslavement of any citizen. The consequence was to secure thereafter the freedom and political capacity of the poorest landholders. Solon proceeded to reduce the political influence of the nobles by establishing four classes of citizens based on income. Only those with the greatest incomes became eligible for the Council (*Boulé*), an organ with executive and judicial functions. Eligibility for election as an *archon* was restricted to members of the upper two classes. Citizens of all classes were permitted to participate in the law-making Assembly (*Ekklesia*) and

19 *See*, e.g., Carl Hampus Lyttkens, "Reflections on the Origins of the *Polis*: An Economic Perspective on Institutional Change in Ancient Greece," *Constitutional Political Economy*, vol. 17 (2006), pp. 31–48.

the courts. Later reforms first under the "tyranny" of Peisistratos (c. 560–510 BCE) but especially by Kleisthenes as *archon* (c. 510–493 BCE) went further. Peisistratos is credited with having instituted loans to farmers, reducing their dependence on local magnates. The question of whether these loans should be classified as personal or governmental illustrates the lack of distinction at this period between personal and institutionalized rule. Kleisthenes, however, moved toward greater institutionalization by reorganizing Athens into 139 demes based on existing rural settlements and urban communities, which were then assigned to one of ten new "tribes" (*phylai*) that were further organized into three Ridings (*trittues*) to include representational urban, rural, and coastal demes. Already organic communities, the demes, each with an Assembly, became the primary unit of administrative organization for purposes of registration for military service and at least putative representation in a new Council of 500 citizens. Subsequent constitutional changes completed the political structure for Athenian democracy. All archons, councilors, and magistrates were elected by lot and served for terms limited to one year. Notably absent were deistic claims to legitimacy for either rule or law.

Despite the later rise of Athens as a major maritime trading and commercial center, its citizens were then and would remain predominantly agrarian landowners, however poor and insubstantial. Except for its value as collateral, landholding, a privilege denied to non-citizens, although still the primary source of wealth became relatively less so. It remained, however, a mark of social status and citizenship. Inequalities in wealth and social status remained a feature of Athenian life, but all citizens, whatever their means or occupation, shared a common legal status. Thus as Athens entered its Classical Period (500–400 BCE), it lacked the fundamental sources of concentrated power and subordination —a small elite ruling class with military power and control over the principal sources of wealth.

What then were the principal sources of wealth for Athens as a polity? Studies of taxation in classical Athens list the principal sources of revenue to include the silver mines of Laurion, direct taxation of resident aliens (*metoikoi*) and freedmen, customs duties, and market polls in addition to the *eisphoré*, a rarely levied direct tax on wealth for emergencies, and the *liturgy*, a contribution by wealthy citizens for public works that was initially viewed as a civic duty, which was apparently solicited and in later stages potentially enforced through a private law process. Finer concludes that, given the meager administrative needs of the city,[20] these sources were sufficient—except in wartime. What most sources tend to overlook are the services and substitute labor provided by slaves and those who were subject to direct regulation.

Athens, as noted, was hardly a democracy as understood today. Half or more of the population were slaves and foreigners (*xenoi* and the *metoikoi*, resident aliens with limited privileges) without citizenship. Assuming that at least another half were women and minors, those who enjoyed status as fully participating citizens in 500 BCE are estimated to have numbered between 20,000 and 30,000 within a population of well more than double that number.[21] As noted, the *metoikoi* or metics were subject to direct taxation. Other merchant foreigners were presumably too mobile for such levies. Slaves, the number of whom had increased significantly as Athens developed, provided the labor for the Laurion silver mines as well as governmental services, including policing. Slave labor presumably performed a wide variety of other services without direct cost for the common good. Athenian "democracy" and its private law system did not reach half the population of Athens. With this in mind, we can now review the principal features of Athenian law.

The history of Athenian legal proceedings seems at first glance to exemplify a progression from mediation to adjudication as chiefs with increasing authority emerge. Vincent Farenga, for example, alludes to the changing role of the *basileus* in "rendering a dike [judgment]" from a mediating headman or chief in the Archaic Period to the adjudicating judge and citizen jury in the Classical Period.[22] Yet, on closer examination, the formal procedures of classical Athenian law might be best described as an institutionalized form of customary community ordering. Lacking an adjudicating ruler, the formal process terminated with a consensual collective community verdict.

Athenians relied on overlapping adjudicatory procedures for law enforcement based in virtually all cases except homicide on citizen initiative and control. It was essentially a comprehensive system of private legal actions. Individual citizens who suffered a wrong could initiate either *dikai idiai* actions to vindicate a personal interest or *dikai dēmosai* proceedings if the wrong also harmed the community. Any citizen could bring a separate *graphai* action to prosecute wrongs against

---

20 Finer, *The History of Government*, vol. 1, pp. 350–351.

21 Some estimates of the citizenry are higher: *see* Ian Morris, *Burial and Ancient Society: The Rise of the Greek City* (Cambridge and New York: Cambridge University Press, 1987), p. 5.

22 *See* Vincent Farenga, *Citizen and Self in Ancient Greece* (Cambridge and New York: Cambridge University Press, 2006), pp. 109, 263.

the community, which thus tended to overlap with *dikai dēmosai* actions. *Graphai* actions were frequently used in cases of official misconduct. Over time, new actions for a wide variety of specified wrongs were added to each category. Drawing from lists compiled by R.G. Osborne and others, S.C. Todd describes the separate *dikai* actions, ranging from assault (*aikeia*) and slander (*kakēgoria*) to debt (*khreōs*) and homicide (*phonos*) as well as other *graphai* actions that could be brought for equally varied offenses, such as "idleness" (*argia*, commonly the failure to maintain land), bribery (*dora*), and proposing illegal decrees (*paranoma*).[23]

In all cases a communal jury functioning as adjudicators often numbering in the hundreds decided the case and entered a non-appealable verdict, although a separate counter action for false prosecution (*paragraphē*, apparently introduced c. 403 BCE) could be brought. The presiding magistrate maintained order but did not participate in the decision. By the fourth century cases involving small sums were referred for a non-binding summary decision to an official arbitrator, a service that all persons eligible for military duty were required to perform. Only citizens could participate as officials, jurors, or, in most cases, litigants. To the extent that foreigners, whom it appears dominated trade and commerce, could not participate, most commercial disputes would have been excluded. Presumably a reflection of the commercial importance of maritime trade, in about 350 BCE the *dikai emporikai* action was created for maritime trade disputes, thereby allowing suits by foreigners who were citizens of another Greek *polis*.

Athenian law also provided for binding private arbitration. The parties to a dispute could always opt to arbitrate and select the arbitrators themselves. By the fourth century, however, cases settled by private arbitration could not by law be litigated again in court. For those involved, binding private arbitration provided a welcome alternative to public trials, which necessarily involved public scrutiny and consequent reputational risks. Indeed, many actions were brought with this aim. As in nearly all legal systems, another benefit of private arbitration was the greater likelihood of remedial relief.

In litigated cases the losing party suffered a penalty that depended on the nature of the action. The most serious offenses could result in a death penalty, imprisonment, exile, or, importantly, deprivation of legal capacity and status (*atimia*) or, more literally, loss of "honor" (*timē*). Fines

---

23 S.C. Todd, *The Shape of Athenian Law* (London and New York: Oxford University Press, 1995), pp. 98–112.

were the most common sanction. In debt actions a debtor could be liable not only for payment to a prevailing creditor but also a percentage of that amount as a fine payable to the *polis*. Claimants who lost were themselves subject to fines. In *graphai* actions the prosecuting parties who did not muster at least a fifth of the jurors' votes had to pay a 1000 drachma fine and lose all or partial legal capacity as citizens (*atimia*). Claimants who failed also forfeited to the *polis* or the prevailing defendant or both deposits made to the court for costs as well as for security based on the value of the claim. In *dikai* actions, self-help through seizure of property or person was the prevailing mode of enforcement.

The Classical Period grew to a close with war and finally the surrender of the city to Sparta in 405 BCE. Its system of citizen rule was restored briefly a year later, but the demands of incessant warfare took their toll on its institutions, although the effects only gradually became evident. Athens as a fully independent polity finally ended with its defeat in 338 BCE by Philip of Macedon and its incorporation into the Macedonian Empire under Philip and his son, Alexander. For our purposes an assessment of the Athenian experience also ends here. Its most telling feature was the reliance on citizen initiative for both making and enforcing legal rules. The procedural nature of the law and the enforcement process in the form of legal actions for specified wrongs with adjudication by a mass citizen jury necessarily precluded the development of clearly articulated substantive legal rules and principles or even a coherent conception of law. The actions delineated the wrongs and claims. The adjudicating jury deciding cases by majority vote could only enter a final verdict. In such a system no reasoned exposition or rationale for the verdict was possible. Nor, lacking judges or jurists with expertise in law, could a coherent system of private law rules develop. Yet as a paradigm Athens suggests what factors are necessary for a private law system or order to emerge.

First and foremost was the diffusion of both authority and power that prevented evolution toward the forms of centralized rule that had been evident in the past and would be in the future in surrounding and ultimately enveloping empires. Religion mattered in the apparent lack of a deistic source for concentrated political authority. Law as *nomos* could have a deistic source but not the law giver or necessarily those who ruled. In turn, geography precluded the concentration of agricultural production and its control as in Mesopotamia and Egypt. It also favored Greece generally and Athens in particular as a center for maritime trade and commerce, ensuring even greater mobility of persons and resources and thereby diffusion of wealth and power. To be sure the Athenian private law order was limited to its citizens. Slaves and others subordinated by Athenians as individuals, households, or the *polis* did not share the equality in legal status and political participation or the mutuality of economic, political, and military dependence on which such diffusion was grounded. For them the Athenian legal system was presumably as regulatory and coercive in effect as any public law system. The question remains whether adjudication as the primary mode of law enforcement and a private law order could evolve or develop within larger, more diverse communities of "citizens" as equal participants in governance or those that lacked such diffusion of authority and power. To answer these questions, we need to consider the influence of rifles and rice.

RIFLES

Rifles (i.e., warfare) as well as rivers were pivotal in defining the polities that emerged in the earliest periods of political organization. One by one the early civilizations and empires formed and fell as a result of military conquest from within or without. Continuous warfare and the consequent need for more human resources and better weaponry also had continuing political and legal consequences. Opportunities for further territorial expansion or threats of conquest invited or forced rulers to use the resources they did manage to control for incessant warfare. Rulers of polities for whom for lack of human or material resources neither a conscripted nor a recruited army was an option could hardly be expected to finance the policing and administrative establishment necessary for an effective regulatory regime. To maintain at least a degree of legitimizing order within the territories under their authority, if not complete or lasting control, rulers in these lands relied instead on adjudicating disputes brought to them by subjects or followers. Adjudication became the primary means of maintaining a semblance of order with a relative handful of adjudicating equals or subordinates. With at least some claim of authority to rule but without comparable power to coerce, as described in Chapters 4 and 5, the warrior rulers of medieval Japan as well as the early kingdoms of Western Europe exemplify such reliance on adjudication for maintaining order and legitimacy with fewer essential officials. Not until a stable political order could be maintained and new sources of revenue acquired could such regimes begin to develop the regulatory structures of a public law order.

Yet, we should note, that through warfare new technologies develop. Thus invention and innovation can be viewed a more positive consequence of continuous warfare. The history of the rifle is especially instructive. From Chinese origins gunpowder, cannon, and ultimately the rifle were improved by European and Japanese warriors so long as warfare remained constant. In Japan, once a prolonged period of peace pertained, innovations ceased and the extant weapon became obsolete. In Europe, war and the resulting technological advances were equally incessant. Readers might pause here to consider the relevance of war among or by the so-called Western Powers (including the United States) to the technological revolutions of the nineteenth and twentieth centuries.

RICE

At least until the age of commerce, the wealth of nations was measured by the agricultural production of sedentary communities. How and what these early settlements produced was also critical. To the extent that the rulers could direct and control the human labor required, agricultural communities could be subordinated or substituted—in other words, compulsory service—military and otherwise—slavery and serfdom—could thrive. In those regions of the world where husbandry or the production of wheat and other cereal grains did not require continuous, intensive labor or cooperative effort, rulers could establish full control by occupying productive land. They could command the manpower and appropriate the wealth. In areas where the principal products did require intensive, on-going labor as well as mutual cooperation and interdependency, as in regions where wet-paddy rice was grown with its requirements for year-round, intensive effort as well as a sustainable cooperative system of irrigation, rulers had less control and reduced capacity to command. To ensure the continued production of the wealth they sought to possess, they could not fully interfere with preexisting community structures and had to allow greater, albeit not necessarily complete, autonomy.

As detailed in Chapters 3 and 4, in southern China and Japan, where wet-paddy rice was the principal agricultural product and source of extractable wealth, rulers seeking to maximize their wealth and control were forced to allow these communities greater participation in local or village governance than in the northern region of China or Western Europe generally. In this respect, southern China and Japan were not exceptional. As Richard O'Connor notes, the argument made here is equally applicable to the rice-producing regions of Southeast Asia.[24]

---

[24] Richard A. O'Connor, "Agricultural Change and Ethnic Succession in Southeast Asian States: A Case for Regional Anthropology," *Journal of Asian Studies*, vol. 54 (1995), pp. 968–996.

Even the rice-producing Muslims of medieval Valencia and African slaves on rice plantations in antebellum South Carolina had greater autonomy and self-governance than other similarly situated communities producing other agricultural products—such as corn, wheat, tobacco, or cotton—or engaged in husbandry.[25] In China as the population and wealth of such regions and the mobility of their inhabitants grew, the relative power and access to resources by those who ruled at the center diminished. One consequence was expansion of a region-centered culture of interdependency and cooperation along with a corresponding growth in trade and commerce that gave rise to a complementary system of ordering within the existing political order but largely outside of governmental control.

Shared habits, values, and expectations—in other words, culture—persist. Even today evidence of the influence of rice production is evident in both China and Japan. Recent studies[26] on differences between southern and northern Chinese patterns of behavior and commercial investment today support the view that the "rice culture" of southern China continues to influence patterns of interdependency and private ordering. However, as indicated in the subsequent studies of China and Japan, other factors profoundly affect prevailing configurations of interdependency. Among these factors are the structures of governance and law. Rice production in Korea, for example, was as predominant as in southern China and Japan. Yet in contrast to both, Korea experienced high degrees of slavery and patrimonialism.[27] Although not as extreme, as detailed below, differences in the effects of "rice culture" between southern China and Japan also existed. Such contrasts among these three nations of Northeast Asia despite a common "rice culture" that fosters interdependency and cooperation are arguably manifest today in patterns of social and economic organization, not to mention law and political

---

[25] On the Muslim rural peasant communities in the post-*Reconquista* Kingdom of Valencia, *see* Thomas F. Glick, *Irrigation and Society in Medieval Valencia* (Cambridge, MA: Harvard University Press, 1970). Also noted in Ostrom, *Governing the Commons*. With respect to rice-producing African slave communities in South Carolina, see Daniel C. Littlefield, "The Varieties of Slave Labor." Freedom's Story, TeacherServe©. National Humanities Center, August 20, 2014. http://nationalhumanitiescenter.org/tserve/freedom/1609-1865/essays/slavelabor.htm. Last visited 29 January 2016.

[26] *See* Thomas Talhelm, et al., "Large-Scale Psychological Differences Within China Explained by Rice Versus Wheat Agriculture," *Science*, vol. 344(6184) (2014), pp. 603–608.

[27] *See* James B. Palais, "A Search for Korean Uniqueness," *Harvard Journal of Asiatic Studies*, vol. 55(2) (1995), pp. 409–425.

structures. As revealed in Gary Hamilton's works, South Korea and Taiwan diverge in patterns of networking and economic organization in commercial organization and networking. South Korean economic organization is notable for an "embedded" lineage-based class hierarchy that enables "coercively" induced cooperation of persons outside of lineage groups in patrimonial organizations while in Taiwan reciprocity based on shared ties outside of familial connections enable horizontal networks.[28] In Japan, as I have argued before,[29] the immobility of rice-producing villagers, their exclusion from governance but local autonomy produced closed communities as well as a widespread "communitarian orientation" that permeates both politics and law today. The need of consensus is a dominant theme in the making of political policy.[30] Seeking the "sense of society" (*shakai no tsūnen*) is among the more distinctive features of Japanese judicial law making.[31]

Whatever the ultimate configurations and patterns of interdependent, cooperative behavior, combined with other factors that have either expanded or limited rulers' control and allocation of resources, rice production has exerted a major influence on law's foundations. Conversely, dependence on the production of wheat and other cereal grains that does not require the degree of interdependency and cooperative behavior has contributed to notably contrasting political and legal institutions and cultures.

---

[28] *See* Gary G. Hamilton, *Commerce and Capitalism in Chinese Societies* (Abingdon, Oxon and New York: Routledge, 2006); Gary G. Hamilton and Robert C. Feenstra, *Emergent Economies, Divergent Paths: Economic Organization and International Trade in South Korea and Taiwan* (Cambridge and New York: Cambridge University Press, 2006).

[29] John O. Haley, *The Spirit of Japanese Law* (Athens, GA: University of Georgia Press, 1998).

[30] *See* Lindy Edwards, *Consensus in Conflict: Competing Conceptual Structures and the Changing Nature of Japanese Politics in the Postwar Era* (Canberra, ACT: Australia Japan Research Centre, 1997).

[31] *See* Daniel H. Foote and John O. Haley, "Judicial Law-Making and the Creation of Legal Norms in Japan: A Dialogue," in John O. Haley and Toshiko Takenaka, eds., *Legal Innovations in Asia: Judicial Law-Making and Influence of Comparative Law* (Cheltenham, UK and Northampton, MA: Edward Elgar Publishing, 2014), pp. 77–122.

RELIGION

An additional, overriding influence must be added—religion. Few would deny the importance of religious beliefs to the political and legal cultures of any community. Certainly no study of the formation and development of the world's two most enduring and influential secular legal traditions can ignore the importance of religion in shaping their underlying structures. Such beliefs are arguably peculiarly resistant to at least rapid change and thus tend to have long-lasting and profoundly instrumental influence.

Among the most noteworthy impact is the extent to which religious norms (and those of less metaphysical belief systems) relate to the legitimacy and thereby, as explored in Chapter 1, the authority of those who govern. Legitimacy as noted is essential for sustained authority to rule. Enduring political and legal orders have had one major feature in common: they reflect commonly shared fundamental values and beliefs of those governed. To the extent that such beliefs and values foster or buttress the authority and power of those who govern or are also shared by legislators, judges, and law-making and -enforcing officials generally, they almost certainly will be reflected in the law.

The world's three monotheistic religions—Judaism, Christianity, and Islam—share a special relationship to law. The one deity of all three is a law-giving God. Within the shared religious traditions of all three, God's law trumps human, man-made law. The tensions have been and continue to be profound. Moreover, even with increasingly secular communities in the West, the residual influence of such religion-grounded "natural law" notions is notable. The claimed universality of moral norms as legal rules without any explicit religious source is evidenced in pronouncements on the applicability of "universal human rights" within "customary" international law. The resulting fusion of law and morality is consequential. On the one hand, it limits the legitimacy of legal rules at variance with widely shared moral norms. On the other, it encourages promulgation of legal rules mandated by similarly shared precepts. In contexts where contradictory moral views are widespread, political conflict becomes virtually inevitable. Even kings have lost their heads in such situations.

By 1900, with the exception of Siam and a tiny cluster of other independent Buddhist states in which arguably law and morality were also joined,[32] only three nations in Northeast Asia—China, Japan, and

---

[32] Rebecca R. French and Mark Nathan, eds., *Buddhism and Law: An Introduction* (Cambridge and New York: Cambridge University Press, 2014).

Korea—remained apart from a world dominated by Christian and Islamic beliefs. Confucian and Neo-Confucian ideology philosophic mandates acutely influenced Chinese, Korean, and, albeit to a much lesser extent, Japanese patterns of governance and law. None conceived of "justice" in terms of a fusion of law and morality. Within the legal and philosophic traditions of all three, law was a "positivist" tool of governance separate from morality. Unlike nearly every other nation-state today, none had a religious tradition in which notions of "justice" included both legal and moral norms.

No religion or religious organization approached the role in political and legal development that the Roman Catholic Church played in Europe. As detailed in Chapter 5, the Church defines the boundaries of Europe even today. The Church also ensured that Latin would be the common written language far beyond the reach of Rome's western empire with imbedded law words denoting concepts of private law that had developed in the Roman civitas centuries before. Unlike any other of the world's major religions, the Church was also a supranational, hierarchical polity incorporating in both language and structure basic elements of Roman governance. As such, as noted, it epitomized a governmental polity with authority but with limited exceptions in territories it controlled, without power. Moreover, like the early European kingdoms and warrior-ruled Japan, it too relied on adjudication with exclusive jurisdiction in family matters as a means of political ordering. The experience of Hispanic America as the first colonial imposition of Western law in non-Western societies, described in Chapter 6, elaborates the full significance of the Church's role.

The organization and beliefs of religious communities after the Reformation and the advent of Protestantism in Western Europe in the sixteenth century had equal significance for political structures and law. Unlike the Roman Catholic, most Protestant, but especially Calvinist, churches were organized as self-governing congregations with shared views on civil society and individual responsibility. Moreover, the seventeenth century English Calvinist philosophers, including Thomas Hobbes and John Locke, in addition to prominent Calvinists of the French and Scottish enlightenments, including Jean-Jacques Rousseau, advanced the idea of a self-ordering civil society distinct from the state. The Western notion of consent of the governed as the basis for legal legitimacy is grounded in the experience and beliefs of the Protestant communities of faith. The story of Western Europe is thus exceptionally one of religion.

3. Rivers, rifles, and rice: foundations of public law and private ordering in China

Until the Industrial Revolution catapulted Europe to center stage in the nineteenth century, China was the most populous, wealthy, and consequential polity on earth. In longevity and influence, its legal tradition rivals that of Rome. A civilization with origins as ancient as those of Mesopotamia and Egypt, by the end of the third century BCE, a centralized bureaucratic polity had emerged that, with intermittent intervals of internal division and fragmented rule, was to endure for over two millennia. In terms of governance by civilian officials, selected by merit from an educated elite versed in a moral philosophy of governance, and subject to oversight under a system of legal rules grounded in clearly articulated principles of proportionality, universality, and equality, China has no historical or even contemporary peer.

China's contributions to the intellectual and political life of the neighboring states of East Asia are difficult to exaggerate. Most fully emulated in Choson Korea (1392–1910) and under Li rule in Vietnam (1428–1788), the institutions and ideological foundations of governance in China provided models that were formally reformed only within the past century. The influence of Chinese civilization is apparent today in art, language, and belief systems throughout Northeast Asia. Here too the world's most highly developed and enduring legal order originated. Based on a carefully reasoned set of fundamental principles, the dynastic codes, which span the history of China, anchored its rulers to a system of administrative principles and prescriptions that remain unsurpassed in coherence and normative justification. With the Chinese diaspora its legacy continues in patterns of political authority, statecraft, legal cultures, and social ordering throughout East Asia. The foundations of these developments are indeed narratives of rivers, rifles, and rice.

RIVERS

No civilization owes so much to its rivers. China, territorially roughly the size of all of Europe, has a network of rivers entirely within its borders that, with the Grand Canal—begun in the fourth century BCE, fully developed by the early seventh century CE, and ultimately completed with restorations to its final form in 1411 and 1415—connected virtually the entire country under the control of a single, centralized polity for roughly two millennia. The rivers of China have provided the highways for military and commercial transport, enabling its historic political unity and its legal achievements.

Chinese civilization originates at the western edges of the fertile plains of the Yellow River (*Huáng Hé*), the third longest river in Asia and the sixth longest in the world. Here the first sedentary agricultural communities known to have existed date from about the fifth millennium BCE. The Yellow River flows eastward from headwaters in the Bayan Har Mountains, looping north, east, and then south as it circumnavigates the steppes of the Loess Plateau. Joined by the Wei, already enlarged by its major tributaries, the Jing to the west of Xian and the Luo to the east, it turns abruptly eastward through the mountains at the intersection of today's Shaanxi, Shanxi, and Henan provinces, where, fed upstream by the Fen, it continues eastward through the mountains and hills of western Shanxi and northwest Henan, where, joined by the Huan (Angang), it enters the North China Plain to form the largest alluvial plain of East Asia. It continues northeastward to end in the Bay of Bohai. Further south is the Yangzi, the world's third longest river. Sourced in the glaciers of the Qinghai-Tibet Plateau, it flows eastward across southwest, central, and eastern China, emptying into the East China Sea at Shanghai. With over 300 tributaries, the Yangzi provides access to nearly all of the southern regions. The major tributaries include the Gan in Jiangxi, the Han in Hubei at the city of Wuhan, the Wu in Guizhou, and the Jialing in eastern Sichuan at Chongqing. Separating the Yellow and the Yangzi is the Huai River. Combined, these three river basins form the world's largest and most fertile set of contiguous plains. By the beginning of the Common Era, by most estimates, they supported a population greater in numbers than the Roman Empire at its peak.[1]

In the valleys and plains of these three rivers, evidence of the first grains in human history, millet in the north and rice in the south, has

---

[1] Walter Scheidel, *Population and Demography*, Princeton/Stanford Working Papers in Classics, Version 1.0, April 2006, p. 9.

been found.[2] Other, competing communities with distinctive cultures also emerged in neighboring regions of the northern steppes, the mountainous southwest, and the Pearl River valley, along the southern coast. Except during intermittent periods of political fragmentation when governed under separate polities, the native inhabitants of these basins have been subject to common rule under Chinese polities, referred to in China as the central "kingdoms" (*Zhongguo*) since the third century BCE.

China is believed today to have been originally occupied by diverse ethnic groups with separate languages. By the second millennium, however, a process of conquest, migration, and assimilation had begun in the millet-producing regions of the north, resulting in the domination of the region and their sedentary peoples by rulers predominantly from the north and west. In the words of Victor Mair, "these same peoples ... were nearly always responsible for the recurrent creation of an Extended East Asian Heartland."[3] With subjection and attendant migrations, Mair argues, until the Common Era a "transfer of culture generally flowed from west to east."[4] Conquerors from the western headwaters and northern frontiers thereby created political and legal institutions and organizational structures—including the foundational justifications and principles of penal and administrative law—that became ingrained in the emerging patterns of governance. From the Common Era onwards in time, however, the institutional transfer began to move in reverse direction from east to west, first from the millet- and later the rice-producing valleys to the mountains and steppes to the west and north.[5] In the process, despite the diversity of ethnic groups and regional cultures, the Chinese managed to create not only one of the first and most territorially expansive but also the most populous, wealthiest, and longest-lived centralized bureaucratic polity in human history.

China's earliest rulers like others had to consolidate both the authority and power necessary for their regimes to endure. Above all they had to establish sufficient control over material and human resources to expand

---

2 Kwang-Chih Chang, "China on the Eve of the Historical Record," in Michael Loewe and Edward L. Shaughnessy, eds., *The Cambridge History of Ancient China: From the Origins of Civilization to 221 B.C.* (Cambridge and New York: Cambridge University Press, 1999), pp. 44–47.

3 Victor Mair, "The Northwestern Peoples and the Recurrent Origin of the 'Chinese' State," in Joshua A. Fogel, ed., *The Teleology of the Modern Nation-State: Japan and China* (Philadelphia, PA: University of Pennsylvania Press, 2005), p. 46.

4 *Id.*, p. 47.

5 *Id.*

and withstand both external and internal threats. The millet-producing settlements of the North China Plain met many of their needs. In terms of both agricultural production and manpower, the resources of northern China surpassed both Mesopotamian and Egyptian empires. As in Egypt they were able to mobilize human resources and to impose controls that both increased the production of wealth and enabled its distribution to those who ruled. Here lived the vast majority of the Chinese population. "North China," as noted by Martin Heijdra, "is characterized by its jointly animal-driven wheat and millet agriculture," with "a resulting social structure with more managerial landlords and sharecropping peasants than elsewhere."[6] Heijdra adds that in the north by the end of the fourteenth century a "centuries-old legacy of numerous small and densely populated counties created opportunities for more penetrating government control and assistance than elsewhere." Here too originated the centralized irrigation projects that figure so prominently in Wittfogel's controversial and contested view of China's "hydraulic society" as a basis for authoritarian rule.[7]

Based on recent archeological discoveries, Chinese institutional history is claimed today to have begun with the late Neolithic rule in two regions at the periphery of the North China Plain—the Longshan region in the west and the Shandong region in the east. A third, notably short-lived culture—the Liangzhu—appears to have developed in the south along the Yangzi River to the northwest of Hangzhou. Based on excavations of the city of Erlitou, just east of the present city of Luoyang, the most significant institutional developments seem to have occurred, however, in the mountainous region at the western edges of the plain sometime after 2000 BCE. Whether this was the center of the historically contested Xia Dynasty of ancient Chinese political "myth"[8] or a "state" as defined by Elman Service and Martin Saline in an evolutionary progression[9] is hardly relevant for our purposes. What does matter is that by all accounts

---

6 Martin Heijdra, "The Socio-Economic Development of Rural China during the Ming," in Denis Twitchett and Frederick W. Mote, eds., *The Cambridge History of China*, vol. 8, *The Ming Dynasty, 1368–1644*, Pt. 2 (Cambridge and New York: Cambridge University Press, 1998), p. 419.

7 Karl Wittfogel, *Oriental Despotism: A Comparative Study of Total Power* (New York: Random House, 1957).

8 Chang, "China on the Eve of the Historical Record," pp. 71–73.

9 For a detailed discussion of Service and Saline's evolutionary argument in the context of Neolithic China, *see* Li Feng, *Early China: A Social and Cultural History* (Cambridge and New York: Cambridge University Press, 2013), pp. 20–22.

these developments occurred along the portions of the Yellow River or one of its western tributaries to the west of the North China Plain. The rulers in this region had both access to copper ore mined in the northwestern mountains (mainly in Gansu and Qinghai), where most deposits in north China were located. Their strategic location thereby gave them potential control over the sources and the distribution the ore required for the improved weaponry of what is commonly referred to as the early Bronze Age.

RIFLES

Sometime during the fifteenth century BCE the Shang Dynasty (c.1554–1046 BCE), China's first fully historical polity, had formed in the most strategic location for dominion over both supply of copper from the west and the agricultural wealth and human resources of the North China Plain. Hereditary warrior monarchs, the Shang kings, are believed to have consolidated control over much of the region by the middle of the second millennium BCE. A lineage- and ritual-based ruling elite emerged to dominate what is believed to have been a partially slave or servile (*zhong*)-based society.[10] At least one of its continuously moving capitals was Yin, in close vicinity to the city of Anyang in the northernmost portion of today's Henan Province. The location is significant. Located on the Huan (Anyang) River, which flows on the eastern periphery of the Taihang mountain range into the Yellow River just as it enters the North China Plain, this last Shang capital was even closer to the central heartland. Shang rulers thus could expand their control over the agricultural settlements of the Plain yet still be able to maintain access to the sources of copper in the Taihang and western mountains and to take full advantage of new Bronze Age technologies and weaponry.

Metallurgists during the Shang era are thought to have determined that adding a small portion of lead to copper produced bronze that could be cast as tools or weapons. Archeological findings provide evidence of

[10] Whether the Chinese term *zhong* is accurately translated into English as "slave" is contested. In any event, whatever the definition, *zhong* were fully under the control of governing elites. David N. Keightley, *Working for His Majesty: Research Notes on Labor Mobilization in Late Shang China (ca. 1200–1045BC), as Seen in the Oracle-Bone Inscriptions, with Particular Attention to Handicraft Industries, Warfare, Hunting, Construction, and the Shang's Legacies*. China Research Monograph 67. Berkeley: Institute of East Asian Studies, University of California, Center for Chinese Studies, 2012.

ceremonial artifacts cast in bronze for elite members of Shang society, including intricately decorated burial objects and massive cauldrons that represent globally the largest metal casting of the second millennium BCE.[11] The Shang produced the earliest discovered Chinese bronze swords, knives, spearheads (some tipped with jade), and axes. In age, they correspond to similar weaponry discovered in the Aegean and elsewhere. Their innovative use of horses and chariots also coincides with their use in Egypt, Mesopotamia, and other early civilizations.

The Shang rulers appear to have attempted to establish the first centralized system of rule in China through a network of residential walled cities inhabited by unilateral kinship groups (*zu*) governed by members of the ruling elite but under the Shang king's direct control in what has been described as a patriarchal clan system.[12] The rulers extended their control by creating new towns, selecting and dispatching the residents by edict.[13] By this means they gained control over both productive land and the inhabitants. The vast majority of the population of the eastern plains was thus subordinated if not enslaved, to become subject to military conscription, collective agricultural production, and labor service.

About 1022 BCE—coincident with the beginning of the decline of the Pharaonic Empire—a frontier warrior chieftain of the Zhou tribe established a new polity centered at the final bend of the Yellow River in the more arid and colder Wei valley of the western mountains, thereby tellingly dominating the most prominent sources and rivers for the distribution of copper ore. Defeating the last Shang ruler at the Battle of Muye (c. 1046) near to the present city of Xinxiang, the chieftain and his sons created the Western Zhou. Ruling for over a millennium, they created China's longest-lasting dynasty—what some have called its "finest and most noble age" and "guiding paradigm."[14]

Sharing language and other features of Shang culture, the rulers of Zhou selectively adopted Shang institutions to extend their rule throughout northern China as they assimilated subject city-centered polities into

---

11 Li, *Early China*, pp. 61–65.

12 Claudio Cioffi-Revilla and David Lai, "War and Politics in Ancient China, 2700 B.C. to 722 B.C.," *Journal of Conflict Resolution*, vol. 39 (1995), p. 470. *See also* Kwang-Chih Chang, *Shang Civilization* (New Haven, CT: Yale University Press, 1980), pp. 210–211.

13 John King Fairbank and Merle Goldman, *China: A New History* (Cambridge, MA: Harvard University Press, 2006), pp. 37–39.

14 *Id.*, p. 15; Edward L. Shaughnessy, "Western Zhou History," in Loewe and Shaughnessy, eds., *The Cambridge History of Ancient China*, p. 292.

a single, centrally controlled kingdom. They were largely successful. With a new political ideology including the "mandate of heaven," superior military technology, and greater capacity to mobilize an effective fighting force, they subdued the various polities within the Shang domain. As described by Cho-Yun Hsu and Katheryn Linduff, "The [Zhou] invaded, conquered, and reconstituted local structures by assimilating the local leaders into the power elite. By doing so they incorporated the conquered into the service of a united state."[15] They also established what Herrlee Creel described as a "proto-bureaucracy" with one of the earliest known governments of civilian officials with specialized functions—including financial administration—albeit supported by grants of land and subordinated laborers in lieu of salaries.[16]

By all accounts, warfare against people in enclaves and at the northern and western frontiers continued, but internal military activity virtually ceased for two centuries of largely civilian rule,[17] albeit buttressed by military power. Although described by some as a "feudal" regime,[18] the early Zhou asserted patrimonial and bureaucratic authority over regional military regimes. Creel asserts that the Zhou kings personally commanded 14 standing armies, garrisoned throughout their empire and in control of all principal roads.[19] Cioffi-Revilla and Lai adopt the term "suzerain system."[20] Most apt perhaps is the label coined by Li Feng in his recent study of bureaucracy under the Western Zhou. Defined by settlements (*yi*) rather than territory, the Zhou polity was, in Li Feng's words, a "gigantic congregation of clusters of *yi* settlements organized into a layered network by the political power" of a "delegatory kin-ordered settlement state."[21]

The available evidence also supports the view that the Zhou kings laid claim to all land, allocating possession and managerial control to the

---

[15] Cho-Yun Hsu and Katheryn M. Linduff, *Western Chou Civilization* (New Haven, CT: Yale University Press, 1988), p. 152.

[16] Herrlee G. Creel, *The Origins of Statecraft in China, Vol. One, The Western Chou Empire* (Chicago: University of Chicago Press, 1970), pp. 101–132.

[17] *Id.*, pp. 194–241. See also Cioffi-Revilla and Lai, "War and Politics in Ancient China," p. 485.

[18] *See* Creel, *Origins*, pp. 317–387.

[19] Herrlee Glessner Creel, "Legal Institutions and Procedures during the Chou Dynasty," in Jerome Alan Cohen, R. Randle Edwards and Fu-mei Chang Chen, eds., *Essays on China's Legal Tradition* (Princeton, NJ: Princeton University Press, 1980), p. 28.

[20] Cioffi-Revilla and Lai, "War and Politics in Ancient China," p. 470.

[21] Li Feng, *Bureaucracy and the State in Early China: Governing the Western Zhou* (Cambridge: Cambridge University Press, 2008), p. 299.

royal household (*wangjia*) and to the "state" subject to management by court-appointed civil officials. From these two sources, the Zhou rulers derived their revenue. Land was also allotted increasingly on a piecemeal fashion as "lineage property," to borrow Li Feng's term,[22] to select aristocratic families, who in turn over time transferred proprietorship and control over portions, producing increasing fragmentation. From royal and state-managed land acquired by conquest and colonization, the Zhou rulers acquired resources necessary for the centralized bureaucratic regime that emerged.

By the tenth century BCE the Zhou rulers had begun to source their claim to political legitimacy in a "mandate of heaven" in addition to perpetual hereditary rule. Thus the authority of the Zhou kings as well as their successors was at least in theory ultimately dependent on the quality of their rule and the welfare of the kingdom. Although the Zhou may perhaps have conceived of "heaven" (*tian*) as some sort of deity,[23] they certainly did not view *tian* as an anthropomorphic, omnipotent law-giving God.[24] Even at this early date, law was substantially regulatory and penal. Although no Zhou "code" or collection of written laws for all of the Zhou kingdom has been discovered, references to regional edicts and their enforcement abound. To fail to enforce or to over-enforce law was evidently viewed as a transgression deserving the loss of Heaven's mandate to rule. Notions that we now think of as "proportionality" had begun to take hold.

In 771 BCE rebellious lords, with access to the land and human resources that had long been allotted to aristocratic families[25] and the aid of frontier warriors, overthrew the last of the Western Zhou rulers, commencing what is known as the late Western Zhou Period, which was soon to be divided into the "Spring and Autumn" (c. 771–481 BCE) and Warring States (481–221 BCE) periods. For over five centuries China remained divided, with protracted warfare among competing city-kingdoms with increasingly bureaucratized, infantry-based, peasant armies. Rulers in the various states—all but three (Chu, Wu, and Yue)

---

22 *Id.*, pp. 156–157.

23 *See* Creel, *Origins*, p. 44 footnote 11, for discussion of *tian* as a Shang deity.

24 Hsu and Linduff, *Western Chou Civilization*, p. 106.

25 *See* Li Feng, *Landscape and Power in Early China* (Cambridge: Cambridge University Press, 2006), pp. 102–107.

centered in northern regions along the Wei and Yellow rivers—mobilized massive armies of tens of thousands to several hundred thousand men.[26]

The first major polities to emerge in the Huai and Yangzi valleys—the Central and South China Plains—occurred during the waning years of Zhou rule. Three deserve particular note. The first and ultimately the most enduring was Chu, believed to have been centered along the upper Han River in western Hubei and southwestern Henan.[27] Its major rival was the Wu polity in the east, which governed the Yangzi Delta with its capital at what is today the city of Suzhou. Both engaged almost constantly in battles for territorial control. For advanced weaponry, the rulers of Chu, like the Shang and Zhou, had access to rich copper and tin deposits in the western region of Hunan and, notably Tonglushan, which is believed to be early China's largest and most advanced copper mine, in southeastern Hubei. The Wu, however, were noted masters of metallurgy.

What is commonly referred to as the iron age commenced here. The earliest cast iron artifacts uncovered in China, dated to the early fifth century BCE, were in Wu. As explained by Donald Wagner,[28] lacking large and accessible copper deposits within the region under Wu control, a cheaper metal for weapons as well as agriculture was essential. Adapting methods for bronze casting learned from the north, the metallurgists of Wu were able to develop less esthetic but equally, if not more, useful white cast iron implements for farming and war. A third major polity, Yue, had formed even further south in the lower Yangzi with its capital near what is today the city of Shaoxing on the southern shore of Hangzhou Bay. Yue is also known for its possible superiority in terms of metallurgy and cast iron weaponry, especially swords. Defeated by Yue, a rival polity to the south, by the end of the fourth century BCE Wu had ceased to exist as an independent polity and Chu had successfully exerted control over its former domain itself to succumb to the might of the Qin. With large deposits of both coal and iron, by the beginning of the second millennium of the Common Era north China was producing over a hundred thousand tons of pig iron each year.[29]

---

26 Patricia Buckley Ebrey, Anne Walthall, and James B. Palais, *Pre-Modern East Asia: A Cultural, Social, and Political History* (Boston, MA: Houghton-Mifflin Company, 2006), pp. 28–30.

27 Barry B. Blakeley, "The Geography of Chu," in Constance Cook and John S. Major, eds., *Defining Chu: Image and Reality in Ancient China* (Honolulu: University of Hawai'i Press, 1999), p. 10.

28 Donald B. Wagner, "The Earliest Use of Iron in China," in Suzanne M.M. Young et al., eds., *Metals in Antiquity* (Oxford: Archaeopress, 1999), pp. 1–9.

29 Fairbank and Goldman, *China: A New History*, pt. 1, 4.

The age of gunpowder, "firepowder" (*huoyao*) in Chinese, also commenced in China. Produced by a mixture of saltpeter, sulphur, and charcoal, gunpowder was apparently used in primitive weaponry from the ninth century CE. By the mid-fourteenth century, through interaction of the West with Central Asia, its explosive potential had been perfected, with hollow shells packed with nitrate-enhanced gunpowder enabling explosive round shot. By the thirteenth century these early cannons and similar firearms were being produced in China. The first use in Europe may have been by the Mongol invaders in the 13th century. With nearly half a millennium of relative peace after the establishment of the Ming Dynasty in 1348 and the Qing in 1644, significant advances in the technology of weaponry in China appear to have ceased. Gunpowder became an ingredient of fireworks not "rifles."

Centralization and Bureaucracy

The Zhou millennium was, in the words of Zhao Dingxin, the age of China's "first wave of bureaucratization."[30] With nearly a millennium of relative political order and peace economic activity also expanded and gave rise to a commercial market economy. As the political system began to fragment and warfare recommenced, new advances appeared in iron weaponry, bronze and casting, coinage, transportation networks, and in agricultural production—all innovations related to the renewed demands of continuous warfare.[31] Intellectually this was also China's axial age,[32] the era of Confucius, Mozi, Mencius, Laozi, and the Legalists inspired by Han Feizi.

Building on preexisting beliefs and practices, these teachers and their followers constructed competing normative visions of proper governance and of law and its role. Their teachings constitute the intellectual foundations of the mainstream Chinese legal tradition and its legacy.

---

30 Zhao Dingxin, "Comment: Spurious Causation in a Historical Process: War and Bureaucratization in Early China," *American Sociological Review*, vol. 69 (2004), pp. 603, 604.

31 *See* Edgar Kiser and Yong Cai, "War and Bureaucratization in Qin China," *American Sociological Review*, vol. 68 (2003), pp. 511–539.

32 The idea of "Axial Civilizations" was introduced by Karl Jaspers. *See* Karl Jaspers, *Ursprung under Zeil der Geschichte* (Munich: Piper Verlag, 1949), cited in S.N. Eisenstadt, "The Axial Age Breakthroughs—Their Characteristics and Origins," in S.N. Eisenstadt, ed., *The Origins & Diversity of Axial Age Civilizations* (Albany, NY: State University of New York Press, 1986), p. 1 fn 1; on China, *see* chapters 13 (Cho-Yun Hsu), 14 (Mark Elwin), and 15 (Tu Wei-Ming), pp. 306–373.

Molded in the context of centralized Zhou rule, both the so-called Confucians and Legalists may have largely articulated prevailing views. Both dealt with the manner and means of governance with a shared acceptance of hierarchies of authority and status in a social order in which each had appropriate place and role. Both rejected any notion of the supernatural but instead embraced a normative hierarchy sourced in a timeless "natural" order that envelops mankind through which those who ruled were properly paternalistic in their concern for the general good. Both condemned self-regarding behavior, envisioning a ruling elite acting for the common good and the welfare of the whole. They differed, however, in their respective views of human nature and the manner and means of rule. The Confucians stressed cultivation of knowledge and habits of mind and ritual based on ancient customs and practices, including filial piety that would engender good governance and social order by example and moral suasion. Rule by an educated elite was manifestly preferable to rule by power or privilege. The Legalists countered with a more pessimistic emphasis on intrinsic human self-regard and the need for clearly defined proscriptive models (*fa*) and punishments (*lü*) to deter bad behavior. They tended to emphasize power and prosperity—"war and agriculture" in the oft-quoted phrase attributed to Shang Yang, whose legal and administrative reforms as the ranking official in Qin Dynasty presaged both the Legalists and the future centralized state. As a deterrent to disorder, good governance thus required well-publicized proscriptive rules of behavior with clearly defined punishments, applicable to all regardless of status (although with differentiated penalties), with group responsibility for their infraction. As described in greater detail below, penalties had to be proportionate to the offense. In Legalist proscription and subsequent Chinese practice can be found even the principles of "legality" prohibiting ex post facto application of criminal laws and requiring legislation for all crimes and penalties, as expressed in the Latin maxims *Nulla poena sine lege* and *nullum crimen sine lege*, for which we today give credit to Beccaria and von Feuerbach.[33]

The Law of Empire

In 221 BCE, Zhao Zheng (259–210 BCE), the king of the western frontier state of Qin, conquered the last of its rival kingdoms and created China's

[33] Jiang Yonglin, *The Mandate of Heaven and the Great Ming Code* (Seattle: University of Washington Press, 2011), p. 44.

first fully centralized political structure with a non-hereditary officialdom. He abandoned the title "king" (*wang*) and instead ruled as Shi Huangdi (literally, China's "first august lord") from his capital at Xianyang near Chang'an (today Xian in Shaanxi Province). Under Shi Huangdi's rule enormous public works projects, including the initial construction of the Great Wall, were initiated with massive conscriptions of manpower and resources. As the Qin armies moved east and then south, logistically aided by the canal they had constructed with conscript labor, the Qin gradually extended rule west to east from the Wei valley to the mouths of the Yellow and Yangzi rivers and north to south from the Gobi Desert to the China Sea. No previous ruler had exercised greater power over so much of what in the West would be known as China.

Confucianism was also ruthlessly repressed. Instead Shi Huangdi relied heavily on proscriptive legal controls as recommended by his Legalist advisors. Archeological finds show "conclusively," in A.F.P. Hulsewé's words, "that in the 3rd century before the Christian era the state of [Qin] possessed an extensive corpus of administrative and criminal law, which was handled by a complex hierarchy of officials"[34] who were now salaried[35] and thus dependent on monitoring officials and authorities at the center. The country was administratively divided into 36 new "commanderies," which were subdivided in turn into multiple counties. Each commandery had a military commander, a civil governor, and a monitoring civil inspector. The regime carried out a massive resettlement program, moving thousands of households to the capital and abolishing all privately held weapons. The process of standardizing Chinese ideographs, weights and measures, and currency was begun. The population was registered and organized into units of five or ten households with collective responsibility for the conduct of each member. Central state revenues were based on a land tax and compulsory labor requirements. State supervision of salt and iron production provided added revenues, but trade and commerce remained effectively untaxed. Some credit Shi Huangdi for instituting an examination system for qualification of civil officials, although it appears that, if this was so, it was never fully implemented, with most appointments made upon

---

[34] A.P.P. Hulsewé, "The Legalists and the Laws of Chin," in W.L. Idema, ed., *Leyden Studies in Sinology* (Leiden: E.J. Brill, 1981), p. 21. *See also* Robin D.S. Yates, "Social Status in the Ch'in: Evidence from the Yün-meng Legal Documents. Part One: Commoners," *Harvard Journal of Asiatic Studies*, vol. 47(1) (June 1987), pp. 219–231.

[35] Li Yu-Ning, *Shang Yang's Reforms and State Control in China* (White Plains, NY: M.E. Sharpe, 1977), p. 67.

recommendation by officials and restricted in any event to members of the ruling elites and the military. In any event, Qin rule ushered in China's "second wave" of bureaucratization that laid the basic foundations for centralized bureaucratic rule on which were erected all subsequent institutions of administration and law.[36]

Upon the death of Shi Huangdi in 210 BCE, Qin rule collapsed. It was shortly replaced by a new, more populist polity known simply as the Han after the river where the founder first gained power. The first Han emperor, Liu Pang, established his capital at Chang'an, near to X'ian. He similarly divided the empire into commanderies and governed through civil officials dispatched from the center. He rewarded his supporters but maintained existing "kingdoms" in most of the empire either with submissive rulers or with replacements selected among favored palace-connected "kings." He otherwise maintained the governing structures of the Qin, albeit with somewhat less ostensible reliance on punitive legal controls. Han rule is notable for a transformational emphasis on Confucian ideology.

While Liu Pang maintained the basic structure of the Qin bureaucracy, his successor, Han Wudi, is credited with having either expanded or, as many assert, introduced the system of examinations based on mastery of the Confucian classics for qualification for government office, candidates usually trained at an academy in the capital established for this purpose.[37] Candidates were generally limited to those recommended by officials in the commanderies. Civil officials were thereby selected from a pool of candidates recommended for direct appointment or for qualification to sit for the examination. Eventually this developed into the "protection" (*yin*) system allowing select officials to designate relatives for direct appointment, thereby by-passing the examinations altogether. In this manner under Han rule the warrior establishment and lineage-based elites were to dominate the central and local offices of governance. Officials were, however, prohibited from serving in their native regions. These officials collected taxes in kind or an equivalent in currency. They also supervised annual registration requirements. At least in the commanderies, the lowest unit of local administration was the district, usually comprising a cluster of several hamlets, whose officials were generally appointed by commandery or county officials. The commanderies also grew in number at the expense of the more autonomous kingdoms as rulers at the center

---

36 Zhao, "Comment," p. 606.

37 Grant Hardy and Anne Behnke Kinney, *The Establishment of the Han Empire and Imperial China* (Westport, CN: Greenwood Press, 2005), p. 124.

consolidated their control. In theory at least, officials trained and selected in the capital were dispatched to government offices throughout the realm to administer the commanderies and counties into which it was divided or to provide centrally appointed officials for oversight in the less autonomous kingdoms.

Militarily the Han emperors extended their rule to the edge of the Tarim Basin to the west and into northern Vietnam and Korea. To secure the frontiers even further they entered into tributary arrangements with bordering tribes and other polities, which in return for at least symbolic allegiance allowed them otherwise to maintain their autonomy. Thus like most subsequent dynasties, except notably the Southern Song, they were generally freed from the resource demands of unrelenting external military threat,[38] a factor that further eroded dependence on and the influence of warrior elites.

The four centuries of Han rule ended in 220 CE. Its collapse ushered in three centuries of fragmented rule with continuous warfare and societal disruption. By the beginning of the fourth century three regional polities had formed—the invading Tibetan Qiang and Di in the northwest, the Toba Turks (the northern Wei Dynasty) in the Yellow River basin in the north, and the Han-dominated southern Qi in the lower Yangzi River basin in the south. In 589 the Sui Dynasty reintroduced unified governance under a centralized officialdom once more selected primarily by means of competitive examinations. In some respects Sui rule appears to have been as coercive as its Qin predecessor, mobilizing labor to restore the Great Wall and to complete the Grand Canal. Yet in the rice-producing regions of the south where optimal production required high levels of intra-lineage local community cooperation, Sui rule was apparently more accommodating. Land was distributed to peasant households, especially incoming families from the north, with state revenues continuing to be based on the rice produced rather than state proprietorship and rents. The Sui warriors thus achieved their southern conquests, in the words of Denis Twitchett, with "the minimum of bloodshed and destruction … consolidated by liberal and imaginative policies which achieved the allegiance of the southern ruling class, and their incorporation into the bureaucracy, while the ordinary people were not saddled with excessive burdens, or brought fully under the northern land system."[39]

[38] *See* F.W. Mote, *Imperial China, 900–1800* (Cambridge, MA: Harvard University Press, 1999), p. 112.

[39] Denis Twitchett, "Introduction," in Denis Twitchett, ed., *The Cambridge History of China: Sui and T'ang China, 589–906*, vol. 3, pt. 1 (Cambridge and New York: Cambridge University Press, 1979), p. 6.

The regime was nonetheless sufficiently repressive to provoke effective opposition. Lasting less than four decades, it was even shorter-lived than the Qin, collapsing in 617 with assassination and insurrection.

In 618 Li Yuan (566–635), whose temple name was Gaozu (high ancestor), became the first Tang ruler. He restored order and ushered in one of the most consequential eras of Chinese history. He reestablished the capital at Chang'an, which at the height of the Tang would become the world's largest city with an estimated population of nearly a million inhabitants.[40] Buddhism, which had been introduced earlier from India, flourished with the invention of block printing, along with literature and art. The Tang rulers instituted a household registration system to be revised annually for tax collection and order. They redistributed land under the so-called equal-field system—notably effective mostly in the north and west—and reinstituted revised systems for conscription into military and labor service. Under the equal-field system, allocated lands were to revert to the rulers upon the death of the occupants but the system was soon revised to recognize what was in effect hereditary possession. At least in the north, as described by Valerie Hansen, the land tenure rules appear to have been followed, except for circumvention of the restrictions on alienation of land by means of disguised transfers.[41] The Tang rulers preserved the Confucian-based examination system for civil office, further fostering a supportive elite of Confucian literati. However, they introduced occupational restrictions as descendants of merchant and artisan families were excluded. Moreover, as under the Han, members of aristocratic families could receive appointment by recommendation without examination. Thus under Tang rule a rather small group of aristocratic, warrior, and civil official elites remained the locus of political authority and influence within the higher bureaucracy.

The most significant law-related achievement of the Tang era was promulgation of the *Tang-lü shu' yi*, generally referred to simply as the Tang Code. The code was revised under his successor, Li Shimin (598–649, temple name Taizong), and twice under his successor, Li Zhi (628–683, temple name Gaozong), his ninth son. The code was revised at least twice under Gaozong's reign. Its most celebrated version was promulgated in 653. As one of the world's first legal transplants in Japan, Korea, and Vietnam, it was China's most influential law-code.

---

40 For a comparison of urbanization in China with other early polities, *see* Tertius Chandler, *Four Thousand Years of Urban Growth: An Historical Census* (Lewiston, NY: The Edwin Mellen Press, 1987).

41 Valerie Hansen, *The Open Empire: A History of China to 1600* (New York and London: W.W. Norton Co., 2000), p. 216.

During the final decades of Tang rule, power at the center began to dissipate as the emperors increasingly became, in the words of Frederick Mote, the "pawns" of warrior rulers.[42] Invasion in 907, again from the north, ended Tang rule. In the following period of the Five Dynasties and Ten Kingdoms, China once more fragmented into a number of relatively small northern and southern polities, more often than not ruled by northern warlords. In the north, continuous attacks by Khitans and Turks resulted in a nearly constant state of war while the southern polities remained generally peaceful and prosperous. A new class of civil officials also began to emerge, particularly in the south, replacing those drawn from the military as well as elite clans and lineages.

Successfully reuniting much of the Tang Empire in 960, the first Song emperor, a professional soldier, Zhao Kuangyin (927–976), temple name Taizu, began a 16 year reign. Establishing his capital at Kaifeng on the southern bank of the Yellow River, Zhao then proceeded to consolidate central control through military engagements against the Khitans in the northwest, wresting control from the northern generals, and conquest of the southern kingdoms. To prevent effective challenge from future warlords, he recruited landless peasants for a salaried, professional army, commanded by officers whom he routinely and regularly transferred to new posts. Also to counter the influence of the warlords,[43] he began to reform the civil bureaucracy. He assigned officials to administer all of the provinces. They too were reassigned to new posts on a regular basis. With similar aims, Zhao and his early successors extended the practice of recommendation or "protection" (*yin*), granting designated officials the privilege of nominating relatives for appointment to civil office. Zhao, with centralizing goals in mind, initiated basic civil examination reforms with the decision to supervise personally the final stage of the process. His successors continued the process of reform, informed, in John Chaffee's words, by "the meritocratic principle of impartiality."[44] By the end of the Northern Song Dynasty (960–1127), the dominance of civil over military officials and the recruitment of civil officials on the basis of objective criteria of merit rather than lineage or patronage had progressed beyond any known previous historical example.

---

[42] Mote, *Imperial China*, p. 7.

[43] See Patricia Ebrey, "Review Article: The Dynamics of Elite Domination in Sung China," *Harvard Journal of Asiatic Studies*, vol. 48 (1988), pp. 493–519, at p. 502.

[44] John W. Chaffee, *The Thorny Gates of Learning in Sung China* (Cambridge: Cambridge University Press, 1985), p. 50.

Conquest of the center by indigenous claimants to the throne or outside (Mongol or Manchu) invaders secured rule over the entire domain. With the exception of Hangzhou from 1129 to 1276 under the Southern Song and Nanjing from 1368 to 1403 under the first Ming ruler, the capital has been in the north—in the northwest, Xian or Chang'an, and in the northeast or Central Plain, briefly Kaifeng under the Northern Song and Beijing from 1403 to the present. Yet by the end of the Han Dynasty China's population was migrating south, claiming unoccupied land in the hills and valleys to the south of the Yangzi plain. With this shift to the south, patterns of rule also changed. More and better warriors and weapons may have won wars, but with respect to rule rice mattered as much.

RICE

For centuries the north had been the source of authority and power. It was home to over half of the population at the end of the eighth century. "Whoever got control over it," in the words of John Fairbank and Merle Goldman, "could rather easily subjugate the other areas, including South China."[45] North China also witnessed the growth of aristocratic families with increasing control over land, especially in the eastern region of the North China Plain, and access to government office. Under the Qin and early Han dynasties, the central authorities had emphasized small farms with individual ownership, thereby establishing direct linkages between ruler and ruled; but by the late Han, war, floods, and the availability of land in the south produced a migration that had begun to shift the center and the culture.

In the north during the Period of the Wei-Jin and North and South dynasties (220–589 CE), large private estates with servile labor owned by a cluster of great families with ties to the court and officialdom became prevalent.[46] Between the eighth and thirteenth centuries a vast migration to the south occurred. By the end of the 13th century, 85 percent of the population was located in the south.[47] As many peasant farmers abandoned their holdings and moved south, the central authorities appropriated the land as state domains. Many of these estates were in turn transferred to an increasingly hereditary military class. In the south,

---

45 Fairbank and Goldman, *China: A New History*, Pt. 1, 4,

46 *See* Mark Edward Lewis, *China Between Empires: The Northern and Southern Dynasties* (Cambridge, MA: Harvard University Press, 2009), p. 31.

47 *Id.*, p. 7.

migrants from the west and north moved into even more productive regions in the south, particularly the eastern Yangzi delta and foothills further to the south, and they encountered and created communities with the shared habits of cooperative interaction and ordering necessary for optimal production of wet-paddy rice.[48] The migration of wealthy families also enabled land reclamation and the creation of new rice-producing communities with privately funded irrigation networks. Soon lineage and family ties mattered less than mutually dependent communities and regional networks.

Wet-paddy rice production, as indicated, requires intensive, year-round, coordinated effort to create, manage, and maintain complex systems of irrigation as well as to plant, cultivate, and harvest the end-product. Unlike the large, centralized irrigation systems of the north, the relative abundance of water made small irrigation efforts practicable. As Francesca Bray points out,[49] individual or cooperating cultivators and households could dig for themselves the necessary tanks and ponds to provide sufficient irrigation for their needs. Arguably at least, the patterns of agricultural production produced shared habits of interdependence and cooperation that significantly influenced prevailing modes of social organization in the region that are still evident today.[50] To the extent that rulers also sought to maximize the wealth they could extract, they were forced to maintain or create such productive communities and thus to yield in varying degrees to local autonomy. Recurrent patterns of regional subjection and accommodation thus emerge as regimes rose and fell to be replaced after periods of political disarray by new successors. In the west and north, the rulers were better able to mobilize the population, to conscript huge armies and forcibly relocate tens of thousands into new city-centers, and to impose direct control over land for its redistribution. In the rice-producing regions in the south and east, however, communities enjoyed greater autonomy with fewer or less onerous burdens for coerced labor. With new migrants lineage became less significant, as communities of "tenant" farmers became more common, but we need to

---

[48] *See* O'Connor, "Agricultural Change and Ethnic Succession in Southeast Asian States," pp. 968–996; Francesca Bray, *The Rice Economies: Technology and Development in Asian Societies* (Oxford: Basil Blackwell, 1986), pp. 170–182.

[49] Francesca Bray, *Agriculture* [Joseph Needham, *Science and Civilization in China*, volume 6, Biology and Biological Technology, Part II] (Cambridge: Cambridge University Press, 1984), pp. 109–110.

[50] Talhelm et al., "Large-Scale Psychological Differences Within China Explained by Rice Versus Wheat Agriculture," pp. 603–608.

keep in mind that "tenancy" did not necessarily mean subservience. A complex variety of customary and administratively recognized possessory interests in land, ranging from proprietorship to leaseholds and mortgages, tied the gentry "landholders" to the communities of peasant "tenants" whose cooperative endeavors for the common good were essential to the production of rice.

In 1127 the Song rulers lost their domain north of the Huai River to Jurchen conquerors from Manchuria, who established the Jin Dynasty (1115–1234). Thereupon the Song emperor relocated the capital to Hangzhou, the southern terminus of the Grand Canal on the coast at Hangzhou Bay, just to the southeast of the site of the Liangzhu archeological discoveries. The move ushered in the era known today as the Southern Song (1127–1279), an era that with a growth of production, commerce, and trade would produce consequential tensions for law and the modes of legal enforcement.

New rice strains introduced from Vietnam had already enabled increased production and agricultural wealth. By 1127 the population, now centered in the south, had grown dramatically, reaching, by some estimates, over 100 million.[51] The growth of the coastal as well as urban population was particularly impressive.[52] Notwithstanding rapid urbanization, the population under the Southern Song remained predominantly rural. Those living in villages and hamlets of a thousand persons or less still outnumbered the total number of residents in prefectural and district capitals.

In terms of administration, the Southern Song rulers abrogated all occupational qualifications for civil officials, opening the examination system to all males. Under the Tang system, there was only one examination. The Song rulers introduced a two-tiered system with a qualifying examination at the prefectural level. Those who passed were entitled to take the "palace" examination at the capital. Even if they failed (or did not take) this examination, those who succeeded at the prefectural level gained status if not office as "degree" holders. Although the extent to which this and other examination reforms promoted social mobility remains a keenly debated issue among scholars,[53] from that time

---

[51] Mote, *Imperial China*, p. 164; John D. Durand, "The Population Statistics of China, A.D. 2–1953," *Population Studies*, 13 (1960), Figure 3.

[52] Sufumi So and Billy K.L. So, "Population Growth and Maritime Prosperity: The Case of Ch'uan-Chou in Comparative Perspective, 946–1368," *Journal of the Economic and Social History of the Orient*, vol. 45 (2002), pp. 96–127.

[53] Ebrey, "Review Article." Chaffee calculates that in 1213, 39.3 percent of all civil officials held their position as a result of imperial "protection" under the

until the first decade of the twentieth century all males at least had the opportunity for access to the highest levels of governing authority. Civil officials were increasingly selected from a pool of persons qualified for service by proven mastery of a corpus of literature on the ideological (Neo-Confucian) foundations of governance, a feat not paralleled by any other ancient civilization nor fully achieved by the vast majority of contemporary states, notably including the United States.[54] Officials were assigned centrally to serve for fixed three year terms throughout the realm at the prefectural (*zhou*) and district (*xian*) levels.

Access to official positions of local authority and influence also expanded under the Southern Song. At the local level the central authorities appointed prominent persons as officials for tax collection, leadership of militia units, and other law-enforcing duties. The system of drawing upon members of local communities to fill village-level posts for clerical and other governmental functions had its origins in the Qin-Han Period, but by the late Tang the status of such local posts was low. By the Five Dynasties Period, in the words of Brian McKnight, "[a]ppointment to this subbureaucratic and village stratum of government became in most cases a feared imposition, borne either by professional workers of low social standing or by those members of the general population who could not find any way to evade service."[55] Under the Southern Song as authorities at higher levels began to appoint the wealthiest and most influential heads of households to fill these offices, they became instead sources of prestige and local influence. One result was to give the most well-to-do households of local communities below the prefectural and district levels at least potential access to offices at both the highest levels of the government through the examination system and in their particular communities. Responsible for registration, tax collection, and various forms of community welfare, these village officials could mediate—legally or extra-legally—between the demands of the rulers and the interests of the local communities they both represented and ruled. The wealthiest households thereby became both more autonomous and more

---

yin system as compared with 27.4 percent of examination degree holders. Chaffee, *The Thorny Gates of Learning in Sung China*, p. 25.

54 Castile was medieval Europe's closest equivalent. As noted in Chapter 6, by the end of the fourteenth century all officials in Castile had to be *letrados*—i.e., to have a university degree (overwhelmingly in civil or canon law, or both). However, appointments to official posts continued to be based on patronage not examination.

55 Brian E. McKnight, *Village and Bureaucracy in Southern Sung China* (Chicago: University of Chicago Press, 1971), p. 13.

fully integrated into the system of governance and law enforcement. In the process they acquired a vested interest in its continuation.

Local Control and Private Ordering

The changes under the Southern Song were not completely novel. In the south successive rulers had increasingly relied on prominent local households for prescribed extractions of the rice and labor, which in turn enabled at least leading households to achieve greater voice in local governance. The first northern governors of the south, the Zhou rulers, had introduced new systems of payment-in-kind taxes for peasant wet-paddy rice cultivators, whose productive capacity increased as they were given greater capacity for more autonomous community and familial cooperation as peasant landholders free from direct oversight and control.[56] As the first major polity centered in the south, the Chu rulers appear to have modified the governing structures borrowed from the Zhou in that they had less authority over kinsmen and did not control large landed estates. Perhaps as a consequence Chu rule also tended to be highly concentrated. Barry B. Blakeley notes these as three distinctive features of Chu governance.[57] Such centralization and, except in the north, lack of ruler-dominated landed estates were to become distinctive features of Chinese rule, allowing future conquests of the center that enabled political dominion without the necessity of direct local governance.

Equally significant, however, was what Robert Hymes calls a "transformation" between the Northern and Southern Song dynasties as a process of "local retrenchment" ensued with elites—especially new migrants—increasingly seeking to establish fixed residences within a specific community, consolidating their home bases, and then through marriage and other means expanding their networks of local contacts.[58] In the process an enduring pattern of familial and clan influence emerged. Local families whose land, wealth, and offices enhanced their elite status began increasingly to turn away from more exclusive pursuit

---

[56] Derek Bodde, "The State and Empire of Ch'in," in Denis Twitchett and Michael Loewe, eds., *The Ch'in and Han Empires, The Cambridge History of China*, vol. 1. (Cambridge: Cambridge University Press, 1986), pp. 27–28.

[57] Barry B. Blakeley, "Chu Society and State; Image versus Reality," in Cook and Major, eds., *Defining Chu: Image and Reality in Ancient China*, p. 55.

[58] Robert P. Hymes, *Statesmen and Gentlemen: The Elite of Fu-Chou, Chiang-His, in Northern and Southern Sung* (Cambridge and New York: Cambridge University Press, 1986), pp. 81, 123, 211.

of offices and entering national networks through marriage. Instead, they began to pursue more localized "strategies" to use Hymes's term,[59] by consolidating their local connectedness through marriage with other local elites. In Song China, we find the origins of what could be dubbed a "three son" approach. One son remains on the land in the local community. Another, presumably perceived to be the most intellectually gifted, is supported in his study for the examinations. The third is dispatched to pursue a career in commerce and trade. Through intra-community marriage the number of uncles, nephews, cousins with established ties and shared habits of mutual cooperation with other members of the community expands. With commerce, as Robert Putnam persuasively argues was the case in northern Italy,[60] such ties of interdependency and cooperation further expand. As Putnam also pointedly notes: "Voluntary cooperation is easier in a community that has already inherited a substantial stock of social capital."[61] We need not wonder why commerce expanded at such a significant pace in the rice-producing areas of southern China. Under Ming rule, evidenced by the proliferation of guilds in trading centers throughout the country based on the shared regional origins of their members rather than their common trade,[62] local network-based commerce expanded throughout China. Commerce in southern China then as now functioned within a customary private order outside of law's domain that was and continues to be held together by networks of regional connections and ties of kinship.[63]

The "three son" approach in Song China had, I believe, another equally profound consequence. With access through the official examinations to political participation and status, the landed gentry of southern China also acquired a notable stake in existing albeit localizing structures of governance. The status quo served them well. We can easily understand their continuing support for whatever regime was in authority—Mongol (Yuan), Han (Ming), or Manchu (Qing). They had everything to lose and

59 *Id.*, at 123.

60 Robert D. Putnam, *Making Democracy Work: Civic Traditions in Modern Italy* (Princeton, NJ: Princeton University Press, 1993).

61 *Id.*, at 367.

62 Christine Moll-Murata, "Chinese Guilds from the Seventeenth to the Twentieth Centuries: An Overview," *International Review of Social History*, vol. 53(16) (2008), pp. 213–247; *see also* Hamilton, *Commerce and Capitalism in Chinese Societies*.

63 For extensive descriptions, see Hamilton, *Commerce and Capitalism*, as well as the essays and references in Gary G. Hamilton, ed., *Business Networks and Economic Development in East and Southeast Asia* (Hong Kong: Centre for Asian Studies, University of Hong Kong, 1991).

little to gain with any radical change other than the steady progression toward greater local control. By the early Qing Period, as described by Paul Smith and others, their assumption of local managerial roles in a variety of governmental functions from tax farming to irrigation had become an "integral" feature of local government. No doubt the process "tended to transform the empire's administrative machinery"[64] without, however, dismantling the fundamental structures of China's public law system.

The Continuity of Chinese Rule

Seeking access to the wealth of the Silk Road and in response to demands for tribute, the Mongol leader, Cinggis Qan (1206–1229), began a decade-long military campaign against the Jurchen rulers in north China. In 1215 Beijing was taken and its inhabitants massacred. By 1234 all Jurchen resistance had ended. The Mongols, having conquered the north, turned south. In 1279 under Qubilai Qan (1215–1294), Cinggis Qan's grandson, they finally overwhelmed the Southern Song rulers and proceeded to form the Yuan Dynasty (1276–1368) as a pivotal, wealth-producing component in what is generally conceded to have been territorially the largest empire in history.

The Mongol Empire at its height extended east to west from the Sea of Japan to Poland and north to south from Moscow to Vietnam. A separate administrative division within this greater Mongol Empire, the Yuan state comprised contemporary Mongolia, China, and Tibet, as well as parts of what would become the Russian Far East. The Korean peninsula under Koryo rule was treated as a tributary kingdom. Within China the new Mongol rulers maintained the basic structures of administration and law. They essentially adapted existing Chinese institutions to serve their interests. They reorganized the administrative and military functions of the central government into three primary offices: a secretariat (*zhongshu sheng*) to which the six ministries for personnel, revenue, rites, war, justice, and public works reported; a censorate (*yushi tai*) that exercised disciplinary oversight over all civil officials; and the chief military commission (*dudu fu*) with command over the armies. They maintained

[64] Paul J. Smith, "State Power and Economic Activism during the New Policies, 1068–1085: The Tea and Horse Trade and the 'Green Sprouts' Loan Policy," in R.P. Hymes and C. Schirolauer, eds., *Ordering the World: Approaches to State and Society in Sung Dynasty China* (Berkeley, Los Angeles, and London: University of California Press, 1993), pp. 125–126, and sources cited in footnote 107.

the examination system although they ensured greater access to official positions by their tribesmen by establishing quotas and revising the examinations to ease their rigor and to allow the Mongolian script to be used. They also found it expedient to continue the Southern Song patterns of local governance under supervision by Mongol-appointed officials (*darughachi*). Yuan rule overall is described as personal, fragmented, and remarkably lax.[65] One consequence was to ensure continuity of local support for the regime under their control and thereby the infrastructure of governance. For our purposes the principal significance of Yuan rule was its continuation of the fundamental structures and institutions of governance that had developed in the north and become ingrained in the Chinese public law order along with modifications and adaptations that had become necessary for effective rule in the rice-producing areas of the south.

Having successfully led a revolt against the Mongol rulers of the Yuan Dynasty, in 1368 a peasant from the southern heartland, Zhu Yuanzhang (1328–1398), proclaimed himself founder of a new Ming Dynasty. Adopting the reign name Hongwu ("Vast Martiality"), he established his capital at Jinling, renamed Yingtian (Nanjing today), the site of his first major military victory, where it remained until moved in 1421 to Beijing in the north under the rule of Hongwu's fourth son and third Ming emperor. Once in authority and with power, Hongwu proceeded with a series of reforms designed to ensure centralized control. At the center, the three offices established under the Mongols were each reformed in an exemplary pattern of division and duplication of functions not only to establish direct supervisory control by the emperor but also to preclude any threatening concentration of authority in a cadre of civil officials or military commanders. The secretariat was abolished, leaving each of the six ministries under its supervision directly accountable to the emperor. The censorate, also initially dissolved, was later replaced by investigating censors who reported directly to the emperor. The central military command was divided into five separate but co-equal agencies, also directly accountable to the emperor. Zhu, whose temple name was Supreme Ancestor (Taizu), instituted hereditary occupational groups, beginning with the military and subsequently extended to the peasantry, artisans, physicians, Confucians, and diviners. One result was to recreate a professional military class subject to command. By the end of the

65 "Introduction", in Herbert Franke and Denis Twitchett, *The Cambridge History of China*, vol. 6, *Alien Regimes and Border States* (Cambridge and New York: Cambridge University Press, 1994), p. 30.

fourteenth century, the Ming emperor would thus directly control an army estimated to have numbered 1,200,000 professional soldiers, six times the size of the Spanish army—the largest in Europe—at the end of the sixteenth century. They were largely assigned to military colonies along the border regions in the north and other peripheral regions of the empire, where allotted cereal-producing land, they would hopefully be relatively self-sufficient but isolated.

Hongwu and his successors are also credited for having fully perfected the Chinese system for recruitment and selection of civil officials. A merit-based civil bureaucracy trained in the moral (Confucian) philosophy of governance became a hallmark of Ming rule. Although the *yin* system of recommendation of officials was continued along with the possibility of direct access to the civil bureaucracy allowed graduates of the national university (*guozi xue*) and the Directorate of Education (*guozi jian*) in the capital, the primary path of entry was the examination route, culminating in the examination under the emperor's personal supervision.

Law making was another Ming hallmark. Unlike his Song and Yuan predecessors, early in his reign Hongwu abrogated the Tang Code and by 1367 had promulgated his own Great Ming Code (*Da Ming Lü*). Although the basic provisions did not differ significantly, the Ming Code reflected an intended break with the past under a new order. The Code under Hongwu's reign was subsequently both revised and supplemented by added regulations (*ling*) as well as pronouncements (*gao*). Only the Tang Code surpassed the influence of the Ming Code and its supplementary rules and regulations in East Asia.[66]

Provincial and district administration was also reorganized with a similar pattern of division and duplication, but the basic structures of local administration remained intact. Based predominantly on Song and Yuan administrative patterns, local communities were reorganized into "hundreds-and-tithings" (*iijia*) with the heads of the most prominent wealthy households deputized as "elders" delegated responsibility for collecting taxes, maintaining order, and enforcing the law. Notably introduced first in the Yangzi valley rice-producing region in 1371, in ideal form a "tithing" or *jia* comprised 11 neighboring households. Each *jia* was headed by a person selected from among the heads of the wealthiest households who served for a ten year term. Eleven "tithings"

[66] *See*, e.g., Dan F. Henderson, "Chinese Influences on Eighteenth Century Tokugawa Codes," in Cohen, Edwards, and Chen, eds., *Essays on China's Legal Tradition*, pp. 270–301.

with a common territory in turn constituted a "hundred" (*li*). Within each *li*, the heads of the ten wealthiest households—presumably one of the wealthiest households of each *jia*—served as captains for the *li*, again on a rotational basis each for a ten year term. Superimposed over them were district "tax captains" (*liangzhang*).[67] The *jia* heads, the *li* captains, and in turn the tax captains were responsible for collecting the individual taxes and enforcing service levies.

Hongwu, like his predecessors, implemented two basic forms of taxation. The overwhelmingly largest source of revenue was a land tax payable in grain—wheat in the summer, rice in autumn—based on uniform rates applied to the predetermined amount of productive land in the territory as measured in *mu* or parcels of roughly 6100 square meters —the fiscal *mu* as well as livestock and other indicia of wealth held by each registered household. The second was a service levy (*i*) to provide the continuous labor necessary for a wide variety of services and the manufacture of materials in addition to ad hoc levies for particular projects based on the size of households. Both the grain tax rate and labor service requirements were allocated based on household size and wealth. All households were registered in three categories based on wealth in what were called the "yellow" registers (*huangce*), with tax rates and service requirements assessed according to wealth. From time to time the government also imposed additional, special ad hoc levies for labor, grain, as well as specialty items and luxury goods. The heads of the *jia* and *li* were responsible to ensure that each *jia* fulfilled its allotted service quota as well as special levies but were themselves along with their household members exempted from routine labor service. They were, however, as households individually liable for the grain and special levies owed by the communities they headed.

The system never worked as planned. Regional and local variations in the productivity of land forced modification of the legal definition of *mu* for fiscal purposes. Population movements and generational changes further complicated the system. Landholding became more dispersed as wealthier households acquired parcels in multiple *li*. With the rise of commerce and cash crops, many wealthier households moved into urban areas, leasing their village land. Immigration into the productive areas of

---

67 Described in detail in Ray Huang, "The Ming Fiscal Administration" and Martin Heijdra, "The Socio-economic Development of Rural China during the Ming," in Twitchett and Loewe, eds., *The Cambridge History of China*, vol. 8, pp. 106–171, 417–576. *See also* Timothy Brook, *The Confusions of Pleasure: Commerce and Culture in Ming China* (Berkeley, Los Angeles, and London: University of California Press, 1998), pp. 22–24.

the south also produced a significant number of landless peasants who along with tenants were not registered. Tax exemptions for degree holders created additional strains as their numbers too increased. Natural demographic changes also contributed. Distinctions had to be made between defunct registered households and unregistered ones that could actually pay the required taxes and satisfy the service requirements. Once again patterns differed region by region, county by county, and especially between north and south. Less formal accommodations, ranging from outright corruption to tacit evasion, produced even greater local variation in compliance. As the burdens on wealthy households, especially those responsible for ensuring community compliance, increased, resort to various means of evasion became more prevalent. Although trade was also taxed and the government had a monopoly over salt, neither proved to be a sufficient source of revenue, especially in light of growing military demands to counter both piracy in coastal regions of the south and the on-going threats in the northern border regions.

In the sixteenth century a number of major reforms were undertaken. In 1580 the government undertook the most extensive and detailed, country-wide cadastral survey of all agricultural land and its productivity undertaken at any time in China and the first since the Song era. A more gradual series of experiments and reforms were also implemented at the provincial and district levels. Among the most significant, allotted service levies were combined with the land tax into a single tax payment based on acreage albeit under standards that differed by locale. Known as the Single Whip Reform (*yitiao bianfa*), the new, amalgamated tax became payable in silver. Other labor and material service levies were also converted into silver payments, the last of which (on deliveries of cloth and refined rice in the north) were collected in 1640.[68] Attempts were made to eliminate or reduce the service exemption for degree holders. Finally, the *iijia* system of local collection was gradually abandoned in favor of direct official tax collection. The *jia* were also redrawn based on land rather than households. Each change was consequential in reallocating tax burdens among the populace, relieving some households of extremely onerous burdens while imposing new taxes on others. Again manifest differences in conditions between the north and south created additional tensions and forced further regional adjustments. In comparison with the south, the north had more compact villages, fewer absentee landlords, more exempt large households, less commercial activity, and

---

68 Heijdra, "The Socio-economic Development of Rural China during the Ming," p. 574.

less silver. Partially because of the inadequacies of the reforms themselves as well as the tensions they produced both south and north, the Ming emperors could not mount an effective defense against the Manchu invaders. Ming rule thus ended in 1644 with conquest and the inauguration of the Qing rule (1644–1911). Yet, the fiscal system of the late Ming era was retained by the Qing and, as reformed but more rigorously enforced, it remained largely in place until the end of the era in 1911.[69]

The policies that Hongwu promoted were designed to create more self-sufficient rural communities under a beneficent and frugal ruling regime. Their effect, however, was to foster interregional trade and even greater commercial growth and economic interdependency. In the words of Timothy Brook, "Hongwu's restoration of agricultural production in the first instance propelled the economy toward production of a surplus that had to be traded."[70] The combination of low tax rates and reliance on the wealthiest local households, primarily in the south, for enforcement ensured the incapacity of the Ming rulers to extract surplus production. Surplus grain had become a commercial commodity that was bartered and increasingly sold for silver to satisfy consumption as well as taxation needs. In the process, cash crops, especially cotton and silk, the production of which the regime had encouraged, also became more prevalent, further expanding commercial activity. An extensive transportation network centered on the Grand Canal was necessary to move the tax grain north to the capital for storage as well as distribution to military garrisons along the border. This network created additional opportunities for commercial activity and the creation of untaxed wealth. Connected to the extensive Yangzi river system in the south, it enabled interregional commercial expansion. Freedom of movement allowed merchants provided further impetus to commercial activity as well as incentive for extended households and lineage groups to encourage their most entrepreneurial members to engage in trade while supporting their most academically able to vie for official status. The growth of guilds (*huiguan*) based on common regional ties (*tongxiang*) rather than a common trade as in medieval Europe from the Ming through the late Qing eras[71] (mid sixteenth through early twentieth centuries) provides

---

[69] *See*, e.g., E.T. Williams, "Taxation in China," *Quarterly Journal of Economics*, vol. 26 (1912), pp. 482–510.

[70] Timothy Brook, "Communication and Commerce," in Twitchett and Loewe, eds., *The Cambridge History of China*, vol. 8, p. 580.

[71] Moll-Murata, "Chinese Guilds."

impressive evidence of the reliance in commercial dealings on familial- and community-based networks stemming from the rice-producing regions of the south.

Internationally Hongwu and his early successors initiated expansive military and commercial policies. Overland they recaptured the Vietnamese city of Annam. Overseas they sponsored a series of naval expeditions that subjected most of the maritime polities of Southeast Asia to tributary status and, commercially, ventured across the Indian Ocean as far as the east coast of Africa. In 1433, however, all naval expeditions were ordered to cease with suddenness that still surprises and intrigues contemporary scholars.

In brief, by the middle of the seventeenth century, the evolving political institutions of China had solidified into a system that fostered the creation and accumulation of private wealth within and dependent upon the structures of an advanced public law order.

Chinese Law and the Legalist Tradition

From the inception of unitary centralized authority in the third century BCE, Chinese law remained almost immutable in fundamental form and substance. Grounded in principles first introduced by the Legalists, all extant examples of legal codes, supplementary statutes, decrees, and edicts share common positivist features and functions. As described above, the Legalists articulated the basic principles that defined the nature of legal rules and their instrumentalist aims in terms that presaged by two millennia the arguments of European Enlightenment reformers from Beccaria to Bentham and the ideological core of contemporary European criminal law.

All legal rules, they asserted, emanate from the emperor (the state). They are designed to serve and reflect state interests—in other words, the interests of those who govern—which include the common good and welfare of the people. They operate through enforcement as a system of incentives and disincentives as well as "teachings" and models. Legal rules thus have a didactic function. They should therefore be sufficiently intelligible and certain not only to enable those responsible for their implementation and enforcement to apply them with predictable uniformity but also widely disseminated to foster respect and voluntary compliance. In addition, by their terms, they should be equally and impartially enforced either by the threat or application of penal sanctions within an administrative structure of officials equally bound by the law. Sanctions were to be proportionate to the applicable infraction—as phrased by the Confucian philosopher and early Legalist, Xun Zi (or

Hsün Tzu)—c. 312–230 BCE—"*xing dang zui ze wei, bu dang zui ze wu*" ("Let the punishment fit the crime").[72] Finally, the ultimate aim of law was to maintain and foster order and prosperity for the common welfare of the empire.

At no moment in Chinese history did the idea of natural law emerge. As an instrument of control, legal rules could and did proscribe conduct deemed by the law makers to be contrary to shared views of moral or righteous conduct. The Legalists had early emphasized that rulers were not above the law.[73] Although legislated rules reflected the norms of various ethical or social philosophies, especially those influenced by China's familial orientations and Confucian beliefs, the idea of law itself remained purely positivist without any claim to deistic origin. As Geoffrey MacCormack has eloquently argued, Confucian values so thoroughly infused traditional Chinese law that they defined its "spirit" and normative emphasis.[74] Qiang Fang and Roger Des Forges thus make a telling argument that notions of "nature" coupled with the influence of various belief systems in addition to Confucianism (Ruism), including Daoism and Buddhism, helped to create a shared understanding that the laws should reflect and further normative goals and that they should apply to ruler and ruled alike.[75] The longevity of the basic patterns and content of the dynastic codes from the Tang through the Qing add support for their view. No one can reasonably question the notion that China adhered to Rule by Law. Whether China can be said to have had a "Rule of Law" tradition, as they posit, is more problematic. The phrase "Rule of Law" itself has become more of a rhetorical catchphrase than a term with analytical value. Nor should Chinese notions of the relationship between law and nature be confused with Western notions of natural law.

The "natural" order that comprised Confucian and other moral norms was entirely separate from the positivist world of law. Even the traditional Chinese notion of "justice" (*yi*)—better understood as "righteousness"—had no legal dimension. Neither of the two characters in the compound (*zhengyi*) that today is used in Chinese (as well as

---

72 *See* John Knoblock, *Xunzi: A Translation and Study of His Complete Works* (Stanford, CA: Stanford University Press, 1988), p. 166.

73 Qiang Fang and Roger Des Forges, "Were Chinese Rulers above the Law? Toward a Theory of the Rule of Law in China from Early Times to 1949 CE," *Stanford Journal of International Law*, vol. 44 (2008), pp. 101–146.

74 Geoffrey MacCormack, *The Spirit of Traditional Chinese Law* (Athens, GA: University of Georgia Press, 1996).

75 Fang and Des Forges, "Were Chinese Rulers above the Law?"

Japanese and Korean) to translate the Latin "*iustitia*" and its equivalent in all Western European languages—all of which in their original meanings bond morality and law—bear any original relationship to law whatsoever. In lieu of a nexus between morality and law out of which conception of "justice" could emerge, the notions of "righteousness" (*yi*) and ethically or morally proper behavior were completely separate from law (*fa*) or legally correct or proper behavior. As Joseph Needham explains: "The harmonious cooperation of all beings arose, not from the order of a superior authority external to themselves, but from the fact that they were all parts in a hierarchy of wholes forming a cosmic pattern, what they obeyed were the internal dictates of their own natures."[76]

The domains of morality and law in China were completely separate. A son who killed to avenge his father's murderers, for example, could without contradiction be both honored as a filial son and concomitantly executed for committing homicide. The rulers' subjects may have had a moral obligation to obey legal rules as their commands arising from their duty of loyalty and obedience. However, they had no moral duty to obey law for its own sake. Law's legitimacy was entirely derivative.

Similarly, lacking a conception of natural law, the Chinese had no notion of morally binding but unlegislated legal rules that constrained either the authority or the power of the emperor. Absent was any conception of an order of binding legal rules or standards not promulgated by those with legislative authority. Those who made the law and issued the edicts were legally bound only by those legal rules that were self-chosen as binding. The idea of justiciable claims against the state could not germinate from belief in the Mandate of Heaven or nature (*tianming*) and in obligations to ancestors. This is not to say, however, that the Chinese emperors were "above the law" inasmuch as they and their predecessors could and did establish legal rules with which they and their successors were committed at least in theory to comply. The natural moral, rather than legal, order of Chinese political ideology governed sovereign as well as subject. Enveloped like their subjects within a system of beliefs that proclaimed a duty of loyalty and respect to ancestors, the Chinese emperors were equally bound both morally and politically to adhere to the applicable promulgated or precedential legal rules established by their predecessors. To the extent that such values were actually internalized by those with political authority, they offered alternative constraints against arbitrary exercises of political power. Built

---

[76] Joseph Needham, *Science and Civilization in China*, vol. II (Cambridge and New York: Cambridge University Press, 1985), p. 582.

thereby into the fabric of the Chinese legal tradition were consequential legal as well as political and social constraints on otherwise unrestricted legal authority and the exercise of power. "From Qin-Han times on," as expressed by Qiang Fang and Roger Des Forges, "Chinese rulers were expected to govern in accordance with customs and models inherited from ancestors, with laws and institutions established in cooperation with officials, and with various Ways produced over time by the interaction of heaven, earth, and humans (i.e., the cosmic process)."[77] Who, however, was to enforce such constraints? Ultimately they were self-imposed and thus depended upon political considerations and self-constraint.

However contestable the claim for the "rule of law" might be, the historical record overwhelms any argument against "rule by law" in China. As an instrument of state control, the idea of law that developed within the Legalist tradition has much in common with the prevailing features of any contemporary administrative state. This is not surprising. With remarkable consistency from the fragmentary evidence of the first known codes and statutes from the Qin and Han dynasties through the great Tang, Ming, and Qing codes, as previously described, Chinese law represented a detailed set of administrative and penal proscriptions with precisely calculated proportionate punishments. Included was a highly rational procedural system with heavy emphasis on confession, albeit coerced if necessary.[78] Confession was considered to be a necessary first step toward rehabilitation and it had the added value of giving the defendant a tool to use against arbitrary state decisions even up to the moment of death by execution. Failure of officials to respect due process was grounds for refusing to confess and might even result in acquittal.

Without claim to transcendent deistic source or divine intervention, the Chinese legal process reflected high regard for rationality and developed into a sophisticated system of fact finding, legal interpretation, documentary proof, and appeals. Review and approval of individual cases by the emperor was common and even necessary as early as the Song Dynasty

---

[77] Fang and Des Forges, "Were Chinese Rulers above the Law?" pp. 145–146.

[78] The system stressed confession and set out complex rules for the degrees of torture permitted for its extraction, if necessary, from both witnesses and the accused. The use of torture was assumed to be legitimate, however, only as a last resort; otherwise it was a sign of administrative incompetence if not tyranny. *See* Alison W. Conner, "True Confessions? Chinese Confessions Then and Now," in Karen G. Turner, James V. Feinerman, and R. Kent Guy, eds., *The Limits of the Rule of Law in China* (Seattle: University of Washington Press, 2000), pp. 132–162.

for infliction of capital punishment. By the second century CE under the early Han, the process for interpreting the law to determine and authorize the application of the prescribed penalty had begun to be separated from the trial process, which developed into a solely fact-finding hearing.[79] By the end of the twelfth century under the Song, it had become routine in cases involving significant offenses for the officials who presided over trials at the local level to send to supervising law-specialists at the prefectural level the written record of their findings for review and authorization for both retrial and sentencing. The record would also be reviewed by assisting legal specialists at the local and prefectural levels. Their function was partially clerical in identifying applicable legal rules but also determinative in their recommendations as to the appropriate penalty. The documentary records of trials and review for serious offenses was subject to further review by officials in the capital. As noted, death penalty cases also required personal review and sanction by the emperor. Moreover, retrials were virtually automatic if the accused recanted a confession or if the family filed a complaint charging official misconduct. In addition, a system of intendant inspectors was charged with oversight of officials to ensure their compliance with the law as well as the potential for collective sanctions for serious infractions. These review procedures continued to be followed through the late Qing. As described by Robert Hegel:

> [T]he judicial system was designed to alleviate the inevitably disastrous effect on an accused person of a prejudiced or insufficiently observant judge or of a false confession given under duress. Because "district magistrates" (*zhixian*) were responsible for determining both guilt and appropriate punishments, these administrators had to justify their procedures, as well as their verdicts in capital cases, to a series of judicial reviewers stretching upward through the bureaucracy of the "prefecture" (*fu*), the "province" (*sheng*), central authorities in Beijing, and ultimately to the emperor himself.[80]

In terms of organization and coverage, the codes also bear a surprising similarity to most European criminal and administrative codes of the nineteenth and early twentieth centuries. All the three known codes—the Tang, Ming, and Qing—are divided into two basic parts. The first covers the general principles of the law. The second includes the most important

---

[79] *See* Hsu Dau-Lin, "Separation between Fact-Finding (Trial) and Law-Finding (Sentencing) in Sung Criminal Proceedings," *Sung Studies Newsletter*, vol. 6 (1972), pp. 3–18.

[80] Robert Hegel, *True Crimes in Eighteenth-Century China: Twenty Case Histories* (Seattle: University of Washington Press, 2009), pp. 9–10.

administrative regulations and provisions for special or more specific offenses. Each offense and the applicable punishment of its infraction are set out with detailed precision. As in most if not all contemporary criminal codes, crimes against the state, such as rebellion, treason, and sedition, are among the most serious and incur the maximum penalties. These are included in part one as three of the Ten Abominations. Among the other "abominations" were crimes against property, such as theft or forgery, as well as murder of lineal ascendants. The codes continue, with variation, with rules governing the imperial household and general administrative regulations, including revenues and military affairs. They conclude with detailed provisions on specific penal offenses and procedures for trials and appeals.

At no time, however, did the Chinese conceive or express a conceptually coherent set of private law rules. While not devoid of rules related to property, contracts, commercial transactions, and familial relations, the Chinese codes, supplementary statutes, edicts, and regulations covered these matters in terms of prescriptive administrative rules as well as penal provisions only to the extent necessary to maintain order and to promote state interests. Law throughout Chinese history remained no more or less than an instrument of governance by administrative processes and enforced by means of penal proscription and punishment. Totally alien was any notion of a comprehensive corpus of legal principles, rules, and categories governing private relationships recognized and enforced within a remedial system of rights and duties or formal adjudicatory processes subject to the initiative and control of litigants. In all legal proceedings the magistrate remained in full control. As succinctly described by William Alford:

> To a far greater extent than even the most inquisitorial of civil law systems, the magistrate—who was, after all, the local representative of the Emperor—was the dominant figure in any trial. In order to discharge his responsibility to ascertain the truth, he was authorized to ask any questions he wished, personally view the scene of the crime, assign staff to investigate and to produce all evidence and witnesses, apply torture (long after it was abandoned as a practice in Europe), and admonish the accused.[81]

Unless a matter was of state concern and therefore subject to official regulation, no mandatory law existed. Other matters were private concerns left to private ordering. Property interests, including proprietorship,

[81] William P. Alford, "On the Limits of 'Grand Theory' in Comparative Law," *Washington Law Review*, vol. 61 (1986), p. 952.

possession, and use were recognized within the administrative system as they are in most legal systems today through registration or recording. What might be considered to be "rights" of contract were thus, as even Philip Huang's study demonstrates, more the creation of custom and practice, recognized at best as "duties" in the interstices of administrative and penal regulation.[82] Their enforcement was left almost fully to extralegal remedies and sanctions applied by community, guild, or family. An ideological emphasis on social harmony, ordered relationships, and observance of ritual, subsumed under the mantle of Confucian ideology, was equally antithetical to the development of private law ordering. Proper behavior and social order were to be maintained more by education and example than by legal rules. All individuals were to act deferentially to superiors and benevolently to inferiors and so as not to disturb a "natural" social order. Conflict was to be avoided. Dispute resolution was not a question of which parties had the "law" on their side; what was important was to suppress conflict and maintain order by making the adversaries understand how to behave according to the norms of Confucian social morality. Better to suffer social wrongs than to seek redress for them, even if they could be punished by law. What are sometimes referred to as "lawsuits" or "litigation" were in fact criminal or administrative proceedings cases initiated by complaints.[83]

Although obstacles of cost, delay, and personal risk confronted litigants in China, they did not deter all parties to private quarrels from resorting to the formal legal process. The threat of a complaint to a magistrate was often used effectively as leverage in negotiating a private settlement. Even such motives as personal revenge might lead to charging acquaintances with commission of a crime. Law remained, nevertheless, a secondary instrument of social control. At least for the strict Confucian, ritual observance and rule by moral example were the ideologically preferred methods of inducing correct behavior.

Political authority in China—the mandate to rule—was based for nearly three millennia on the quality of governance for the public good and common welfare. Only the limits of power, however, prevented full

---

[82] *See*, e.g., Philip C.C. Huang, *Civil Justice in China: Representation and Practice in the Qing* (Stanford, CA: Stanford University Press, 1996).

[83] On the threat or actual filing of criminal complaints for retribution or other personal motives, *see* R. Kent Guy, *The Emperor's Four Treasuries: Scholars and the State in the Late Ch'ien-lung Era* (Cambridge, MA: Harvard University Press, 1987).

law enforcement and restricted the exercise of such "totalitarian" authority.[84] In this context law was essentially an instrument of "good" governance—a carefully crafted and articulated set of rules made and enforced consistently through prescribed procedures by a corps of officials whose status was based on tested education and merit. No polity until the modern era enjoyed as perfected a system of rule by law. With nearly absolute authority and only intermittently contested power, administrative and penal law (public law) prevailed.

However, the lack of private law rules left routine arrangements for commerce, contracts, property, and associations to be managed through expanding familial, clan, and regional networks. These patterns of private ordering were most notable with the expanding commercial activities within and emanating from the rice-producing regions of southern China. Illustrative of the expanding scope of such commerce was the growth of region-based rather than trade-based guilds (*huiguan*) into major commercial centers and the capital city.[85]

One consequence was negation of need for contract law as the glue that binds merchants to their deals or that encourages commercial expansion and complexity by fostering transactions between strangers. The experience thus seriously challenges the argument made notably by Nobel prize laureate Douglass North that "personal ties" and "voluntaristic constraints" do not suffice as "more complex" patterns of trade and commerce emerge.[86] At least in China, contract law was not an essential ingredient of economic growth. Even the institutional rule-making of the Mediterranean and European merchant guilds was missing. In other words, "customary private ordering" based on trust and reputation prevailed in the enduring rice-culture of southern China with its shared habits of mutual dependency and cooperative community effort.

Still today the influence of (predominantly southern) Chinese experience remains. Customary private ordering, including relational contracting, appears to be an intrinsic feature of economic activities in southern China—as exemplified by contemporary patterns of foreign investment from Taiwan. Even today among southern Chinese private law remains a

---

[84] Benjamin I. Schwartz, "The Primacy of the Political Order in East Asian Societies: Some Preliminary Generalizations," in S.R. Schram, ed., *Foundations and Limits of State Power in China* (Hong Kong: Chinese University Press, 1987), p. 1.

[85] *See*, e.g., Moll-Murata, "Chinese Guilds."

[86] *See*, e.g., Douglass C. North, "Institutions," *Journal of Economic Perspectives*, vol. 5 (1991), pp. 97–112.

less favored alternative.[87] North may have the last word, however. As investors from Taiwan venture further north where their regional contacts and connections are weak and dealing with "strangers" becomes more common, they have begun to seek legal protection in order to secure legal property and contract rights that make bargaining in the shadow of the law feasible.[88] In other words, "private ordering" and other aspects of a "rice-producing culture" continue to prevail among Chinese from the south.

---

[87] *See*, e.g., Kao Cheng-sha, "'Personal Trust' in Large Businesses in Taiwan: A Traditional Foundation for Contemporary Economic Activities," in Hamilton, ed., *Business Networks*, pp. 66–76.

[88] *See* Weitsheng Chen, "Arbitrage for Property Rights: How Do Foreign Investors Create Substitutes for Property Institutions in the Developing World?" *Washington International Law Journal*, vol. 24 (2015), pp 47–97.

4. Rice and rifles: foundations of private law and private ordering in Japan

China illustrates how the earliest centralized bureaucratic regimes developed and thereby established public law orders. In order to achieve their goal of centralized regulatory governance, the rulers had to acquire sufficient resources and be able to allocate them to the administrative structures and personnel necessary to maintain their bureaucratic regimes. The pivotal factors for China, like Egypt, were control over major rivers and the wealth and human resources of their basins along with extended periods of relative peace and security.

We now begin to explore the political foundations of private law orders. Our initial focus is early and medieval Japan. Few if any societies of comparable population and territorial size replicate the Japanese experience. For nearly two millennia from at least the third century CE to 1945 CE, the four main islands of the Japanese archipelago did not experience any transformative intrusion from external sources either by migration or by conquest. Japan thus represents a rare if not unique example of political and legal development based exclusively on internal influences and self-selected borrowings from abroad. For our purposes, the Japanese experience also illustrates the correlation between the institutional constraints within political systems and both customary and institutionalized mechanisms of private ordering.

To summarize the main conclusions at the outset: Japan's political environment was shaped decisively first by lack of any sizable rivers or broad, contiguous river plains as in China over which centralizing rulers could directly control the principal sources and producers of wealth. The result was competition for power, the emergence of competing warrior bands, and ultimately warrior hegemony. Moreover, whoever did gain power was dependent on rice for revenues. Produced by expanding clusters of sedentary agricultural households, collective cultivation of wet-paddy rice remained the principal source of redistributable wealth until at least the nineteenth century. Thus, without rivers, Japan's story of political development is one of rice and rifles.

Three enduring features stand out: The first was the incapacity of successive rulers to establish a fully integrated polity controlled directly from the center. Despite political and legal structures borrowed from Tang China with an imperial institution at the center as a locus of authority, the initial effort to form a unified national polity out of a confederation of independent chiefdoms was never complete. With dissipation of control over resources, the power of the first imperium soon disintegrated. Privatization of public office and revenues and related recognition of an array of private entitlements to rice rather than land led to increasing numbers of relatively autonomous centers of power and control. In the chaos, warrior rulers emerged. Yet, these local centers of independent power were paradoxically sustained by the authority of the sinofied imperium. This disjuncture of centralized political authority from administration with fragmentation of power remained characteristic of the Japanese polity through World War II.

The second feature was the development and endurance of private ordering. Rice production was, as noted, the principal source of sustenance and wealth but, unlike the experience of southern China, its producers were denied access to political authority or power within the structures of governance. Their mobility was also constrained. Instead, these communities developed an unparalleled degree of autonomy along with collective, extralegal strategies for survival that enabled them to resist without overt noncompliance externally imposed controls. Reliance on rice-producing communities as the primary source of wealth coupled with the exclusion of these communities from political participation within a status-based structure for governance in turn led increasingly to closed, self-governing villages outside of law's domain. The rice-producing village thus provides, as I have argued previously,[1] the paradigm of social ordering in Japan.

With authority but limited power, the warrior rulers utilized adjudication as their primary means of maintaining order, first within the context of warrior bands and later between villages. With order maintained and commerce beginning to thrive, adjudication also became a major means of ordering within an expanding merchant community.

These three features of political development had determinative influence on the legal institutions that developed in tandem. With the advent of warrior rule, the paradoxical disjuncture of authority and power made adjudication a prevailing mode of law enforcement. Successive warrior rulers relied on adjudication as a primary mechanism for settling disputes

---

1 *See* Haley, *Authority without Power.*

among their followers as well as disputes related to village oversight and related claims to revenues. Adjudication as an expression of authority furnished the least costly means for maintaining order. Once peace and political stability were established with the advent of Tokugawa rule at the dawn of the seventeenth century, the predominant configurations of law and governance reverted to Imperial Chinese patterns. From the perspective of the warrior rulers and their newly established fortress enclaves, Japan had all of the trappings of a highly developed regulatory state. Yet, adjudication remained a principal means of governance. The consequent mix of adjudication and private ordering enveloped by a conceptual system of regulatory law distinguished the Japanese experience from both its advanced imperial neighbor on the continent and, as detailed in Chapter 5, Western Europe. With peace restored, internal trade and commerce expanded. Within this context emerged a nascent private law system and the institutional foundations for Japan's successful transplantation of Western law in the late nineteenth and early twentieth centuries.

RICE

Japan comprises an archipelago of narrow, volcanic islands that stretch over 1500 miles from Hokkaido in the northeast to Okinawa in the southwest. The main island of Honshu alone extends over 700 miles from the northeast to the southwest. Its widest point, however, is only 170 miles. Japan has many rivers, but they are short and run fast. Only 20 percent of the land is arable, 70 percent of which is upland plateaus. The largest lowland areas include the Kanto plain, by far the most extensive, which surrounds what is today the capital city of Tokyo (formerly Edo). It is followed in size by the plains of the Kinai (Osaka-Kyoto), Nobi (Nagoya), Echigo (north-central Honshu), and Sendai (northeastern Honshu) regions. None are contiguous. Mountains and other natural barriers separate them all. An island nation, Japan has not experienced any significant migration from the Asian mainland since Paleolithic times (c. 35,000–13,000 BCE). Nor until 1945 were the islands ever subject to conquest and occupation by any outside invader.[2] The areas closest to the Asian mainland are separated

[2] For a controversial contrary view, *see* Oka Masao, Yawata Ichirō, and Egami Namio, "Nihon minzoku bunka no genryū to Nihon kokka no keisei," *Minzokugaku*, vol. 13 (1949), pp. 207–277. In English, *see* Gari Ledyard, "Galloping Along with the Horseriders: Looking for the Founders of Japan," *Journal of Japanese Studies*, vol. 1 (1975), pp. 217–254.

by over 120 miles of sea as compared with the 21 miles of the English Channel at the Straits of Dover, the shortest point between England and France. Topography similarly precluded the establishment of any political regime with uncontested control over the entire archipelago until the seventeenth century. And not until the mid nineteenth century were any of the ostensibly centralized regimes in full control. Rivals for power at the periphery with effective dominion over critical resources have been recurring themes of Japanese political history.

As evidenced in China and the earliest civilizations of South and West Asia (the "Near East" from a European perspective), the development of political organization and law commenced with the emergence of political authority in sedentary agricultural societies. Such communities were commonly defined by kinship and coalesced by virtue of interdependency based on the mutually recognized need for cooperation for both physical and economic welfare. As these agrarian communities expanded, political authority emerged. Polities developed either from within or by conquest from without. What we know of ancient Japan fits this pattern.

Japan's prehistory is generally divided into three post Paleolithic periods—the Jomon (c. 13,000–300 BCE), the Yayoi (c. 300 BCE–300 CE), and the Kofun (c. 300–600 CE). The first rice-cultivating settlements appeared at the end of the Jomon Period, becoming increasingly numerous during the Yayoi Period in lowland plains along the slopes of rivers. By the end of the Yayoi Period, rice cultivation and metallurgy had spread throughout the western and eastern coastal regions of the archipelago. The archeological evidence indicates that small predominantly kinship-based settlements dependent on the cultivation of adjacent land for rice had become the prevailing social organization by the beginning of the Common Era. These settlements, often only hamlets with a half dozen or so households, were commonly established on hillsides overlooking rivers and streams separated from neighboring communities across rice-producing paddy fields. Socially constructed, it appears, predominantly along cognate rather than patrilineal lines, at least from the mid to late Yayoi Period, these communities were subject to continual armed incursions. They developed defensive ditches and embankments and could call upon sibling ties for loyal manpower to provide armed resistance. The disappearance of such defensive fortifications is taken to indicate a degree of political consolidation and externally imposed security during the Kofun period.[3]

---

[3] *See*, e.g., Obayashi Taryo, "Uji Society and Ie Society from Prehistory to Medieval Times," *Journal of Japanese Studies*, vol. 11 (1985), pp. 3–27.

The Kofun period is named for the burial mounds that began to appear during the third century CE. These burial sites indicate greater social and political stratification and the emergence of chieftains as well as an elite economic and governing class. During this era, smaller agricultural communities are believed to have begun to coalesce into larger territorial units that in turn had forged mutual alliances. In the process, the clan-based chiefdoms—the *uji*—that characterize the late Yayoi and Kofun periods took form. Swamps were cleared and dikes built, new paddy fields were opened and developed, and new rice-producing settlements were established. The introduction of iron tools from the Asian mainland and their augmented availability by local manufacture enabled the development of the uplands primarily for cereal production and husbandry, resulting in further expansion of settlements, additional sources of wealth, and new forms of social organization.

As the process of consolidation continued, a confederation under a single ruler emerged. As described by a Chinese source in the earliest known writing on Japan, by the end of the Yayoi era in the third century CE a "queen" (*nii-wang*) known as Himiko reigned (perhaps with a male co-monarch) over a confederation of "countries" (*guo* in Chinese, *kuni* in Japanese) that had joined together after seven or eight decades of war.[4] The emergence of these larger *uji*—held together by mutual interest and cognate kinship (often fictive or created by adoption)—may have been, as Carl Steenstrup suggests[5] a first attempt at the reorganization and subordination of smaller agricultural communities—the old and newly formed villages and hamlets of protohistoric Japan. Among the most likely explanations for this process was a need for greater security. Smaller communities simply banded together and submitted to chieftains and others in return for protection against similarly confederating rivals. Also appearing were the more clearly subordinated artisan *be*, whose members apparently became responsible for producing a variety of

---

[4] The Record of Wei (*Wei chih*), quoted in Joan R. Piggott, *The Emergence of Japanese Kingship* (Stanford, CA: Stanford University Press, 1997), p. 15. *See also* Gina L. Barnes, *State Formation in Japan: Emergence of a 4th Century Ruling Elite* (Abingdon, Oxon and New York: Routledge, 2007), pp. 83–103.

[5] Carl Steenstrup, *A History of Law in Japan until 1868* (Leiden, New York, Copenhagen, and Cologne: E.J. Brill, 1991), pp. 15–16; Delmer M. Brown, "The Yamato Kingdom," in Brown, ed., *The Cambridge History of Japan*, vol. 1, pp. 133–140.

products from weaponry to burial mounds.[6] Seemingly absorbed, pre-existing settlements are most likely to have remained essentially intact productive components of these newer polities. They were probably surpassed as sources of revenue and wealth, however, by new settlements established in the continuous expansion of rice cultivation through an almost endless process of land reclamation.

During this period, the first significant influences from the Asian mainland began to penetrate into Japan. Whether the result of expanded contacts through emissaries to China and skilled migrants from southern Korea or, less probable, "horse-rider" conquest of parts of Kyushu and western Japan, the impact on language, technologies, and ideas proved to be profound. Mainland influence politically accelerated the process of confederation of *uji* chiefdoms into a centralizing polity under what is today referred to as the Yamato kings. The acquisition by elites of what Gina Barnes describes as "prestige goods," such as bronze bells, iron implements and weapons, even gold seals as gifts from Han Dynasty rulers to Japanese emissaries in return for pledges of allegiance, assisted the process.[7] The adaptability of the Chinese ideographs to disparate spoken languages enabled the introduction of a sophisticated writing system in the fifth century and the expansion of literate, hereditary elites. In royal sponsorship of Buddhism and the ceremonial trappings of an Imperial Chinese court—to which emissaries were now routinely sent—centralizing rulers also found new sources of political legitimacy, more advanced weaponry, and, in law, tools of governance.

A more direct onslaught on the autonomy of local polities and their constituent rice-producing communities came with the imposition of sinofied administrative rule beginning with the adoption of the *Ōmi* Code in the 660s and the *Kiyomihara* Code two decades later, the first of four codes promulgated during the *Taika* reforms from the middle of the seventh century. As these reforms were implemented, Japan underwent an institutional and cultural transformation.

Centered on the Yamato plain near Nara, successive rulers recreated fundamental institutions and structures of governance and law based on models from China, already, as we have seen, one of the most institutionally advanced centralized polities. This era of Japanese history is commonly referred to as the *ritsuryō* period by virtue of the legal

---

[6] J. Edward Kidder, "The Earliest Societies in Japan," in Delmer M. Brown, ed., *Cambridge History of Japan*, vol. 1, *Ancient Japan* (Cambridge: Cambridge University Press, 1988), p. 139.

[7] Barnes, *State Formation in Japan*, pp. 37–40.

institutions that were adapted and imposed—a system of criminal proscriptions (*ritsu*) and administrative regulations (*ryō*) based on Imperial Chinese law, particularly the Tang Code. The legal reforms commenced, as noted, in the 660s with a set of administrative regulations, supplemented later with penal proscriptions. The first known fully integrated *ritsuryō* Code was the Taihō *ritsuryō* promulgated in 702. The only complete extant code, known as the Yōrō Code, followed in 757 (drafted in 718).

Political legitimacy was an essential element of governance that Chinese models could not fully provide. Unlike China, the new Japanese imperium lacked the historical or embedded philosophical foundations for a normative claim to rule. Instead, as in other early kingdoms and empires, Japan's rulers based their political authority on claims to deistic origin rooted in indigenous folk-beliefs as well as identification with Mahayana Buddhism, a recently introduced and rapidly expanding belief-system. Joan Piggott argues persuasively that Japan's rulers purposefully constructed their legitimacy commencing with initiatives undertaken at the beginning of the seventh century. In addition to the cultivation of Mahayana Buddhism as an official cult, they emulated the Imperial Chinese palace and system of court ranks. The 17 article "constitution" on the principles of governance promulgated by Prince Shotoku in 604 provided what Piggott calls the "third pillar" of legitimacy.[8]

Until the eighth century both old and new agricultural communities appear to have been largely self-governing. Outside of the ambit of formal law, customary modes of private ordering presumably continued to function as the primary means of maintaining internal order. Stratification of political and social authority had, however, also advanced, although presumably rudimentary and relatively weak. Family hierarchy (some suggest matriarchic tendencies[9]) and accepted claims to religious authority appear to be the common sources for legitimacy. Custom and customary processes appear to have prevailed. Law as related to institutional processes had just commenced as governing hierarchies developed, especially in those areas closest to mainland influences and settlers. The most advanced of the known communities appear to have been

---

[8] Piggott, *The Emergence of Japanese Kingship*, p. 82.

[9] Steenstrup, *A History of Law in Japan*, p. 11; Torao Toshiya, "New Economic and Social Institutions," in Brown, ed., *The Cambridge History of Japan*, vol. 1, p. 429.

highly collectivized.[10] Slavery existed but, as in southern China, it is believed never to have been a significant source of agricultural labor.[11]

Unlike the Mediterranean civilizations, Japan had no history of enslavement through conquest. Those who can be described as slaves were apparently primarily young children who, for whatever reason, were sold or bartered by their parents. The population remained relatively unsubordinated with collective action and mediation as the prevailing means to resolve social conflict and maintain order within mutually interdependent communities.[12] Mutual need and interdependence between those who ruled and cultivators also ensured that a degree of cultivator possessory proprietorship and autonomy became intrinsic features of the social and political environment.

By the end of the eighth century the rulers in the capital cities of the new sinofied imperium (from 710 to 794 Nara; Kyoto thereafter until 1869) had put into place an administrative system that enveloped all four main islands. On paper Japan was a unified realm, divided into provinces, each with a provincial capital and appointed governors with six year terms, as well as unifying circuits. The rulers at the center asserted imperial proprietorship of all land. Censuses were taken; households duly registered, and communities reorganized or simply reformulated as administratively defined units of 50 families (*gō*). Rice-cultivated land was surveyed and redistributed plot by plot (*kubunden*). In the uplands, land was granted to households without restriction or qualification based on composition or status. Cultivators allocated land were subject to both payments to the authorities in kind (rice) and mandatory labor, including military service. However, the new regime by law also distinguished "private land" with entitlement to perpetual personal possession and production from unallocated "public land" possessed by agents of the imperium. Much of the public land represented newly developed land and reclamation projects, especially in the uplands. Coinage was also initiated, laying the foundations for a monetized economy. Taxation replaced tribute. With payment principally in rice but also other produce and products, notably silk, a commodity barter trade began to develop along

---

[10] Kidder, "The Earliest Societies in Japan," p. 93.

[11] Toshiya, "New Economic and Social Institutions," pp. 425–426. For a contrary view on the extent of slavery, see Kozo Yamamura, "The Decline of the Ritsuryō System: Hypotheses on Economic and Institutional Change," *Journal of Japanese Studies*, vol. 1 (1974), pp. 3–37, at Appendix, p. 30. Whatever the extent in the era of *uji* chiefdoms, Yamamura agrees that slavery was on the wane by the ninth century.

[12] Steenstrup, *History of Law in Japan*, pp. 22–24.

with concomitant proliferation of attendant practices and institutions. Included, despite attempted proscription, were private loans in money or rice.[13] Also introduced to encourage agriculture was a system of public loans of seed rice (*suikō*) repayable at harvest with interest.

At the local level many of the centralizing reforms were short lived. The rulers in the capital failed to implement an examination system for qualification for appointment as an imperial official—among the most critical features of the Imperial Chinese model. Kinship, clan status, and hereditary office continued to be the determining criteria for imperial appointment.[14] Powerful local chiefs or their kin received imperial appointments and ceremonial offices as officials, administrators, and courtiers with heritable entitlements to stipends and revenues. Local elites with familial ties to the court occupied key posts and increasingly exercised independent control over local resources, especially new lands being reclaimed and cultivated under their supervision. Politically favored temples and shrines also received reclaimed, tax-exempt lands. Other means of co-option also existed. Despite legal prohibition, intermarriage of officials and immigrant nobles with local elites was common.[15] By such means, "as local chieftains were drawn more strongly toward the center," Joan Piggott notes, "their relations with their home communities—the very relations on which the center depended for integrating the realm and mobilizing its fruits—were put at risk."[16]

The allotment of plots to individual cultivators and households created acute tensions within the most populous regions, particularly the *kinai* plains near the capital. There was simply too little land for too many people. The plots were small and, if in less productive areas, were simply abandoned. In addition, the opening of new fields for rice in the lowlands and cereal cultivation as well as pasturage in the uplands and their allocation to local elites, temples, shrines, and others with close ties to the throne also created tensions. New lands meant an increasing demand for agricultural labor. The consequence was a movement of households into less densely populated areas as well as a concomitant process of

---

13 Torao Toshiya, "Nara Economic and Social Institutions," in Brown, ed., *The Cambridge History of Japan*, vol. 1, pp. 444–451.

14 Naoki Kōjirō, "The Nara State," in Brown, ed., *The Cambridge History of Japan*, vol. 1, pp. 224–226.

15 Cornelius J. Kiley, "Provincial Administration and Land Tenure in Early Heian," in Donald Shively and William H. McCullough, eds., *The Cambridge History of Japan: Heian Japan*, vol. 2 (Cambridge and New York: Cambridge University Press, 1999), pp. 236–240, at p. 335.

16 Piggott, *The Emergence of Japanese Kingship*, p. 234.

bargained-for agricultural labor—ostensibly agricultural tenancy—as *kubunden* cultivators supplemented the output from their allotted plots with share cropping and similar arrangements to cultivate neighboring land for absentee proprietors. In less populated areas such negotiated tenancy with multiple households presumably led to the creation of altogether new agricultural settlements. Murakami Yasusuke, Kumon Shumpei, and Satō Seisaburō argue, for example, that in newly reclaimed land in the eastern Tōgoku region (comprising today Aichi, Nagano, and Toyama Prefectures) with its extensive uplands, collaborative mixed communities of cultivators and warriors emerged forming what they have coined a "proto-*ie*" society dominated by hereditary, hierarchal warrior households and their retainers.[17]

Provincial governors and favored families in the capital with long-standing local ties also began to subvert the centralizing process first by skimming off tax revenues, including repayment of often fictitious *suikō* loans, in addition to appropriating labor services for their own use. Removed from public policing and the tax rolls altogether were the continuously expanding areas of rice cultivation. Under the patronage of noble houses and Buddhist institutions in the capital, newly reclaimed and adjacent land became subject to commendation as tax-exempt estates (*shōen*). The *shōen* typically comprised disparate villages and hamlets clustered around newly reclaimed land as well as existing cultivated fields that for purposes of control and revenue extraction were designated in clusters as *myō*, the smallest administrative unit within a *shōen*. The new estate holders, mostly in Nara and Kyoto, held offices (*shiki*) with entitlements to revenue from land that continued to be cultivated by both existing holders and paid laborers, many of whom had possessory entitlement to adjacent fields.[18] Along with the steadily growing number and expanse of these estates, preexisting patterns of social organization and tenure also began to change. A blend of traditional and newly evolving forms of social organization, landholding patterns, and local control reshaped basic structures of authority and power within local and regional governance. Although the authority of the center remained, its coercive capacities, already constrained, were further weakened in a spiral of inexorable decline.

---

[17] Murakami Yasusuke, Kumon Shumpei, and Satō Seisaburō, *Bunmei to shite no ie shakai* [Ie society as a pattern of civilization] (Tokyo: Chūōkōron Sha, 1979), summarized in English in Murakami Yasusuke, "Ie Society as a Pattern of Civilization," *Journal of Japanese Studies*, vol. 10 (1984), pp. 281–363.

[18] Toshiya, "New Economic and Social Institutions," p. 450.

At the height of centralized *ritsuryō* rule in the ninth century, Japan had evolved politically to resemble China in important ways. Its political and legal institutions were adaptations of Chinese models. Political authority, albeit unlike China, was defined in deistic terms vested in a ruling sovereign at the center. Perhaps the most telling feature was a notable reliance on written records and documentation. From China, Japan had received not only conceptions of administrative governance but also a written language as its tool. Registers and written records were thereafter to have a determinative role in governance. The extant household and land registers of the seventh and eighth centuries are one legacy.

Fundamental patterns of social organization reflected the shared predominance of wet-paddy rice cultivation. Most Japanese continued to live and work in territorially defined communities—the *sato*[19]—in which, albeit stratified, most cultivating households retained at least a vestige of autonomy and freedom from direct central oversight and control. Nor did cultivation depend on a servile peasantry. Wage labor and commodity markets had also appeared.

Equally fundamental contrasts were also apparent. No massive relocation of the peasant population was undertaken. Except for the building of Tōdai-ji and the capitals at Nara and Kyoto,[20] there was apparently no significant mobilization of labor. Compulsory labor service (*zōyō*) was limited to 30 days per year. Recruited labor tended to be either for local projects or military service. The Japanese cultivator, at least within household or lineage groupings, retained an apparently increasing degree of dominion over the land that produced the rents and revenue parceled out as entitlements of office (*shiki*). Economic and status stratification

---

19 Apparently the earliest indigenous term for village, *sato* had multiplied with the reclamation and development of new lands into clusters of villages and hamlets surrounding the "mother" settlements. Despite the administrative denomination of 50 family units—usually encompassing two or three *sato*—as *gō* during the *ritsuryō* period, there is no evidence of their displacement as a natural community. As noted below, villages within the *shōen* were administratively defined in clusters as *myō*. By the fourteenth century, designated as *sō*, they had acquired a politically meaningful degree of formal autonomy and self-governing authority. This self-governing autonomy but absent any legal authority continued during the Tokugawa era. The word *mura* as the prevailing term for village seems to originate in the sixteenth century. *See*, e.g., Nakada Kokichi. "Gōrisei no shikō to sonraku," *Rekishigaku kenkyū* [Journal of Historical Studies], no. 550 (1986), pp. 30–38; Harashima Reiji, *Nihon kodai shakai no kiso kōzō* (Tokyo: Miraisha, 1968), pp. 18–21, 76–77; Ōshima Takehiko, et al., eds., *Nihon o shiru jiten* (Tokyo: Shakai Shisōsha, 1971), pp. 68–101.

20 Piggott, *The Emergence of Japanese Kingship*, pp. 263–279.

among cultivating families within the *shōen* had likewise expanded, with more prosperous cultivators themselves becoming managers or independent farmers, acquiring in the process entitlements to revenues. *Shōen*, *shiki*, and the complex patterns of land use and tenure that were rapidly expanding in the tenth and eleventh centuries had no apparent counterparts in Imperial China.

Moreover, unlike China, the vast majority of Japanese had no access to officialdom or membership in the ruling elite. Except by deserting the land to become outlaws or foot soldiers, Japanese cultivators were locked into their status as wealth-producing subjects. By the late sixteenth century even these avenues for exit had closed. In addition, a dynamic process of divorcement of power from authority was fully underway. The rulers of Japan's *ritsuryō* imperium had never enjoyed full capacity to command and coerce. Without such power, adjudication of private claims became a routine function of governance.

The expansion of *shōen* coincided with the development of a complex system of proprietorship based in part on the recognition of *shiki* as transferable claims to the revenue or produce of cultivated land.[21] Cultivator submission of a portion of their produce and labor to those who governed was grounded in the political legitimacy as well as coercive powers of those who ruled. With the development of *shōen*, the offices with rights to revenue from rice-producing communities proliferated. By the end of the eleventh century, the entitlement to revenue had separated completely from any particular office. The recognition of such newly defined *shiki* as transferable private entitlements to the produce of land was a major conceptual innovation. The creation of a transferable claim to such revenues also in effect represented the "privatization" of taxation. To the extent that rulers recognized the claims of those who held *shiki* either by virtue of an original grant of office or its transfer, they in effect created an enforceable property interest. S*hiki* were thus conceptually transformed into a novel form of intangible but still contingent property. This recognition of a transferable private claim to such revenues also represented a significant step in the development of a private law system.

The validity of such entitlements required continued formal recognition and enforcement by those with political authority. *Shiki* holders enjoyed independent access to wealth at the expense of the ruler but remained paradoxically dependent on the ruler's authority for recognition

[21] *See*, e.g., "shiki," in *Iwanami Nihonshi jiten* (Tokyo: Iwanami, 1993); also in *Kokushi daijiten*, vol. 6 (Tokyo: Yoshikawa Kobunkan, 1985), pp. 688–689.

of their entitlements. As *shiki* proliferated an increasing number of actors moved beyond the coercive capacity of the rulers at the center but also continued to have a significant stake in the political legitimacy of the institutions of governance and the maintenance of the political and social order. Disputes multiplied and claims to these entitlements had to be adjudicated. The combination of these factors—the paradox itself—thus helped to foster the development of the adjudicatory institutions of early and medieval Japan.

As proprietary entitlements, it should be noted, *shiki* did not exclude the more fundamental claim to possession and the entitlement to cultivate the land in question. As detailed by Kan'ichi Asakawa in his 1925 collection of documents from the Iriki region of southwestern Kyushu,[22] "men held on to the soil of the land, but divided and disposed of part of the income."[23] At least in the most productive and prosperous regions of west central Japan nearest the capital in Kyoto, Asakawa identifies five cultivator status groups that persisted into the twelfth century—the *myōshu*, local land managers who held proprietary claims within the *myō*; *kobyakusho*, small cultivators with landholding entitlement; *zōmen-byakusho*, less numerous small cultivators subject to *myōshu* direction; *mōto*, transient agricultural laborers; and *genin*, the least numerous whose status was closest to chattel slavery and who served primarily the *myōshu* and other *shōen* officials.[24] At the apex of the hierarchy was the principal proprietor—the *honjo*—commonly a temple or court noble, usually an absentee. Below the *honjo* was the "lord"—the *ryoshū* or *ryoke*—who exercised local oversight and control.

The expansion of *shōen* estates combined with aggregation of official office and private interest by provincial officials also promoted a provincial elite with growing autonomy in local governance. Along with exemption from taxes, the *shōen* proprietors enjoyed exemption from entry by provincial officials. They became as a result territorially expanding, self-governing communities with internally developed means of ordering. In the words of John Whitney Hall:

---

[22] Kan'ichi Asakawa, *The Documents of Iriki* (Westport, CN: Greenwood Press, 1925).

[23] *Id.*, at 71.

[24] Nagahara Keiji, "The Medieval Peasant," in John W. Hall, Marius B. Jansen, Madoka Kanai, and Denis Twitchett, eds., *The Cambridge History of Japan: Medieval Japan*, vol. 3 (Cambridge and New York: Cambridge University Press, 1990), pp. 306–310.

> Under the proprietor, the *shōen* came to embrace a regular system of customary law deriving in large part from those aspects of imperial local administration which had been displaced by the immunities granted the proprietor. As the various levels of proprietors, managers, cultivators, and tenants worked out their relationships by agreement with each other, and as the increasing acquisition of immunities placed more and more of the responsibility of government into the hands of the proprietor, a virtual system of local administration came into being which looked to the *honjo* as the ultimate authority.[25]

With self-governance came responsibility to maintain order and security. *Shōen* proprietors as well as provincial officials thus began to recruit and command warriors (*tsuwamono*) as armed guards. By the end of the tenth century the conscript imperial army had been replaced by small, independent units increasingly employed by provincial governors and *shōen* managers to maintain internal order and protect against external encroachment.[26] The abandonment of a paid professional military with a conscripted peasant army under central control was one more example of the disintegration of centralized *risturyō* governance. The growing number of *shōen* administered by local managers further reduced both effective control over wealth-producing resources and revenues by those who governed at the center. Local managers as *ryoshu*, many of whom were warriors, were also able to extract more from the cultivating communities within the *shōen*, which led to an escalating number of futile complaints and petitions to absentee principals for redress. In the wake of this spiraling disintegration of effective rule, piracy, brigandage, and forced dispossession of land reached critical levels. Faced with mounting insecurity, smaller proprietors in record numbers started to commend their *shiki* holdings to Buddhist temples, shrines, and larger and more powerful families in return for the protection that the imperial regime could no longer guarantee.[27] Small armies controlled by the largest landholders as well as provincial officials with ties to the court were a consequence.

---

[25] John Whitney Hall, *Government and Local Power in Japan: 500–1700* (Princeton, NJ: Princeton University Press, 1966), p. 112.

[26] Takeuchi Rizō, "The Rise of the Warriors," in Shively and McCullough, eds., *The Cambridge History of Japan: Heian Japan*, p. 647.

[27] *See*, e.g., Mikael Adolphson and J. Mark Ramseyer, "The Competitive Enforcement of Property Rights in Medieval Japan: The Role of Temples and Monasteries," *Journal of Economic Behavior and Organization*, vol. 71 (2009), pp. 660–668.

As a result of such catalysts, historians agree, within a relatively short time warriors had seized or otherwise acquired control of revenue-producing land, not only in the frontier regions of the northeast where they and reclamation projects were most numerous,[28] but throughout Japan.[29] Beyond the rice-producing lowlands, a new pattern of patrimonial organization emerged. Many of the emergent warriors had local kinship ties. Others were more recent settlers, especially in areas such as the Kanto plain in the northeast, where arable public land was reclaimed and effectively privatized.[30] Obayashi attributes their rise in part to the availability of upland pastures, especially in the northeast, which were ideal for raising horses.[31] Murakami, Kumon, and Satō identify newly created, warrior-led agricultural communities especially in the more remote regions of the "east country" (*Tōgoku*) with a new form of "house-based" (*ie*) social organization.[32] Whether aptly described as indigenous "horse-riders" or not, the emergence of a professional warrior (*bushi*) caste and hereditary warrior houses was the consequence. More often than not in command, however, were scions of noble families who as *shōen* proprietors or their kin or provincial governors had control over land and men as well as access to military office. The privatization of governance proceeded to its militarization.

RIFLES

As consensually constructed local rule accelerated the displacement of centralized governance, a parallel but centripetal process of centralization was also occurring among the emerging warrior houses. By the end of the twelfth century, a totally restructured dual polity had formed. Warrior houses had the capacity to coerce but the imperial court remained the ultimate source of political legitimacy. The consequence was warrior governance within the steadily enfeebled ambit of imperial authority,

---

[28] Takeuchi Rizō, "The Rise of the Warriors," p. 647.

[29] Hall, *Government and Local Power*, pp. 187–190.

[30] *See* Judith Frőhlich, "Land Administration in Medieval Japan: Ito no shō in Chikuzen Province, 1131–1336," *The Historical Association* (Oxford: Blackwell Publishing Ltd., 2003).

[31] Obayashi, "Uji Society and Ie Society," p. 21.

[32] Murakami Yasusuke, Kumon Shumpei, and Satō Seisaburō, *Bunmei to shite no ie shakai* [Ie society as a pattern of civilization] (Tokyo: Chūōkōron Sha, 1979), summarized in English in Murakami Yasusuke, "Ie Society as a Pattern of Civilization," *Journal of Japanese Studies*, vol. 10 (1984), pp. 281–363.

lasting with only one brief interval from the twelfth through the mid nineteenth century.

The construction of warrior rule began, as noted, with the creation of private militia under the personal command of provincial officials as well as *shōen* estate holders and their managers. Local warrior houses organized around newly created agricultural communities. The formation of warrior bands into forces capable of effective rule, however, required an ascending order of allegiances and alliances that would eventually parallel the structures of centralized governance of the *ritsuryō* imperium. This was achieved by means of a hierarchy of consensual undertakings framed within shared patterns of cooperation. Each level formed on the basis of reciprocal bargains. In return for loyal service were promises of protection and land—more accurately a share in the wealth produced by the land's cultivators. Binding these bargains were familiar forms of relational ties and sanctions—fictive familial ties and threats of supernatural sanctions.[33]

By the middle of the twelfth century two patterns of warrior rule had evolved. Warriors from the western regions led by the Taira dominated the imperial system through a process of infiltration by official appointment combined with the capacity to command armed coercion. The challenge to a unified imperial system dominated by western warriors came from the eastern provinces. By means of direct recruitment, alliances, and other consensual undertakings, all with the promise of reward, the warrior house of Yoritomo Minamoto—also personally tied by kinship to the court—was able to command an armed force centered in eastern Japan that became the supreme warrior organization. The defeat of the Taira in a series of military engagements ending with the victory at Dan-no-ura in 1185 left Yoritomo without a major warrior rival. Yoritomo was named *Seii Taishōgun* (or simply *shogun*) in 1192. Not until after his death (1199) and the Jōkyū War of 1221 was control over the archipelago by the eastern warriors, now commanded by Yoritomo's Hōjō heirs, ensured. Kamakura became the administrative capital of Japan, a position it retained until 1333, when the Kamakura *bakufu* ("tent government") fell victim to the same forces that had fatally eroded the *ritsuryō* system.

Granted the authority to appoint allied warriors in each province as constables (*shugo*) and stewards (*jitō*), not to replace but to serve alongside provincial governors appointed by the imperial government, the

---

[33] *See* Joüon de Longrais, *L'Est et L'Ouest* (Tokyo and Paris: Maison Franco-Japonais, Institut de Recherches Histoire, 1958), pp. 143–156.

warrior rulers in Kamakura created an administrative structure that paralleled and ultimately overwhelmed the imperial system but did not fully displace it. Adhering to sinofied administrative models, neither office was to be filled by warriors from the province to which they were assigned—a rule that also justified the transfer of loyal warriors from the eastern provinces to the domains of defeated rivals in the west. Neither office, however, received a stipend that might have made the holders dependent on the *bakufu*. Instead the holders of both offices had to extract from local sources the means for their support. Their intensified oversight, control, and outright appropriation restricted cultivator as well as centralized—imperial or warrior—dominion nationwide. In addition to earlier prescribed taxes, even interest from *suikō* rice loans, whether actually extended or not, had become simply another tax, now collected and appropriated by office-holding warriors. The incentives created by the system fostered the rise of local warrior houses that would eventually challenge once again the authority and power of those who ruled from the center. As before, control over resources determined Japan's political development as warriors at the periphery, particularly the *shugo* constables, gained in power.

In 1333 the Emperor Go-Daigo attempted to end the duality of rule and to restore imperial rule. The Kamakura *bakufu* was sufficiently weakened by the diffusion of resources under the effective control of the *shugo* constables for the so-called *Kenmu* Restoration under Go-Daigo to be briefly successful. The attempt faltered three years later with the advent of a new *shogun* and *bakufu* regime under the Ashikaga house, which now centered *bakufu* headquarters in the Muromachi district of Kyoto. Never fully capable of reigning in the disparate warrior houses that had proliferated throughout Japan, the Ashikaga presided over a century-long era—known alternatively as the Ashikaga or Muromachi periods—of civil war and general disorder.

The *shōen* system itself collapsed during the fourteenth and fifteenth centuries as warriors increasingly took over *ryoshū* offices. The ensuing conflicts were predictable. Some non-warrior *myōshu* and other cultivators resorted individually and as communities to petitions pressing *shōen* principals for redress. They had little apparent success, and the disintegration of effective rule from the center accelerated. Between 1467 and 1493, competing warlords (*daimyo*)—most of whom held hereditary *shugo* office—fought a series of battles mainly near the capital in Kyoto, commonly referred to as the *Ōnin* wars. From these armed conflicts a new set of warlords emerged. The majority of the victors had no claim to delegated or sub-delegated imperial authority as either *shogun* or *shugo*. As a result of military success as well as compensation for the loss of revenues from dispersed holdings, they began to acquire direct control over sources of revenue in territorially contiguous agricultural communities. They then proceeded during the next century to consolidate their power and position over the territorially defined land and people they now effectively governed.

Concomitantly, agricultural communities underwent a third administrative identity. At least some, now administratively recognized as *sō*, gained formal authority for self-governing administration. They selected leaders and began to develop rules for internal order. With common interest in resisting external control and the more effective extraction of any agricultural surplus, they also began to band together in leagues to resist.

The sixteenth century was medieval Japan's pivotal era as the new class of Warring States warlords (*sengoku daimyo*)—controlling, by one estimate, 150 territorially defined domains[34]—individually began to implement policies that by accident or design avoided the errors of past rulers. One by one they initiated reforms that would have national significance by the end of the century. First and foremost, they took stock of the resources under their territorial control with plot-by-plot cadastral surveys based on tiller households and the yields of agricultural land under their cultivation. Closely related, they also required personal registration of all inhabitants. Neither of these measures was novel. Both had antecedents in the Taika reforms of the seventh century. Secondly, they began to convert existing fortresses or to build new ones at sites of strategic importance to serve as their personal residences and headquarters. They also began to legislate, promulgating codes for their "countries" (*kuni*) with general applicability to all persons within their territorial control. Not since the seventh century had any rulers claimed so broad an authority to legislate. The fourth reform was the most transformative. They began to remove their warrior retainers out of the villages, compelling them to reside in the environs of their newly constructed fortresses, often turning small villages into urban centers—the "castle towns" of sixteenth and early seventeenth century Japan. In return, the warrior retainers were to receive monetary stipends based on their previously acquired claims to the product of the lands over which they had oversight and control. As warfare subsided, these warrior retainers became the administrators for their overlords who ruled. Those

---

[34] Mary Elizabeth Berry, *Hideyoshi* (Cambridge, MA: Harvard University Press, 1989), p. 26, citing Nagahara, et al., eds., *Chūsei-shi handobukku* (Tokyo: Kondō Shuppan-sha, 1973), pp. 397–402.

who chose to remain lost their warrior status, presumably preferring status as members of local, wealthy landholding elites within the peasantry. These individual transformations in governance were replicated and consolidated nationally over the course of the century under the three successive "unifiers"—Oda Nobunaga, Tototomi Hideyoshi, and finally Tokugawa Ieyasu.

The contribution of innovative weaponry to the unification process is difficult to access, but credit is given to the use by Nobunaga of the matchlock rifle or acquebus with Japanese-designed improvements at the decisive battle of Nagashino in 1575. The European matchlock rifle had been introduced into Japan in 1543 with the accidental arrival of the first Portuguese to Japan on a shipwrecked Chinese junk on the island of Tanegashima, southeast of Kyushu. On board were two or three Portuguese adventurers with muskets. When the daimyo of the island, Tanegashima Tokitaka, saw the muskets and witnessed a demonstration of their use, he is said to have immediately realized their potential and purchased one or two of the newly named *Tansegashima-teppō* rifles. He then ordered an island smith to make a copy. Within four months, Tokitaka is reported to have used the new weapon in his successful campaign to retake the neighboring island of Yakushima.[35] Matchlock rifles are also considered to have been instrumental in Hideyoshi's first and only successful invasion of Korea in 1592.[36] In the end, Korean control of the sea with "Turtle boats" equipped with technologically less advanced cannons proved to be decisive and Hideyoshi's forces were forced to withdraw back to Japan.[37]

By the start of the Tokugawa hegemony in 1603, a national cadastral survey had already been completed. Also completed was the exit of warriors from the village. By separate decrees in the 1580s, Hideyoshi disarmed the peasantry, required all warriors to reside in castle towns, and restricted movement out of one's registered domain (*han*) without

---

[35] *See* Olof G. Lidin, *Tanegashima: The Arrival of Europe in Japan* (Copenhagen: Nordic Institute of Asian Studies, 2002), pp. 1–6. Noel Perrin, *Giving Up the Gun: Japan's Reversion to the Sword, 1543–1879* (Jaffrey, NH: David R. Godine, 1988), pp. 5–7.

[36] Delmer Brown, "The Impact of Firearms on Japanese Warfare, 1543–98," *Far Eastern Quarterly*, vol. 7 (1948), pp. 238–253. *See also* Kenneth Swope, "Crouching Tigers, Secret Weapons: Military Technology Employed During the Sino-Japanese–Korean War, 1592–1598," *Journal of Military History*, vol. 69 (2005), p. 22.

[37] For a detailed account, *see* Samuel Hawley, *The Imjin War: Japan's Sixteenth Century Invasion of Korea and Attempt to Conquer China* (2nd ed., n.p.: Conquistador Press, 2014).

official permission. Castle towns now marked Japan's new and future urban centers.

The Tokugawa settlement in the aftermath of the Battle of Sekigahara in 1600—a battle in which the victor, Ieyasu, had a telling supply of matchlock rifles—ended the civil wars and ushered in two and a half centuries of peace, order, and both commercial and agricultural advancement. Further advancements in weaponry, however, came to an abrupt halt.

Japan was unified in effect as a confederation of 200 to as many as 625 warrior domains (*han*)[38] under the Tokugawa shogunate with its headquarters in the now central castle town of Edo (Tokyo). Most *han* were quite small. Only four or five can be considered major. Ieyasu's principal rivals among these were relocated into domains at the periphery in southern Kyushu and western Honshu. Allies—the *fudai* daimyo—were granted preferred lands, while those with kinship ties to the Tokugawa house were given control over the more strategic of these choice domains. The shogunate itself, however, directly controlled about a quarter of all wealth-producing land and established direct control over the three most important castle towns—Osaka, Niigata, and Shizuoka—in addition to the imperial capital at Kyoto, the ancient capital and center for Japan's oldest temples at Nara, and Nikkō, where Ieyasu's mausoleum was to be located. Also under direct Tokugawa house rule were the only two ports through which foreign trade would be permitted—Nagasaki and Hakodate—and Sado Island, the locale of Japan's principal gold deposits. All were designated as special districts.

All of the great overlords (*daimyo*) were required to maintain an official residence in Edo with their wives and children serving, in effect, as hostages. Every two years each was also required to return from their personal domains to reaffirm their allegiance and loyalty to Ieyasu and his successors as supreme overlord. Disregarding the advice of some neo-Confucian advisors, who urged Ieyasu to justify his political authority, however acquired, in the manner of Imperial Chinese dynastic change by appeal to a Mandate from Heaven, Ieyasu chose to construe his

---

[38] Dan Fenno Henderson, *Conciliation and Japanese Law: Tokugawa and Modern*, vol. 1 (Seattle: University of Washington Press, 1965), p. 30. By most accounts whatever the actual number in 1600, the number of *han* had significantly increased by the early eighteenth century. See Harold Bolitho, "The Han," in John Whitney Hall and James L. McClain, eds., *The Cambridge History of Japan: Early Modern Japan*, vol. 4 (Cambridge and New York: Cambridge University Press, 1991), p. 201.

legitimacy in traditional Japanese terms—kinship with the Minamoto and imperial appointment as shogun.[39]

The Tokugawa regime also reverted to older models and began the recreation of a regulatory order. The administrative institutions within Tokugawa domains represented a blend of new and old. Under Hideyoshi the last formal vestiges of the *shōen* estates had been dismantled with the elimination of older village units—such as the *myō* and *sō*—and administrative reorganization of the country into provinces (*kuni*), districts (*kōri*), urban centers (*machi*), and villages, now designated by a common appellation as *mura*. For each district, which included the special districts under direct Tokugawa control, a warrior-official was posted as *daikan* to function like an Imperial Chinese magistrate with full administrative and judicial authority. The Tokugawa rulers similarly reinforced other sixteenth century reforms. They added to Hideyoshi's division of the population into a hierarchy of five, permanently fixed, hereditary status or caste groupings—warriors at the apex, followed by cultivators, artisans, merchants, and "non-persons" (*hinin*) at the bottom. Inter-status mobility ceased completely. They also introduced three additional castes—the nobility (*kuge*), Buddhist and Shintō priests (*sōni* and *shinkan*), expanded the formal groupings of five households, and promulgated new registration requirements. Births, adoptions, marriages, and divorces had to be recorded in the personal registry (*ninbetsuchō*) maintained in each urban district and village. In addition, as a means to enforce the ban on Christianity, all households had to maintain a registry with their local Buddhist temple.

Topping the administrative structure were three commissions located in Edo, each with responsibility for supervision and oversight: the Temple and Shrine Commission (*jisha bugyō*), the Edo Town Commission (*Edo machi bugyō*), and the Finance Commission (*kanjō bugyō*). Headed by *fudai* daimyo, the Temple and Shrine Commission was the most prestigious. The Finance Commission was the most important. In addition to fiscal responsibilities that included supervision of tax receipts, the Finance Commission was responsible for most ordinary adjudication as well as oversight of the *daikan* under shogunate control.

39 *See* Haley, *Authority without Power*, pp. 52–54.

Community Ordering and Commerce

On a nationwide level these reforms had lasting influence. Most important, they further reinforced village autonomy and mechanisms for self-governance outside of the domain of law. Any possibility of integrating village autonomy within a legal structure ended. Historians can only speculate what might have occurred had the self-governing structures and political authority of the *sō* developed. Instead, by the beginning of the seventeenth century, the village as *mura* had become a self-governing administrative unit whose *daikan*-appointed headsmen and councils were collectively responsible for maintaining order and, above all, the previously allotted quota of rice or equivalent in money. Left to them were the means to prevent open conflicts and collect the rice or specie from the village community.

Despite an ever burgeoning array of edicts regulating residence, dress, treatment of strangers, and all manner of behavior, even how to save rice by mixing it with other grains for meals, without continuous oversight within the village, the vast majority of Japanese were free at least collectively to order their own lives outside of the law's domain. So long as the village community remained outwardly submissive and law abiding, they could manage their household affairs almost at will, including how to deal with any surplus that exceeded allotments based on older surveys. Moreover, effectively untaxed were other sources of wealth. And such untaxed wealth grew. The more entrepreneurial or enterprising households accumulated surpluses that enabled them to acquire land as much as a symbol of status as a source of wealth. Rural sake brewers avoided the licensing and tax burdens of their urban competitors. Enterprising cultivators found new crops to grow and new ways to increase their yields. Peasant artisans found additional sources of income in a variety of skilled manufactures. Under such conditions, few communities had much incentive to seek political change. The consequence was to reinforce the political equilibrium of the Tokugawa settlement, which contributed further to the maintenance of peace, order, and economic growth. Yet, these same forces also stimulated economic stratification both within and among village communities.

Within villages the collective mechanisms of social ordering provided the means for orderly adjustment. With wealth and new community status came added burdens. As members of the community, their reputations and status, their full acceptance and leadership depended on their willingness to shoulder responsibilities for the common welfare. Intra-village conflicts presented different problems. Some villages prospered less than others, or did not prosper at all. Those in the more remote regions and more distant from the urban centers and well-trafficked highways lacked the sources for manufacture and trade available to others located more favorably. Those with less advantageous natural conditions for agriculture could not as readily introduce new crops or gain untaxed surpluses. Others were simply not as lucky in their entrepreneurship and enterprise of their constituents. When negotiated settlements failed, the only recourse was adjudication.

Villagers were not alone in advancing collective mechanisms of private ordering. Among the most economically significant institutions to develop during the Tokugawa era were various cooperative associations for the mutual benefit of their members. As in the case of the village, such associations of merchants, often in the form of *kabu nakama*, were licensed and promoted by the authorities as efficient (cost-free) mechanisms for maintaining order and payment of taxes. They were the counterpart of the medieval trade guilds in Western Europe. Although, as noted below, suits by members related to the distribution of profits from these and other associations were recognized, they were disfavored. Instead, the authorities preferred to allow them to thrive and serve self-policing functions. Tetsuji Okazaki argues persuasively that the security of transactions they provided contributed meaningfully to Japanese economic growth in the eighteenth and early nineteenth centuries.[40] Membership in the *kabu nakama* took the form of a proprietary share or *kabu* that could be used as collateral or transferred (ordinarily only with membership approval) by inheritance, sale, or loan.

Adjudication

Formal mediation and adjudication have been integral features of governance from the beginning of Japan's political development. We can only surmise the manner and means for the resolution of disputes in prehistoric periods. As chiefdoms appeared and the authority and capacity for coercive ordering developed, communal mediation was as likely in Japan as elsewhere to have yielded to adjudication. Reliance on customary norms and community sanctions may similarly be presumed to have been replaced by decisions by chiefs and elites based on rules that they made and enforced. The introduction of advanced conceptions of law and law enforcement from Imperial China, however, enabled new forms of

[40] Tetsuji Okazaki, "The Role of the Merchant Coalition in Pre-modern Japanese Economic Development: An Historical Institutional Analysis," (unpublished paper, 1999), http://www.computer-services.e.u-tokyo.ac.jp/p/cemano/research/DP/documents/coe-f-33.pdf. Last visited February 3, 2016.

regulatory law making and law enforcement. Unlike Imperial China, however, the combination of decentralizing forces with the expanding complexity of individual, household, and corporate entitlements to land and its produce fostered increasingly complex mechanisms for adjudication of land-related disputes. By the ninth century adjudication of land disputes had become an integral feature of governance.

At the center in Kyoto were the principal offices of governance, again based on Imperial Chinese models. One, a Bureau of Records (*Kirokujo*), had administrative functions as an office for record keeping and documentation. As the office for formal recognition of documented claims to imperial grants of offices, land, and related entitlements, the *Kirokujo* began to adjudicate competing claims to these entitlements conferred under the *ritsuryō* regime. It thereby progressively acquired judicial functions and soon became the office for civil suits. With jurisdiction for all criminal matters, the Bureau of Police (*Kebiishicho*) in contrast functioned along familiar Imperial Chinese patterns as a criminal court—although, unlike Imperial China, criminal law enforcement was never a defining feature of Japanese governance. The work of *Kirokujo* was a form of what might best be called "administrative adjudication" in that it principally involved determining the validity of conflicting claims on the basis of the presentation and authentication of documents evidencing conferrals or transfers of entitlements. As its decisions were based on precedents, the *Kirokujo* appears to have acquired in the process a significant law-making function as exemplified by the recognition of *shiki* as a transferable property interest.

To maintain order and to consolidate their capacity to command were high political priorities for the Kamakura rulers. Public order under their control and at least partial command were essential for purposes of enhancing both their political authority and power. Most important was their capacity to reward and protect allied warrior houses. The nature of their rule through layers of consensual undertakings between overlords and subordinate warrior retainers with reciprocal obligations for protection and a promise of reward in return for loyalty and service meant that, by definition, like their imperial predecessors, no warrior rulers could fully control. Without the resources to provide stipends to agent administrators, those who ruled at the center also suffered from weakened means for control and also created additional incentives for officials at the local level to expropriate local resources for their own benefit. As officials in the provinces gained control over wealth-creating resources, they were to establish independent bases for power. Thus for lack of more effective options, the Kamakura and Muromachi overlords at the center, like their *ritsuryō* predecessors, relied extensively on adjudication, particularly over land claims (i.e., control of revenue-producing territory) to maintain order as well as enhance their authority. In the process Japan's rulers established the necessary and sufficient structures for a fully developed private law system. By the end of the thirteenth century, an institutional structure for adjudication of private claims and recognition of applicable legal rules had almost fully evolved. Functioning within conceptions of law and governance borrowed initially from Imperial China as modified and adapted for warrior rule, the consequence was a legal order that included what we can describe as an incidental system of judicial precedents and private law rules within an essentially administrative order.

Under the Kamakura *bakufu*, adjudication became the primary means of maintaining order and control. A system of predictable procedures based on both edict and practice had fully emerged. The sources of decisional rules and principles included recognized customary practice, administrative precedent, and proscriptions legislated by both imperial and *bakufu* authorities. The process required outside complaint or accusation generally, and remained dependent on the petitioners' initiative and direction. The warrior adjudicators in Kamakura and those acting under imperial authority in Kyoto functioned as neutral arbiters.

Without the means for direct supervision and control or the resources necessary for direct policing and coercion, adjudication was the only alternative as a means of control over the warrior class with increasingly independent sources of wealth that still buttressed *bakufu* authority. Yet also by giving those subject to warrior rule some voice in the principal means for maintaining order and positioning those who ruled as neutral arbiters applying precedent, custom, and reason (*dōri*) as the primary source of legal rules, *bakufu* officials helped to legitimize their rule.[41] "The system was effective," Mass concludes, "because the Bakufu served as arbitrator, not as prosecutor, within an exclusively accusatorial process. Kamakura thus remained outside and above the suits it sought to resolve, and in the process insulated itself from undue partisanship and criticism."[42]

As the *bakufu* strengthened, the warrior officials at the center began to issue a growing number of orders and instructions to subordinates and future officials responsible for administration and the adjudication of disputes among the men-at-arms under *bakufu* jurisdiction. The most

41 *See* Tom R. Tyler, "Legitimacy and Legitimation," *Annual Review of Psychology*, vol. 57 (2006), pp. 375–400.

42 Jeffrey P. Mass, *The Development of Kamakura Rule, 1180–1250* (Stanford, CA: Stanford University Press, 1979), p. xv.

complete set of such instructions were contained in the *Goseibai Shikimoku*, known in English as the *Jōei* formulary of 1232, with hundreds of supplemental orders. Its promulgation was an exercise in legitimization as a set of rules for the warrior class with nationwide applicability. The legitimizing function of this law-making effort was even more apparent in its successor a century later, the *Kenmu* formulary (*Kenmu Shikimoku*) issued by the Ashikaga shogun in 1336, which has been described aptly as "an attempt to legitimize his coup d'état."[43]

Neither formulary was a "code" in the contemporary sense. Both are brief. The *Jōei* formulary has 51 articles; the *Kenmu* formulary, only 17. Both, however, were supplemented by edicts with an increasing number of legal rules (*tsuikahō*). They combined admonitions and commands based on precedent and customary norms within the warrior community. The *Jōei* formulary is foundational. It comprises a collection of general instructions to the *bakufu* warrior officials with respect to a variety of issues. The formulary begins with exhortations on the maintenance and repair of shrines and temples. Most, however, relate to the handling of cases brought to the authorities for adjudication. The primary purpose was to set out the basic rules on how to proceed—such as the necessity for documentary evidence—as well as substantive rules and principles to be applied, including interstitial identification of criminal offenses of concern. As supplemented, they constituted the written corpus of *bakufu* law. By its terms the *Kenmu* formulary and supplementary instructions were intended to restore order and compliance with the instructions of its *Jōei* predecessor. They reflect an overriding need to restore and maintain order in the wake of increasing lawlessness by warriors in particular. The 17 articles of the formulary deal with the decorum of warrior officials, the selection of able officials, and finally the need for access by commoners for hearings and redress of grievances. The supplementary laws lack organization and conceptual coherence. Missing are the general proscriptions and related penalties that constituted so conspicuous a feature of Imperial Chinese law. They are for the most part a collection of particularized commands ordering miscreant warriors to comply with precedents and prior commands to vacate improperly acquired lands, relinquish illegally claimed offices, to return misappropriated goods, or to pay taxes or revenues in default. Included also are provisions to protect with regulation of interest the supply of credit by money lenders with

---

[43] Kenneth A. Grossberg, *The Laws of the Muromachi Bakufu* (Tokyo: Monumenta Nipponica, 1981), p. 8, quoted in Haley, *Authority without Power*, p. 43.

pledges of commodities and goods. Lacking is any apparent coercive element. Coupled with the repetition of suits and appeals this suggests that the *bakufu* in fact lacked the means to compel compliance. The actual enforcement of *bakufu* judgments was, it appears, left to a combination of their consensus-creating legitimacy and self-help.

Whatever *bakufu* adjudication seems to have lacked in coercion, procedurally it functioned within a well-developed structure pursuant to well-defined evidentiary rules. Disputes classified as *shomusata* were tried in both Kamakura and *bakufu* offices in Kyoto. What would today be classified as criminal actions involving rebellion, theft, brigandry, homicide, rape, violent assaults, and similar conduct were tried by special *bakufu* offices in either Kamakura or Kyoto under *shomusata* procedures. The third category of miscellaneous cases, referred to as *zatsumusata*, encompassed various claims to property, other than land, arising from interest-bearing loans, bills of exchange, mortgages, and sales. At least by the fourteenth century these suits were being tried in Kamakura before the *monchiijo* under direct control of the *bakufu.* Documentary evidence of official appointment or investiture as well as commercial and other contractual instruments relating to debts, land, and distributions of property nevertheless determined the outcome of the vast majority of cases. Thus the Kamakura and imperial magistrates continued the development begun at least by the tenth century of law making by adjudication through precedent based on documentation or what might best be called "notarial" law.

Legislated rules, precedent, and documentary evidence were not the only bases for judicial decisions. Resort to "reason" or *dōri* was always an option. An open-ended principle that could be used whenever deemed necessary to fill gaps or to justify deviation from legislated rules or precedent, *dōri* represented in effect the consensus or sense of the warrior community. Although *dōri* provided a means for the recognition of community values, it was not a substitute for a conception of principled judicial reasoning or a belief in any universally applicable set of norms. Unlike Rome or China, no notion of universally applicable, transcendental norms, whether conceived as natural law or a separate moral order, took hold in Japan. Historically Japanese culture did not include shared belief in universal values nor a dichotomy between "good" and "evil." Despite the influence of universalistic modes of thought advanced in Buddhism and Neo-Confucianism, particularistic values remained primary. As expressed by Robert Bellah, "It [is] the particular system or collectivity of which one is a member which counts, whether it be family, *han* or Japan as a whole. Commitment to these tends to take precedence over universalistic commitments, such as commitment to truth and justice."[44] Assessing similar observations, S.N. Eisenstadt views Japan as a "de-Axializing" culture in which the universalistic and transcendental orientations were muted, segregated, and bracketed out.[45] As a result, no conception could have taken root in Japan of universally applicable legal rules or principles, especially ones against the legitimacy or "legality" of those imposed by rulers. Nor did Japan's reliance on Imperial Chinese conception of law as a set of ruler-determined administrative regulations and criminal penalties allow for the development of any generalized conception of private or civil law. In their place was an emphasis on *dōri*, community consensus, "harmony" (*wa*), and the legitimacy of those who governed as benevolent rulers maintaining the common "public" welfare as overriding social and political values. Without such conceptual framework, Japan's embryonic private law order could not, therefore, evolve beyond a basic institutional framework.

The emphasis on adjudication as a primary means of maintaining order and social control continued into the nineteenth century as the systematic adjudication of claims based on precedent developed even more fully under Tokugawa rule (1600–1867). The consequence was a growing volume and variety of rules and practices that constituted private law in all but name. By the eighteenth century Tokugawa edicts had recognized two types of adjudication—one labeled "inquisitorial," the other "adversarial" (in translation)—differentiated by the subject matter of the complaint and the extent to which the matter in dispute related to the interests of the Tokugawa overlords.[46] Japanese adjudicatory procedures further differentiated "adversarial" suits into four categories: "main suits" (*honkuji*), those related to land and water (*ronsho*), "money suits" (*kanekuji*), and mutual affairs (*nakama-goto*).[47] *Honkuji* was a generic category for all private law claims other than those that came within one of the three particular categories. *Ronsho* cases had special importance for the regime in that this category of suits covered disputes over irrigation entitlements. *Kanekuji* were essentially claims by creditors seeking to collect on defaults of loans with or without collateral but in

---

44 Robert N. Bellah, *Tokugawa Religion: The Values of Pre-Industrial Japan* (Boston: Beacon Press, 1970), p. 13.

45 S.N. Eisenstadt, *Japanese Civilization: A Comparative View* (Chicago: University of Chicago Press, 1996).

46 *See* Henderson, *Conciliation and Japanese Law: Tokugawa and Modern*, vol. 1, pp. 99–125; Yoshirō Hiramatsu, "Tokugawa Law," *Law in Japan: An Annual*, vol. 14 (1981), pp. 1–48.

47 Henderson, *Conciliation and Japanese Law: Tokugawa and Modern*, vol. 1, p. 102; Hiramatsu, "Tokugawa Law," p. 27.

context they involved various commercial transactions and instruments. Earlier forms were being adjudicated, however, at the outset of the Tokugawa era.[48] The Tokugawa authorities had little interest in adjudicating *Nakama-goto* suits in that they involved disputed distributions of profit within an association, which Tokugawa officials regarded as best resolved internally.

As influenced by Imperial Chinese law—particularly the Ming Code—these classifications and the differential treatment each received reflected a decision to allow official discretion and claimant voice in cases involving matters deemed less significant to the interests of the rulers. As in China, the outcome of disputes left to the initiative of claimants was considered to be of so little concern to the ruling authorities that they could receive official attention but could and indeed should be settled quickly, preferably by some mutually acceptable compromise. Unlike the discretionary enforcement of "private law rules" in China, however, in Japan these suits, particularly commercial suits, became increasingly common fare as they were resolved through well-established adjudicatory procedures. With the frequency of like claims, a system of private law rules established by precedent developed. By the end of the seventeenth century the adjudicating officials of the Tokugawa regime had developed "by judicial precedent," in the words of John H. Wigmore, "a body of native law and practice, which can only be compared with the English independent development after the 1400's."[49]

The political consolidation of Japan had been completed at the end of the sixteenth century. A balance among the competing warrior houses had been achieved within a decentralized framework that would last for two and a half centuries. Despite a formal and extensive order of regulatory law, most Japanese enjoyed a significantly greater autonomy than any comparable polity in size and wealth. The life of the majority, living in rural villages and hamlets, was ordered predominantly outside of the domain of law by local custom and private ordering. Consensual arrangements were commonly used to avoid or to circumvent administrative requirements.[50] Even in Japan's growing urban centers, the regulatory

---

[48] *See* Jimbo Fumio, "Edo bakufu deirisuji no saiban ni okeru honkuji-kanekuji no bunka ni tsuite [Differentiation between main suits and money suits in adjudication of adversarial suits under the Edo bakufu]," *Hōseishi kenkyū*, vol. 45 (1995), pp. 1–38.

[49] John Henry Wigmore, *Panorama of the World's Legal Systems* (St. Paul, MN: West Publishing Co., 1928), p. 504.

[50] *See*, e.g., Dan Fenno Henderson, *Village "Contracts" in Tokugawa Japan* (Seattle: University of Washington Press, 1975).

reach of shogunate and daimyo law was limited. For city dwellers as well, private ordering prevailed. Disputes and conflicts that could not be resolved within individual communities, particularly intra-village disputes and between individuals from separate communities, were left to the administrative adjudicatory mechanisms of the shogunate and individual domains.[51] Hence despite stratification and diffusion of wealth that could have created pressures for political change, the structural equilibrium of the Tokugawa settlement held to await catalysts from the outside in the mid nineteenth century that revealed the regime's full weakness and set into motion the full forces of political transformation of the Meiji Restoration.

---

[51] *See* Henderson, *Conciliation and Japanese Law: Tokugawa and Modern*, vol. 1, pp. 162–163.

5. Rivers, rifles, and religion: the primacy of private law in Western Europe

The Western legal tradition is today the paramount source of perceptions of law worldwide. Conceptions and processes, which for Europeans by the nineteenth century identified the attributes of law in all "civilized" nations, have become universally accepted. Hand in glove with prevailing notions of statehood, the understanding of law as predominantly a system of private law enforced through litigation was evidenced in the centrality of civil (private law) codes and judicially constructed common (private) law. Today law faculties throughout the world continue to treat private law—contracts, civil delicts (torts), property—as law's core components. In law schools in the United States, multiple fields of regulatory public law—with the notable exception of criminal law—are sporadically taught as electives. Seldom if ever is any distinction as described in Chapter 1 noted between the manner of private and public law enforcement. This is in part the result of the pervasive influence of private law institutions. The role of judges and judicial processes, not to mention the emphasis on "rights," are private law borrowings that have become fundamental features of the Western legal tradition. They shape all fields of law. We might well ask how could this be if in developmental terms public law orders represent the more advanced prototype as evidenced in the contemporary expansion of public law in all legal systems.

Why Western law succeeded globally is a relatively easy question to answer. The processes of legal transplantation varied, but colonization by Western European states and imposition of their municipal law were overwhelmingly the most common. This was a story of rifles. Extending throughout the Americas and the Philippine islands, the Hispanic colonial empire, as detailed in Chapter 6, represented the first, territorially most expansive, and longest-lasting external extension of Western European law. The combined kingdoms of Castile and Aragon also represented at the dawn of the seventeenth century the most advanced legal order in continental Europe. Castile had enacted the first private law code influenced by the *Corpus Juris Civilis*—the *Siete Partidas*—which, along with one of the earliest post-Roman statutes of Western Europe, the Visigothic *Fuero Juzgo*, was foundational for its empire and its remnants to the end of the nineteenth century. During the preceding two centuries English common law as well as French and Dutch civil law similarly spread with colonization. By the end of the nineteenth century, as noted, only a handful of countries outside of the Ottoman and Russian empires, including the most institutionally developed polities of Northeast Asia, remained independent. Beginning with the United States, nearly all post-colonial regimes retained their former colonial legal institutions and orientations[1]—a pattern that continued through the twentieth century with the exception of the lands formerly under Ottoman rule. All, however, ultimately succumbed to Western military, industrial, and cultural dominance and within a generation had reformed traditional political and legal institutions and structures along Western European patterns—patterns that derived from Western Europe's own peculiar institutional experience.

To understand the development of Western law and the primacy and global reach of private law with its related emphasis on adjudication, we need to look back in time to examine the historical foundations on which Western legal tradition rested. The most commonly given reasons are the reception of the *Corpus Juris Civilis* and subsequent expansion of Roman private law as the *ius commune* of continental Europe. Left unanswered—and for the most part unquestioned—is why the discovery of a long-neglected, ineffective, five-century-old *codex* had the influence that followed its rediscovery. What formative influences and political structures enabled its initial reception and propelled its subsequent expansion as the primary basis of European law? To answer these questions, the comparison with Japan suggests several cardinal factors.

As in Japan, the political and legal institutions of Western Europe evolved in the context of competing centers of authority and power, the emergence of warrior overlords, and centuries of continuous warfare. The aim of those who governed was twofold—to gain control over sources of wealth and to maintain order. As we have seen with respect to both China and Japan, to appropriate wealth, centralizing, kingdom-creating rulers

---

[1] Latin America is a notable exception. The new states of Spanish America upon independence in the first decades of the nineteenth century uniformly rejected at least wholesale adherence to Spanish colonial institutions in favor of the most available "modern" models. They thus adapted the United States Constitution and French Civil Code as more suitable than wholesale adherence to Spanish law. *See* M.C. Mirow, *Latin American Law: A History of Private Law and Institutions in Spanish America* (Austin, TX: University of Texas Press, 2004).

and their challengers had to control human and wealth-producing sources. Initially, as elsewhere, these were sedentary, agricultural communities. Over time, with the growth of commerce, they faced the more daunting task of controlling and appropriating wealth from highly mobile sources. The two objectives were interrelated. To assure the continuous creation and redistribution of wealth, they needed local order and stability. In order to maintain order and defend against challengers, they needed a surplus of both human and material resources for military use. As again in Japan, within the principal polities that had emerged by the dawn of the modern era—England, France, and the kingdoms of the Iberian peninsula (first Portugal, then Castile and Aragon)—balances were finally achieved between those who ruled from the center and their regional challengers. More precarious were the mutual needs to fill royal treasuries and to maintain order. Various resolutions were reached—more lasting in Japan than in Western Europe, where to the end of the twentieth century rulers continued to confront external threats from within the continent. In both, those with a meaningful degree of wealth-creating autonomy—in particular, the rice-producing villages of Japan and the merchant communities at the mouths of Europe's major rivers and the merchant-dominated city-states of Italy—produced and kept for themselves significant gains in wealth. Also as in Japan, adjudicatory processes constituted the principal means by which rulers maintained internal order. Within the warrior communities, as Marc Bloch observed, "the right to sit in judgment on his subordinates, to the exclusion of other courts, alone enabled a lord both to protect them and to maintain effective control over them."[2] By the twelfth century, adjudication had become the primary mode of dispute resolution and law enforcement in each of Western Europe's early kingdoms as well as, importantly, by the Church. In other words, several centuries before the rediscovery of the *Corpus Juris Civilis*, various systems of private law rules enforced through adjudication extended throughout Western Europe and its constituent communities.

Unlike the China-sourced notions of law that dominated Japan, the legal conceptions that became constituent features of Western Europe's legal culture by the twelfth century fit perfectly the prevailing adjudicatory structures. As these concepts were recreated and spread, adjudication with its principal actors—first priests, then overlords, and finally judges—became even more embedded in the structures of governance.

2 Marc Bloch, *Feudal Society*, vol. 2 (Chicago: University of Chicago Press, 7th ed., 1968), p. 359.

The discovery and study of the *Corpus Juris Civilis*, the reform of canon law, as well as the development of natural law theory between 1050 and 1350 had no counterpart in Japan—neither did a view of *justice* with universal and morally binding applicability.

For the history of Western Europe, the twelfth century may have been, in the words of Harold Berman, "*the* legal century, the century in which the Western legal tradition was formed."[3] Within Europe, perhaps uniquely, even earlier a legal culture had already begun to evolve within which law was conceived as a system of rights enforced by their holders through judicial processes along with a notion of justice that included universally mandatory principles. The consequence was a synergy that led in the eleventh and twelfth centuries to an institutional transformation and deep implantation of shared understandings about the essential nature of law itself. Law came to define the sources and boundaries of authority. It enveloped within its terms what might otherwise have remained forms of private ordering and public law duties as in China and Japan. Above all, for our purposes, nowhere else on the planet was law's direct and derivative legitimacy, its consensus-building capacity, or its domain so extensive.

RIVERS

Three distinct factors—geography, war, and the Roman Catholic Church—define the institutional borders and political orders that formed in Western Europe. The first is geography. Western Europeans had ready access to the sea. All but one transcontinental river—the Danube—flow northward; none but the Rhône, directly into the Mediterranean. The interior terrain is marked by mountains, hills, and valleys, interlaced over a dozen major rivers, each with multiple tributaries. Finally, Western Europe is blessed with a temperate climate. All combined in the first millennium of the Common Era to facilitate south and westward tribal and coastal invasion, small cohesive settlements in interior regions, grain agriculture, husbandry, and a continuously expanding movement of persons, goods, and ideas.

The Atlantic Ocean and the Norwegian and Mediterranean seas circumscribe the western, northern, and southern borders of Western Europe. The North and Baltic Seas separate out the Nordic regions. The British Isles are left in splendid isolation. Only the eastern borders have

[3] Harold J. Berman, *Law and Revolution: The Formation of the Western Legal Tradition* (Cambridge, MA: Harvard University Press, 1983), p. 120.

been historically in contention. Mountains stretching from the Schwabish Alps along the north side of the Danube through the Carpathian mountain range, which curves back toward the Danube east of contemporary Belgrade, form the principal natural border on the east. Along the northern coast a flat plain stretches from the Pyrenees to the Urals. To the south, hill country intersected by rivers begins west of the Elbe.

Again rivers mattered. Four paradoxically constituted both barriers and significant means of connection. One, the Danube, flows eastward into the Black Sea from the mountains of the Black Forest. Its headwaters are within less than a hundred kilometers of those of the Rhine, which like the Elbe combined with the Valtava, one of its principal tributaries, flows north into the North Sea. A fourth, the Oder, flows out of the Sudeten Mountains northward into the Baltic Sea, within a few kilometers of the Elbe. The Rhine, the Elbe, and the Oder thus facilitated transport and communication from interior regions to the North Sea and the Baltic with the Danube similarly connected interior southeastern settlements with the Black Sea and the Eastern Mediterranean. Of the major transnational rivers only the Rhône, with headwaters in the Alps and valleys circumscribed by mountains and hills, flows into the Mediterranean. It is the only river that provides access into the interior of Western Europe from the Mediterranean. Not coincidentally was it the Roman republic's principal military highway to its northwestern domains. No single political regime, including Rome, was able fully to dominate one, much less all, of these continental thoroughfares. None would ever succeed in fully controlling access to the sea.

Within continental Europe the Danube and the Rhine marked for the Romans the northern and northeastern extent of civilization and their rule.[4] The lands to the north and to the east beyond these two rivers were left to sedentary agricultural tribes. Wealth in grain, livestock, and goods was generated in the east and south—from Anatolia around the Mediterranean through the Fertile Crescent and along the Nile and coastal North Africa, and back across narrow straits at Gibraltar into the Iberian peninsula. The Mediterranean was a natural highway. Until the end of the fifteenth century goods and produce from all adjoining regions could be transported for comparable distances more efficiently by ship in the Mediterranean than almost anywhere else in the world. The centers of

---

[4] The province of Dacia Triana is the one exception. It stretched from the Danube northwards to include several regions of what is today Romania and even, for a while, into Moldova. The province was held by the Romans following Trajan's defeat of the Dacian kingdom in 106 until abandoned to the Goths in 275.

wealth and population were thus to the east and the south. Western Europe was a backwater. Dense forests, few extensive arable plains, and even fewer available agricultural workers gave the Romans little incentive to extend the frontiers of their rule to the east beyond the Rhine or north beyond the Danube, their most defensible natural northern borders.

As in China, the first enduring political regimes to develop in Western Europe had full control of the rivers within their territory. Control by the kings of Wessex over the Severn and the Thames enabled their unification of England as a single kingdom in the third decade of the tenth century. France formed later. The largest and most fertile river plains in continental Europe are those of the Seine and the Somme, the Loire and the Garonne, along with their tributaries, all flowing northwestward into the Bay of Biscay or the English Channel. As rulers gained dominion over these rivers, the first significant medieval polities of continental Europe developed. With control over the Rhône from Lyons to Arles in the fourteenth and fifteenth centuries the basic boundaries of contemporary France were established.

Portugal was exceptional. By 1200 Portugal was fully established as the first still-extant territorial polity on the Iberian peninsula, second only to England in all of Western Europe, with full control over six of its nine major rivers—the Lima, Cávado, and Mondego in the north; the Sorraia and Sado in the center; and the Mira in the south—and partial but dominant control over two of the longest rivers—the Douro and the Tagus (or Tejo). All originate in Spain but exit into the Atlantic in Portugal. The longest is the Tagus, which flows westward from Sierra de Albarracín in the east between the Sierra de Gredos and Montes de Toledo in central Iberia to the Atlantic through Portugal with Lisbon at its mouth. The Portuguese rulers also controlled all major tributaries. The only exception is the Guadiana, which flows east to west through Spain, then south where it forms the Spanish–Portuguese border. It too ends in the Atlantic at the Gulf of Cádiz. Thus, unlike all but one (Galicia) of its Iberian neighbors, Portugal had full access to the Atlantic but none directly to the Mediterranean.

Equally significant in the Iberian peninsula is the Ebro. It flows southeastward from the Cantabrian Mountains through the lower Pyrenees into the Mediterranean, forming midway between Barcelona and Valencia the largest wetland delta on the Mediterranean. Both the Tagus and the Ebro have historically delineated the borders of competing regimes. In the early medieval period the kingdoms of Aragon and Castile controlled the headwaters of each. Until the fifteenth century only the Tagus was fully controlled by a single ruler, first under the Emirate (756–926) and then the Caliphate (929–1031) of Córdoba.

East of the Rhine and along the Danube are regions that have been in continuous territorial flux. Except along the northern coasts, stable, territorially defined polities did not develop until the nineteenth century, except perhaps for Hungary in its mountain-protected valley. Into the twenty-first century, the territories along these river valleys—particularly the Danube—have remained the principal contested regions of Western Europe.

Also defining Western Europe is the diversity of the descendants of the region's first inhabitants. They include the first tribal settlers, the Romans, and later arrivals, as well as invaders through several centuries of settlement, migration, conquest, and varying degrees of assimilation. Some, like the Franks and Alamani in the north, are believed to have lived for centuries in well-established settlements along the Rhine. Others were relative newcomers. Jutes, Angles, and Saxons had moved into England from the coastal areas along the North Sea, driving the Celts, among the earliest tribes of the continental heartland, even further to the periphery. Tribes from northeastern and central Europe, like the Burgundians, had migrated to the Roman borders, pushed by competing tribes, particularly from the Baltic regions and the east, but also pulled into the Roman political, economic, and cultural orbit by its wealth and opportunities for advancement.

By the fourth century, Rome had begun its prolonged withdrawal in the northwest, inviting occupation of former territories by various regional tribes. Roman occupiers retreated entirely from the more remote, sparsely populated areas of their Western Empire. In more populated regions, they were gradually assimilated. In the most populous areas at the core of Roman rule—the Italian and Iberian peninsulas and southern France—the process of assimilation was reversed with the tribal peoples and their leaders acquiring the language and habits—including law—of those whose lands they now ruled.

To the east the Goths, having migrated southwards from the Baltic in different tribal groupings, had settled and established kingdoms from the Baltic to the Danube and Black Sea. Constantinople and the Eastern Empire withstood their raids and invasion, and peaceful interaction and accommodation ensued. Hunnic invaders from the central Asian steppes under Attila (406–453) ruptured these relationships and transformed the Gothic kingdoms. Split into two regional groupings—the Visigoths and the Ostrogoths—they renewed their efforts to enter the empire either as refugees fleeing from or invaders subject to Hunnic domination. The population and overall military superiority of the Eastern Empire ultimately prevailed. Prevented from occupying the rich and well-populated lands of the eastern Mediterranean but freed from Hunnic control after

Attila's death, the Visigoths led by Alaric (395–410) moved eastwards into the heart of the Western Empire. They were followed at the end of the century by the Ostrogoths, who established control over much of Italy. The Vandals allied with the Suebi and Alans entered Iberia at the dawn of the fifth century. In the northwest corner of Iberia, the Germanic Suebi took over the Roman province of Galicia, establishing a kingdom ruled from Braga (today in Portugal). Although the Roman Senate was still meeting in the sixth century,[5] the Visigoth sacking of Rome in 410 marked the end of the Roman Empire in the West as well as the birth of Western Europe. Initially enlisted to assist Roman recovery of the lost Iberian provinces, the Visigoth kings within the next two decades had established full dominion over most of Iberia but for the Suebian northwest and a cluster of other northern territories along the Atlantic.

By the end of the fifth century, the Visigoths controlled much of southern Gaul and Iberia. They established a kingdom that at its height under the reign of Euric (466–484) stretched from the Loire River to Gibraltar, with Toulouse its capital. The victory of Clovis at the battle of Vouillé in 507 reduced the kingdom to the Iberian peninsula, with a new capital at Toledo. An Ostrogothic kingdom under Theodoric dominated the Italian peninsula. Another Germanic tribe, the Vandals, had allied with the Romans as well as the Visigoths. Crossing the Straits of Gibraltar in 449 they had established control over the Roman provinces of North Africa. In the north the Franks under Clovis established control over much of Roman Gaul—not coincidentally the region most comparable to China with the continent's largest and most fertile contiguous river valleys unprotected by natural barriers. Only the Iberian Visigothic kingdom endured for long. Protected by the Pyrenees in the north, threats to it came from the south. Neither of the unified kingdoms established by Clovis or Theodoric outlasted their founders. By the mid sixth century, imperial rule from Constantinople under Justinian had been briefly reestablished in Italy, North Africa, and southeastern Spain, only to be relinquished by the end of the century in northern Italy to the Lombards, and their Bavarian, Bulgar, Gepedae, and Saxon allies. Clovis's Frankish kingdom was divided among his sons and later grandsons. Although ostensibly the kingdom remained intact, fratricidal wars resulted in its fragmentation. The Kingdom of the Franks was not fully reunited until the first half of the eighth century under Charles Martel.

---

5 O.F. Robinson, T.D. Fergus, and W.M. Gordon, *An Introduction to European Legal History* (Abingdon, Oxon: Professional Books, 1985), p. 17.

RIFLES

A second factor—warfare—also shaped the borders and profoundly influenced the structures of the political regimes that emerged and matured throughout the continent in the wake of Roman rule. The migrating tribes were predominantly headed by warrior chiefs whose rule was based on military success. As one tribe in search of land or plunder pressed against another, those whose leaders were better able to mobilize resources and warriors to win battles, and to occupy and hold land for their followers, were able to establish and organize sedentary agricultural settlements and polities. As these and subsequent warrior-chiefs-turned-warrior-kings sought control over larger territories and more peoples or simply to defend the territories that they had acquired, they required larger military forces and greater resources. To achieve either goal, they had to compromise their autonomy and capacity to coerce by forging internal and external alliances, creating in the process complex structures of mutual dependence. Even the most successful, however, often lacked the means to ensure the capability of progeny. This failure throughout Western Europe to resolve the ultimate problem of succession—the peaceful transfer of their personal authority and power—led to repeated internecine conflicts among rival claimants. Facing unrelenting external as well as internal threats, no early ruler could marshal the resources necessary to create a corps of officials who were ultimately accountable to them in the administration of the emergent kingdoms, whether in the collection of taxes or enforcement of other laws. Nor could they extract wealth—especially the mobile wealth generated by commercial activities with rivers and especially uncontrollable sea lanes—by mere command. They were therefore forced to seek the revenues they required through consent. One outcome was the development of representative assemblies throughout Western Europe from the Catalan Cortes to the English Parliament.[6]

---

[6] On the relationship between warfare and the development of representative government in Western Europe, *see* Thomas N. Bisson, "The Military Origins of Medieval Representation," *American Historical Review*, vol. 71 (1966), pp. 1199–1216; Brian M. Dowling, "Medieval Origins of Constitutional Governance in the West," *Theory and Society*, vol.18 (1989), pp. 213–247; and Edgar Kiser and April Linton, "Determinants of the Growth of the State: War and Taxation in Early Modern France and England," *Social Forces*, vol. 80 (2001), pp. 411–448; David Stasavage, "War, Geographic Scale, and Constitutional Control," unpublished manuscript, January 2009. http://politics.as.nyu.edu/docs/IO/5395/geographic_scale.pdf. Last visited February 5, 2016.

RELIGION

Religion was the third factor. No single feature of early Western European history rivals the foundational influence of the Roman Catholic Church. Within the diversity spawned by European geography, migrations, and warfare, it supplied the one constant, unifying feature. Around the Bishop of Rome a new order formed. Adapting administrative structures and the language of the Western Empire, the Church emerged as its principal organizational and cultural remnant. With dedicated personnel and an overriding evangelical mission to the pagan tribes, within a millennium the Latin Church under the Bishop of Rome had extended the Christian faith and its organizational reach throughout the former Western Empire well beyond the Roman frontiers. The Latin Church replicated the structure of the empire. As Roman control waned, the Church reestablished a hierarchical administrative system that remains unique even among organized religions. It was from inception centered in Rome with territorial subdivisions—dioceses under the authority of bishops and parishes under priests—that by the end of the tenth century stretched from the Atlantic to beyond the Wistula and from the North Sea to the Mediterranean. By the middle of the fourteenth century its reach extended from Portugal and the Straits of Gibraltar through the lands bordering the Baltic Sea, defining Western Europe even today.

The Church also inherited the language of the empire. By adopting Latin, the Church provided a common written language for all of Western Europe and also ensured access to the written legacies of the Roman Empire—including law. All early written laws were in Latin and thus by default the customary norms and legal rules of the Germanic tribes and other non-Romans had to be expressed in the legal terminology of Roman law. This process in itself ensured Roman legal influence. The Church also hosted the centers of literacy and learning. Its missionaries and priests provided early political rulers with their primary initial access to written communication and to a pool of talent on whom Europe's first post-Roman rulers drew. Long before the twelfth century the Church had already nurtured a European legal culture dominated by conceptions and the language of Roman law that permeated territories that had never been subject to Roman rule or its law.

For our purposes two fundamental aspects of the Church's influence need to be stressed. The first is that the Church epitomizes a regime with authority but without coercive power. Not coincidentally, as in early and medieval Japan, such regimes tend to rely on adjudication of disputes brought by litigants as a primary means for the enforcement and recognition of legal rules. Ecclesiastical courts throughout the Church's domain played a foundational role from inception in the development of adjudication and private law. The availability of a supranational system of courts also enabled the making of a continental *ius commune* that encompassed both adjudication and private law with the additional emphasis on a conceptual system of natural legal rights as reformulated by twelfth and thirteenth century canon law jurists and theologians.

A second contribution of the Church was its competitive role. The Church functioned in all meaningful respects as a political competitor for allegiance and resources with all of the emerging political regimes in Western Europe. Until the Papal Revolution at the end of the eleventh century, the demarcations of authority and jurisdiction between the Church and secular political authorities were uncertain and contested. In places the Church was a territorial ruler. Throughout Western Europe, it collected its own tax—the tithe—and controlled in addition vast sources of wealth and wealth-creating activities. Its omnipresence and supranational authority were sufficient to restrict secular control. Moreover, by the twelfth century the Church also asserted overriding authority and adjudicatory jurisdiction over a category of matters (*ratione materiae*) of core importance to secular rulers, as, for example, ecclesiastical jurisdiction over marriage and divorce. The Church's separate claim to jurisdiction "by reason of persons" (*ratione personarum*) provided at least a legal justification to protect various categories of persons, particularly clergy and their households but also students and "travelers," particularly merchants and sailors, from regulation by secular political authorities. With canon law allowance for removal from secular to ecclesiastic courts based on the ecclesiastic court determination of some "default" in secular adjudication,[7] adjudicatory jurisdiction became the focal issue of many of the most critical competitive political contests. To the extent that such jurisdictional claims were recognized, the Church effectively constrained both the authority and the power of secular rulers within territories they otherwise controlled. Unlike the political regimes of Eastern Europe as well as Asia, the Church thus imposed significant competitive structural as well as ideological constraints on all emerging political regimes in Western Europe.

---

7 Berman, *Law and Revolution*, p. 223.

Law and the Early Kingdoms—c. 450–650 CE

At the dawn of the seventh century an astonishing variety of political orders had formed. A few—Visigothic Iberia, a Frankish kingdom under Clovis (c. 466–511) in France, the first Swedish kingdom—presaged the formation of future nation-states. Each evidenced law's main developmental progression from essentially consensual, communitarian systems based on custom and consensus with rulers acting more as responsive mediators to institutionalized legal orders in which rulers actively redefined and enforced legal rules. As the invaders and their descendants settled and established kingdoms, they initiated a separate trajectory—or a step backward—as relatively primitive polities replaced the much more advanced, centralized administrative structures of the Roman Empire. In their interaction, customary norms applicable to communities with common ancestors gave way to rules made by those who governed and applied through the territory under their control. Equally if not more significant for the argument offered here, rulers throughout Western Europe replicated patterns of ancient kingdoms. As in Japan, with limited authority as well as the capacity to coerce, they resorted to adjudication as a primary mode of law making and enforcement. What differed was the Church and the legacy of Roman law.

Across Western Europe the warrior rulers and the territories they ruled acquired some of the trappings of the vanished empire. In need of authority as well as augmented power, rulers sought sources for both. With conversion of entire tribes, the Church provided one source of legitimacy and law another. The Church was the principal source of Western European unity. Pope Gregory I (c. 540–604) had expanded the Church's missionary and political role. By the eighth century papal coronation functioned as a critical legitimating ceremony. With that legitimizing role, the Church in effect defined kingship. Under its tutelage throughout the region, kings emerged as justice-dispensing adjudicators as an integral feature of royal governance.

To redress the grievances of petitioning subjects, the early kings and their delegates relied on communal custom, biblical admonition, and their own edicts, all mixed in varying degrees with vestiges of Roman law. As described by Julia Smith: "All the kingdoms that emerged on the Continent in the fifth century relied directly on these inherited techniques of ruling. By appropriating traditional mechanisms of government for their own use, fifth- and sixth century warrior kings asserted legitimacy, collected revenue, made law, and proclaimed their power."[8]

The appropriation of Roman models of governance was almost immediate in the early kingdoms established by the Goths and the Franks in Italy, Spain, and, at least, central and southern France where native Roman inhabitants outnumbered their new rulers. Roman landowning elites were increasingly drawn into the new political orders. Law like language reflected predominant Roman influence. Principles and practices of Roman law rapidly pervaded these kingdoms. In Italy, Theodoric was recognized both as Gothic king and, with Constantinople's recognition, legitimate ruler of Italy. Roman legal institutions thus simply continued to be recognized. Roman aristocrats, such as Theodoric's *amanuensis* Cassiodorus, as Michael Richter puts it,[9] were co-opted. The rulers of the Gothic kingdoms in Iberia and southern France were among the first to legislate (of course in Latin) on Roman models, presumptively for the Roman population.

Western Europe's first law makers, however, were the Visigothic kings of the Iberian peninsula. King Euric (456–484) is believed to have issued the earliest Visigothic law book, the *Codex Euricianus*. Praised by Ernst Levy as the "best legislative work of the fifth century,"[10] Euric's code is believed to have been promulgated c. 476. In 506 Euric's son and successor, Alaric II (484–507), issued his own set of laws, known best as the *Lex Romana Visigothorum* or simply the *Brevarium Alarici*, apparently based on the Theodosian Code. Whether territorial or personal in scope—their application remains contested—neither appears to have significantly influenced subsequent Iberian law.[11] The legislation of Spain's earliest kingdom with lasting influence was the *Liber Judiciorum* or *Fuero Juzgo* (also known as the *Libro de las Leyes* or *Lex Barbara Visigothorum*) that was developed over four reigns—Kings Chindasvinth (641–652), Reckesvinth (652–672), Ervig (680–687), and Egica (687–701). Also written in Latin, the *Fuero Juzgo* continued to be applied with

---

[8] Julia M.H. Smith, *Europe after Rome: A New Cultural History, 500–1000* (Oxford: Oxford University Press, 2005), p. 29. *See also* Peter Heather, *The Goths* (London and Malden, MA: Blackwell Publishers, 1998), pp. 194–195.

[9] Michael Richter, *The Formation of the Medieval West* (New York: St. Martin's Press, 1994), p. 60.

[10] Ernst Levy, *Gesammelte Schriften*, vol. 1 (1963), p. 209, quoted in P.D. King, *Law and Society in the Visigothic Kingdom* (Cambridge: Cambridge University Press, 1972), p. 7.

[11] *See* E.N. van Kleffens, *Spanish Law until the End of the Middle Ages* (Edinburgh: Edinburgh University Press, 1968), pp. 67–70, 66.

modification in Castile and later all of Spain and its empire into the nineteenth century.

Clovis and England's Saxon kings also made law. Clovis's *Pactus Legis Salicae* is generally believed to have been compiled during his reign in about 496. As a collection of royal decrees and legal procedures applicable in the Frankish region between the Loire and the Rhine, Roman influence in its content, except for language, is much less apparent. Like other written laws of the period it specifies the compensatory monetary payments to be made for various wrongs, including payment to plaintiffs by defendants for failing to answer a summons. The earliest known written laws in England were the decrees issued by Ethelbert, the King of Kent (c. 560–616) in about 602, listing the penalties for a long list of offenses. Like the *Legis Salicae*, most were fines to be paid to the person who suffered the harm, but many were payable to the king as, for instance, a freeman's theft from freeman for which the fine was three-fold the value of the goods or the goods themselves payable to the king.[12] Later that century King Ine (688–726) issued what is believed to be the first written set of laws by a Wessex king.[13]

The content of the general laws of the early kingdoms evidences the foremost concerns of the kings who made them. Their emphasis on wrongs and penalties reflects social stability and order as their prime purpose. The civil and criminal fines they collected were also, it might be noted, a handsome addition to their revenues. Whatever their motivations, they thereby laid the foundation for a core conception of law as a system of rules designed to redress "private" grievances through an adjudicatory process that at its core excluded more direct regulatory controls. Once developed, however, the law-enforcing structures that were constructed on this foundation became the chief means for enforcing all legal rules.

Notably absent are comprehensive rules for the imposition and collection of revenues. One explanation is that such rules were simply stated in incremental edicts not general law, which most contemporary historians tend to ignore. Another, not inconsistent explanation, is that our contemporary understandings of "taxation" as a governmental, public law imposition conceptually simply did not exist. As noted previously, Roman private law, much less public law, had not matured into coherent conceptual systems. Claims to revenues by both the early European kings

---

12 *See* Dorothy Whitelock, ed., *English Historical Documents*, vol. 1, *c. 500–1042* (New York: Oxford University Press, 1955), p. 357.

13 *Id.*, p. 364.

and local magnates therefore were best conceived as proprietary interests in the lands they governed. A roughly similar process, as detailed in the preceding chapter, occurred in Japan with the development of *shiki* as officially (i.e., legally) recognized transferable claims to revenues for designated land separated from the governmental office to which the entitlement was originally connected. The conceptual basis for claims to revenue by those who ruled claims was thus a private proprietary interest in the land and thus a claim for "rents" as revenue. Without a conception of "public revenue," all income to those who ruled had to be construed as private property, thereby further reinforcing the primacy of private law.

Political Consolidation, Fragmentation, and Reconsolidation— 700–1200 CE

By the end of the eighth century a political and economic revival had commenced. In northern France the Carolingians under Charlemagne (747–814) replaced the Merovingian kings to create an invigorated united kingdom that grew into the largest united political domain of the medieval period, incorporating a large portion of both western and central Europe, even briefly including much of the northern Italian peninsula. Crowned Holy Roman Emperor by Pope III in 800, Charlemagne represented Western Europe's first and grandest effort to replicate the extant Roman Empire in the East.

Legal developments evidenced their progress. An apparent transition to a public law regime commenced. They had begun to transform civil delicts (torts) into public law crimes as they replaced compensatory sanctions with fines and punishments. Seventh and eighth century Alamanic Laws (*Lex Alamannorum*) as well as Bavarian laws (*Lex Baiuvaiorum*) had typically provided for a specified amount in compensation to be paid as *wergeld* to those harmed by specified wrongs. The Capitularies of the Carolingian kings similarly identified specific wrongs but tended to replace compensatory sanctions with fines to be paid to those who ruled. Nonetheless the criminal process depended upon complainants and private prosecution. In the Carolingian domains as well as other parts of Western Europe, adjudication thus remained the primary mode of law enforcement and maintenance of order.

Invasions on all sides during the eighth and ninth centuries arrested this progression. Vikings and Danes in North and West, Magyars from the East, Islamic invaders from the East and South placed even greater demands for military resources to maintain control and order on each of these emerging regimes. Once again rifles determined Europe's future course. By the end of the second decade of the eighth century Visigothic

Spain—Western Europe's largest and institutionally most advanced regime—had been successfully invaded and conquered by Islamic Berbers from North Africa. By the mid ninth century Viking and Danish raiders had made significant territorial conquests in Ireland and Scotland, as well as France and southern Italy. They temporarily ruled England under Cnut and established a permanent settlement in France that as Normandy stills bears their name. At the end of the ninth century the Magyars had entered the Carpathian basin and commenced their enduring settlement. Unable to gain new territory and resources and increasingly unable to maintain control within territory previously acquired and ruled, the early Western European political regimes collapsed as a new form of governance emerged. With incessant warfare and overriding demand for security, in their place systems of decentralized rule based on consensual alliances among those with sufficient military prowess to make credible promises to provide security and reward in return for loyalty and service intensified into what is commonly referred to as European feudalism. The relationship between lord and vassal, a participant in the ruling elite—and, by extension, subject and ruler—was now conceived as founded upon a consensual undertaking with reciprocal and conditional obligations. One immediate consequence for Western Europe was that Roman law conceptions of both ownership and contract now became the basis for claims by those who ruled. And, as in Japan as well as republican Rome, formal processes for adjudication of competing claims among the ruling elites became all the more necessary.

On the eve of the tenth century a complex network of diverse, competing systems of autonomy and control characterized all of Western Europe. From urban centers in the South and North, to isolated agricultural communities in interior regions, a remarkable variety of political orders had emerged. Warfare and insecurity, along with the collapse of a money-based economy and disruption of established trading routes and networks, led to declines in population and urban life. European communities became increasingly isolated into nucleated villages, local trading zones, and subsistence-based agricultural households. Even the Church seemed to follow suit as the monastic orders appeared as essentially self-contained communities.

Access to the sea enabled the growth of relatively autonomous city-states, generally ruled by merchant oligarchies, which, largely free of external political control, were able to develop into thriving commercial and banking centers and both customary and institutionalized systems of private ordering. Without the means for expansive administrative regulation, few if any political regimes could subject merchant communities to their control. Throughout Western Europe merchants, like their southern Chinese counterparts, were able to establish largely autonomous means of private ordering. Until the eighteenth century European *lex mercatoria* consisted largely of rules and practices established and enforced by merchants themselves.

The sedentary inhabitants of agricultural areas were much more constrained. Warrior-kings and their vassal-delegates, whose control over productive land allowed direct supervision of agricultural labor, enabled a new system of subordination to develop. Such local manorial rule was made possible, however, by recognition of both ruler and cultivator proprietary interests in the land, on the one hand, and allegiance to overlords above them, on the other. For them, access to judicial enforcement of their proprietary rights was a means to protect and to consolidate their sources of wealth. For the peasant cultivator and herdsman, the limited recognition of proprietorship and possession that they may have gained cost a concomitant degree of freedom as constraints on their mobility were imposed and enforced by private law.

The heirs of Clovis and Charlemagne presided over a continuously fragmenting domain. The empire split into separate territorial polities. Menaced on all sides by Vikings, Magyars, Slavs, even the heirs of Constantine, not to mention a rising threat from Muslim invaders, Charlemagne's son and heir, Louis the Pius, barely managed to maintain its borders. Internally, the empire had begun to come apart. Again paralleling the Japanese experience, territorial governors—the Carolingian counts assigned the responsibility for military defenses, maintaining order, and collection of taxes on Charlemagne's behalf—succeeded in appropriating royal revenues for their own use and subverting their agency to become largely independent rulers. Throughout the continent royal power was forfeit to local magnates, both lay and ecclesiastical. In the process, although not entirely eclipsed, centralized royal authority greatly diminished. The empire was formally divided into three separate kingdoms by Louis' three sons. To Charles the Bald went the lands roughly west of the Scheldt, Meuse, Saóne, and Rhône rivers; to Louis, those east of the Rhine and north of the Alps; with Lothar left to rule the remaining strip of territory from the North Sea through northern Italy. Their kingdoms soon disintegrated even further. By the eleventh century, the German territories had divided into multiple, competing polities. The Kingdom of the Franks itself was effectively governed by several largely independent duchies only nominally subject to the king. Territorially combined, they constituted nearly the entire kingdom: Aquitaine, Burgundy, Gascony, Normandy, Provence. The king was left with little more than the Île de France under his direct rule. Not until the reign of Louis XIV (1638–1715) was France to be fully unified under the king.

The early kingdoms reached the nadir of fragmentation at the end of the tenth century. By the middle of the eleventh, processes of reconsolidation had already made their mark. A glance at the political map reveals that in terms of territorial dominion at least three future nation-states had emerged—the kingdoms of Sweden, Portugal, and, above all, England.

In England, Alfred the Great (849–899) had defeated the Vikings and united warring Angles and Saxons under Wessex-based rule as an Anglo-Saxon Kingdom, interrupted only by the brief interval of Danish rule (1018–1035) under Cnut (c. 985–1035). Among Alfred's most enduring contributions to English institutional development was the introduction of fortified centers, known today as the "burghal system" for purposes of defense. With the influx of traders, these provided regional marketplaces that would become centers for trade and commerce. The Anglo-Saxon kings also introduced the territorial division of England into shires, "hundreds" as well as "tithings," which, as in China and Japan, established a system of vicarious liability for the designated groupings of ten adult men (households in China and Japan). As units of governance under the king, the shire and the hundred acquired combined administrative and judicial functions. By the time of the Norman Conquest (1066), relatively extensive and well-developed structures for local governance and adjudication were in place. As elsewhere, adjudication had become the prevailing means for maintaining order in Saxon England.

The Norman kings also inherited a structure for royal administration and revenue. Surrounding the Saxon monarchs was a cluster of officials—seneschals, chamberlains, marshals, and stewards—all nobles, who collectively constituted the peripatetic royal court. Permanently posted in the countryside and town were the reeves who administered the royal estates and the ealdormen assigned to districts comprising one or more shires. The ealdorman was the local representative of the king, with both military and judicial responsibilities. Their treasuries relied almost exclusively on rents from their personal estates, payments made in place of military or *corvée* service, customs, various special taxes, and, whenever possible, extractions from the nobility.

They also found a common law of the kingdom. Credited with promulgating the Deemings, or Book of Dooms (Book of Laws), Alfred, as other kings before and since, had used law as a means of unification. Also as in other early kingdoms, the rules did not distinguish between civil and criminal wrongs. Essentially a compensatory system, they typically provided for payments to the injured party or kinsmen based on the wrong committed and, if homicide, *wergeld* based on the value by fixed social class of the decedent. An edict attributed to Cnut made membership in both a tithing and a hundred mandatory for standing to defend oneself against a charge of wrongdoing or recovery of *wergeld* in a hundred court.[14] Shire courts, which had been functioning since at least the last decades of the seventh century, heard appeals and were the principal vehicles of local control, exercised through the ealdorman (later the sheriffs) appointed as the royal officials responsible for administration and adjudication in each shire.

The first Norman rulers faced the immediate need to subdue a conquered people within their new realm and to defend against threats from without by Scots, Welsh, and above all Danes. Their consequent concern for security made them particularly vulnerable in their dependency on their Norman warlord vassals who had made the Conquest possible. Coupled with familial rivalries, the forces of decentralization robbed them of many of the benefits of the preexisting structures of local governance. However, the final conflict between Stephen and Matilda ended in the accession in 1154 of Henry II of Anjou (1133–1189) and ushered in an era of foundational consolidation and reform.

Attributed to Henry II is a transformation of the adjudicatory institutions of medieval England. Making use of existing institutions, Henry and his agents created a unified system of governance and royal justice that has gained him a permanent place of honor in English legal history. Royal revenue was a paramount concern. W.L. Warren makes the point: however "precocious and justly admired," government under Henry II "was predatory."[15] The other, closely related, aim was to restore order after years of civil war. Among Henry II's earliest actions within his English realm were to reform coinage, create a more orderly system of administration, and to gather information. At the beginning of his reign Henry commanded his tenants-in-chief to account for their sub-tenancies and service duties. Such information was a means to determine misappropriation of land and rents. Inasmuch as proprietary royal lands produced much of the king's revenue, the objective, as many of those who resisted correctly perceived, was to restore royal revenues to pay the debts incurred in his accession and refill his coffers, and not incidentally those of his closest associates. At the end of his reign his itinerant judges

---

[14] *See*, e.g., Peter Hunter Blair, *An Introduction to Anglo-Saxon England* (Cambridge: Cambridge University Press, 2nd ed. 1977), p. 235.

[15] W.L. Warren, *Henry II* (Berkeley and Los Angeles: University of California Press, 2nd ed., 1983), p. 257.

were delegated a similar task. The king thus benefited as much as his subjects from ensuing reforms of the adjudicatory procedures that enabled the return of land and revenues to their rightful owners. Similar motivations prompted him to encourage *scutage*, a monetary payment in lieu of military service, which allowed him to use hired troops under his command instead of reliance on warriors mustered by the barons.

Henry II's other administrative and legal reforms were more lasting. They commenced with the assertion (attributed to Ronulf Glanvill, his chief justiciar) of ultimate royal jurisdiction by right of removal or appeal over all free tenements and exclusive jurisdiction over all criminal cases. Both jurisdictional claims were justified as customary but neither reflected existing practice. Henry's pronouncements significantly augmented the authority of the sheriff as the king's chief local representative. By the removal of the majority of all serving sheriffs under the Inquest of Sheriffs of 1170, Henry also assured that the office would not become proprietary and would remain subject to his approval and direction. This, together with the institution of royal "assizes" as an alternative to manorial courts, reliance on trial by juries, and the reaffirmation of royal rather than baronial protection of towns, combined both to extend and cement royal authority. Henry similarly—and famously in his conflict with Thomas Becket—asserted final jurisdiction in cases viewed by the Church as matters for ecclesiastical adjudication and subject to final appeal to the Pope. Adjudicatory jurisdiction thereby became the central focus of political competition and conflict between the Crown and both the nobility and the Church.

On the Iberian peninsula, a very different process of consolidation, conquest, and reconquest was taking place. There in the wake of Roman disintegration, as noted, the Visigoths had formed the first consolidated kingdom of Western Europe. During the course of two centuries Roman and Goth intermarriage had produced a remarkably homogeneous population. Its rulers, as noted, were among the first in Europe to use written laws as a means of national unification. It had also resolved the problem of succession through election by nobles and clergy rather than heredity. The process implicitly recognized kingship as an office and made the political legitimacy of its holder dependent on the will and welfare of the community, thereby combining features of both the Roman and Gothic communities. A primary function of the king in Visigothic Spain, as other Western European kingdoms, was the role of a supreme adjudicator for the community. The Visigoths had begun to restore Iberian prosperity with agriculture and trade within the Mediterranean ambit. All to naught, however, as the kingdom ended abruptly with the Muslim conquest under

Jabal al-Tāriq in 711 and the establishment of the Umayyad province of al-Andalus ruled from Damascus. This was Iberia's transformative event.

The making of medieval Spain begins with the *reconquista*, the seven century-long recovery of the peninsula from its Muslim rulers by the separate polities that formed in the wake of the Umayyad conquest. The process began in the eighth century in the northern reaches of the peninsula that remained beyond Muslim control. Along the Bay of Biscay and the Cantabrian mountains, in the foothills of the Pyrenees, and, at their eastern edges, along the Mediterranean coast took shape a cluster of tiny, independent kingdoms. The first in time was Asturias—later consolidated with Galicia and named Léon, after the capital city on the southern flank of the Cantabrian Mountains. Their rulers initially sought legitimacy by claiming Visigothic ancestry. In the center was the breakaway vassal kingdom of Castile. A third, Aragon, represented a consolidated group of Carolingian counties that separated under counts-turned-autonomous rulers at the turn of the century. Nestled in the southern Pyrenees between Castile and Aragon was Navarre. Finally, closely tied to Aragon, with a long history of relative independence under the Carolingian Empire, was the County of Barcelona in Catalonia. By the beginning of the tenth century, two centers had formed, one in the west by Léon and Castile, now united; the other in the east by Aragon, Navarre, and, on occasion, Barcelona. Castile and Aragon were thenceforth to lead the crusade to recover the peninsula from Muslim rule and to dominate all of Iberia. (During this period Portugal was a semi-autonomous county under the sovereigns of Léon and Castile. It did not become a fully autonomous kingdom until the twelfth century.)

Ousted from Damascus by the Abbasids, the Umayyads in 756 created the autonomous Caliphate (initially as emirs) ruling Iberia and North Africa from Cordova as its capital. The Caliphate proceeded thereafter to establish al-Andalus as one of the wealthiest polities in the world over nearly the entire peninsula. Improving existing irrigation systems, the agricultural production of the prior Roman and Visigothic regimes expanded. Introduced were crops unknown in Roman or Visigothic times—apricots, cauliflower, cotton, eggplant, grapefruit, honey melon, jasmine, oranges, lemon, mulberry/silkworm, safflower, sorghum, spinach, sugar cane, watermelon, and rice.[16] Linked by trade throughout the Islamic world with regimes that extended from Spain through North

[16] Karl W. Butzer, Juan F. Mateu, Elizabeth K. Butzer, and Pavel Kraus, "Irrigation Agrosystems in Eastern Spain: Roman or Islamic Origins?" *Annals of the Association of American Geographers*, vol. 75 (1985), Table 1, pp. 502–503.

Africa into Central South Asia, the merchants of al-Andalus may have been the first to trade Spanish silver for Chinese gold and silk. Having introduced mulberry and silkworm, al-Andalus in turn became a major producer and exporter of silk into Muslim markets in the eastern Mediterranean. At the close of the tenth century the city of Cordova was the world's largest in population. By then, however, the Umayyad Dynasty had neared its end. This did not, however, assure immediate military decline. Caliphate raiding parties under Al-Hajib Al-Mansur (c. 938–1002), better known as Almanzor, who by this time controlled the Caliphate in all but name, sacked both the city of Barcelona in the east (in 985) and Santiago de Compostela in the west (in 997). In 1031, the Caliphate split into various belligerent *taifa* entities. Al-Andalus was reunited in 1056 under the Almoravids who, having conquered Morocco and portions of Algeria, annexed and ruled Muslim Iberia for another century. The Almoravids were in turn overthrown by Abd al-Mu'min (1094–1163), who established the Almohad Empire as its first Amir, ruling al-Andalus from Marrakech in Morocco. The Almohads were Iberia's final Muslim rulers.

Law's Eleventh Century Foundations: Adjudication

By the eleventh century, adjudication had become the predominant mode for maintaining order and enforcing legal rules at all levels of medieval European society. Within extended families, settlements, and communities all across Western Europe as elsewhere, mediation and arbitration had been from their inception the means chosen by communities and their leaders for ensuring the peaceful resolution of grievances as an alternative to private vendettas and violence. As political structures evolved, in Western Europe as in Japan, formal adjudication similarly became the preferred means for such redress. In the process, unlike Japan, lawyers, and notaries—whose documentation provided proof and finality—rather than administrative officials were becoming primary actors in law's enforcement. Latin as the common written language and language of the Church ensured a vocabulary of law and the Bible much of its content. As noted previously, the Church had led the way.

Parish priests and bishops had long functioned as local arbitrators and judges for both informal and formal resolution of grievances and redress of wrongs. As rulers extended and sought to consolidate their territorial jurisdiction, they also began to establish structures of governance, commissioning officials to collect rents and to mobilize military defenses. In the process, they also established more accessible mechanisms and procedures for formal adjudication. To maintain peace and do justice had, as noted, become prime requisites of kingship. Ecclesiastical coronation had become universal, with monarchs promising, as in the words of the Wessex king Ethelred (c. 968–1016), "that God's Church and all Christian people in my dominions shall keep true peace … that I promise and command justice and mercy in all judgments."[17] As a system for maintaining order, formal adjudication by those seeking to maintain or expand their political authority, lawsuits had compelling advantages. First, they empowered rulers by reinforcing their authority as adjudicators to find facts, identify and apply the appropriate rule, and thereby determine the outcome of submitted disputes. Their superior status over the parties was also acknowledged by virtue of either prior mutual consent as in arbitration or some sort of officially recognized authority. Most importantly, adjudication required fewer resources than other forms of law enforcement. Lacking sufficient resources for a constabulary or overseeing officialdom, medieval kings and other rulers had little choice but to rely on a few designated officials as adjudicators who thereby maintained a sense of lawful order and also expressed and enhanced their political authority. Thus as early as the tenth century formal adjudication of private claims had become the prevailing mode of law enforcement throughout Western Europe.

The seventh century Visigothic *Fuero Juzgo* exemplifies the early emphasis. The king is viewed above all as a dispenser of fair justice through royal courts, even admonished to order judges "to practice moderation" in their adjudicatory functions (Book Twelve, Title One).[18] Law's enforcement was presumed to be adjudicatory. The second book set out in detail the requirements for adjudicatory procedures, the role of judges, lawyers, and witnesses, as well as authentication of documents. No distinction was made between civil and criminal offenses. Both were enforced within essentially the same adjudicatory framework.

Throughout the continent similar premises prevailed. Courts and adjudicatory assemblies at all levels—royal, seigniorial, local—proliferated. Most had, without distinction, merged judicial and administrative functions. Many administered tax assessments. With increasing trade, merchant guilds institutionalized the rules of their private orders and expanded private arbitration for commercial disputes. Throughout Western Europe adjudication had become virtually the sole mode for the formal settlement of disputes and the enforcement of law.

---

[17] Dorothy Whitelock, *The Beginnings of English Society* (Baltimore, MD: Penguin Books, 1952), p. 53.

[18] Quoted in Van Kleffens, *Spanish Law*, p. 77.

Law's Twelfth Century Renaissance: Roman Private Law

The two centuries between 1050 and 1250 constituted an era of rationalization, renovation, and renewal of law and adjudication. Although commonly viewed from a European or Western perspective as a period of developmental transformation,[19] few if any altogether new or novel structures or institutions were introduced. Rather, as argued throughout this chapter, existing legal rules and conceptions were reformulated and the means for their enforcement rationalized and recast to serve better the processes of consolidation of authority and power of both kings and popes. The consequence was the formation of the Western legal tradition as we understand it today, with a core emphasis on the conception of law as a system of rights to be enforced by judges through adjudicatory procedures. The era commenced with the reforms undertaken first within the Abbey of Cluny in southern France, then followed within the papal curia under the leadership of Hildebrand and continued under his leadership as Pope Gregory VII (1073–1085).

Legislation in the consolidating polities, as exemplified by the Castilian *Siete Partidas*, described in greater detail below, may have included provisions related to transactions, but aside from matters of Church and Crown, their primary focus was on a rationalization of procedures for adjudication of private claims for the redress of wrongs to both property and person and crimes. Barely any distinction was made between civil and criminal offenses except in terms of procedures for initiating criminal prosecutions by accusation rather than complaint and the availability of non-compensatory sanctions, such as corporeal punishment. At this point Western law could have taken a very different developmental track. Had the authority of rulers become more secure and the resources at their disposal more abundant, their capacity to expand the administrative structures of their realms and thereby their capacity to coerce would also have grown. Had they developed in such fashion, one might have expected a growing emphasis on administrative regulation with an expansion of criminal law and ruler-controlled prosecution—in other words, a progression toward a public law system similar to that in Imperial China. In fact, quite the contrary occurred. The legal structures in Western Europe evolved along a very different path, with private law adjudication its hallmark. The path actually taken throughout Western Europe was politically determined by challenges that beset the consolidating kings from barons, townsmen, and, importantly, the Church. The process began with the institutional reforms

---

[19] *See*, e.g., Berman, *Law and Revolution*, p. 120.

taking place within the Church and continued with the establishment (or recognition) of degree-granting universities, which were largely autonomous or under the protection of the Church.

The Church's jurisdiction rested on two broad, fundamental claims: its authority over the sacraments and sin. On the basis of such authority, the Church asserted jurisdiction over marriage and much of family law as well as all "moral" wrongs. Ecclesiastic jurisdiction extended in addition to all cases, as noted above, involving persons in designated categories that included the clergy, students, and "travelers." Its jurisdiction also extended to cases that arose within and without the Church, thus encompassing issues of property, contract, and corporations and other legally constituted associations. No area of canon law or jurisdiction was as critical or extensive as adjudicatory process and procedures.

The canon law reforms included rationalization of judicial procedures for both civil claims and prosecution of criminal offenders. By the thirteenth century complaints and accusation had to be in writing. Each had to include short statements of alleged facts. Written records of the proceedings as well as the judgments had to be kept. Rules to ensure the materiality and trustworthiness for both documentary and oral evidence had been introduced. Oral testimony was admissible only under oath with false testimony a punishable offense. Other rules related to proof regulated legal presumptions, restricting their applicability in cases involving criminal offenses. Judges were charged with responsibility for determining truth and thus were equipped with broad authority to conduct the fact-finding process through direct interrogation of witnesses and evaluation of documentary evidence.

Balancing the reforms in canon law from the perspective of the secular rulers was the rise of universities and the rediscovery of classical Roman private law. The university movement began not coincidentally in northern Italy, where small, urban polities governed by their mercantile and land wealthy elites had appeared. In these and other urban centers of trade and communication, young men gathered to be taught by prominent scholars. Thus were the first institutions to be called universities formed. In 1088 the University of Bologna was the first to be recognized. It was followed by the University of Paris in 1150, Oxford University in 1167, and the University of Modena and Reggio Emilia in 1175. Nearly two dozen additional universities were formed during the thirteenth century in Italy, France, Spain, England, and Portugal. By the end of the fifteenth century, double that number had been established throughout Western Europe. They had been formed, many earlier as schools, and recognized, often by papal Bull, in nearly every major city or urban center in Western Europe from Aberdeen to Zadar, Pisa to Pècs.

More telling was their common disciplinary emphases and curriculum. Theology, medicine, and, above all, law were the primary disciplines. Notably in Italy, law became the primer discipline. The discovery of fragments of the three books of *Corpus Juris Civilis* and their compilation and use as a basis for legal learning in Bologna by Irnerius (c. 1050–1125) ushered in a new age. The reception of classical Roman private law in the West had begun.

Because adjudication, as described in Chapter 1, is a process through which persons with a cognizable claim have access to its recognition and enforcement, some core conception of enforceable claims against others —some conception of "rights" and correlative "duties" or their equivalent —is notionally necessary. In other words, the legal rules enforced through adjudication become by definition private law rules. Moreover, within a legal culture that had long centered on adjudication and private law, no wonder that the discovery of fragments of a sixth century-old set of books that restated and explained the conceptual formulations of classical Roman private law could have produced an intellectual transformation and set into motion the creation of the *ius commune* of continental Europe and foundational features of the Western legal tradition. The books of the *Corpus Juris Civilis*—the Digest, the Institutes, and the Novella—had at best some limited currency in the isolated areas of the Italian peninsula over which Justinian and his successors managed temporarily to hold or temporarily regain control. Even in the Eastern Empire at the time of their making, they probably had little if any actual application except as academic texts that, written in Latin, few of the Greek-speaking populace could even read. It is even more doubtful that they had any meaning as "living" law in the politically advanced, highly bureaucratic public law system of the late Eastern Empire or the regions of the eastern Mediterranean that remained under its control. Their fate is aptly described by Manlio Bellomo:

> We know that only a very few copies of the *Institutiones* continued to be known, occasionally read, and modestly annotated. The Codex was dismembered: the last three books dealing with the administration of the empire fell into neglect; the text of the first nine books was abridged into an extremely rare and incomplete *Epitome Codicis*. The *Digesta* and the *Novellae* were totally lost, save for a few extremely rare fragments of the latter.[20]

[20] Manlio Bellomo, *The Common Legal Past of Europe, 1000–1800* [Lydia G. Cochrane trans.] (Washington, DC: The Catholic University of America Press, 1995), p. 40.

The *Corpus Juris Civilis* would have been completely lost or ignored as an ancient artifact of late Roman rule had it not been rediscovered over half a millennium later in the political and academic context of the eleventh and twelfth centuries. Saved by the ready reception of Roman private law in the eleventh and twelfth centuries, during the course of the next millennium the *Corpus Juris Civilis* instead was to provide the conceptual foundations of private law around the globe.

Roman private (civil) law and canon law constituted the universally accepted core of the legal curriculum, which soon became the pursuit of preference for students in all of the universities in the south. The numbers are impressive. The oldest and most prestigious universities attracted students aspiring to posts in the consolidating polities, including the Church, by the thousands from across Europe to cities with populations less than half that number. Then and now, as young men who could afford to spend years in study, most were from affluent families. With the notable exception of England, as law graduates they found ample career opportunities as judges in the ecclesiastical and secular courts and officials in the chanceries and other governmental offices that were expanding throughout the continent. Only in England did a university degree in law not ensure access to the legal profession. English judges reached the bench as barristers through apprenticeship and practice, not academic legal education—a prime factor in the separate development of English Common Law from the continental Civil Law tradition.

The era also began and ended with perhaps its most influential innovation of all—a reconception of natural rights within a universally valid and mandatory hierarchy of legal principles and rules. Gratian (dates unknown), the twelfth century canon lawyer in Bologna, initiated the change. In the *Concordia discordantium canonum* (*Concord of Discordant Canons*), or simply the *Decretum*, he articulated an understanding of law that drew on the studies of the *Corpus Juris Civilis* and scholastic methods to reconstruct and rationalize the existing and often conflicting corpus of canons. The era concluded with the work of Thomas Aquinas (1225–1274), a thirteenth century Dominican friar. Related to royalty in Germany, France, and Spain, Aquinas began his career as a student at the University of Naples. Assigned to study as a friar under Albertus Magnus, he continued his studies at Cologne. In about 1252, he began to teach theology as a sub-regent at the University of Paris. There he began (around 1265) and barely completed before his death his major work, the *Summa Theologica*, as a manual for students. Gratian and Aquinas shared a common vision of law within a hierarchical system of principles and rules with God's law as supreme. Ruler-made legal rules were subordinate. Written in Latin, law was by definition a system of rights. For Gratian at least, customary rules were also law. Private law rights—right to property, of contracts, to compensation for wrongs—were at least implicitly core elements of any system of laws. Within the theological context within which they wrote, their schema was both universally applicable and mandatory. Western European understandings of law as a system of legal rights were thenceforth to have an evangelical cast.

Political Consolidation and Law—Spain, 1200–1492 CE

The rulers of the remnant Iberian kingdoms, as small as their domains seemed to be, were among the most successful consolidating polities in the early middle ages, particularly the kings of Castile. As leaders of military campaigns with fervent religious justification and papal support, within their domains they exercised authority and, initially, a significant degree of centralized control. Their military successes further enabled them to control and redistribute both land and tribute from the polities into which the Caliphate ultimately fragmented. With the notable exception of the capture of Toledo in 1065, until the thirteenth century the *reconquista* had hardly progressed. The Tagus and Ebro rivers marked the borders between the Catholic kingdoms in the north and the newly established Almohad Empire. The efforts of the Iberian kingdoms in the north amounted to little more than periodic raids on all sides. In 1212 the kings of Aragon, Castile, Navarre, and Portugal defeated the caliph, al-Nāsir at Las Navas de Tolosa. Encouraged by the apparent Almohad weakness, the Banu Nazari (Nasrid) began their ultimately successful revolt. The Iberian kings took immediate advantage, capturing Mallorca (1229), Valencia, Alicante and the Balearic Islands (1235), and finally Cordova and Seville in 1248. By mid century, the *reconquista* was largely complete. By 1294 only Granada under Nasrid rule survived as the sole Islamic polity on the peninsula, paying tribute to both Castile and Aragon, until 1492 overwhelmed by a united Spanish force under the joint rule of Queen Isabella of Castile (1451–1504) and Ferdinand II of Aragon (1452–1516).

In the initial phases, the kings of Castile redistributed conquered land and granted tax immunities to those equipped with horses who served as cavalrymen along the frontiers. One consequence was the creation of commoner-knights (*caballeros-villanos*) and a growing class of small peasant landholders. Thus Castile and the other realms of Spanish Iberia did not experience the early centripetal fragmentation of French royal authority and power. Only later in the later stages of the *reconquista* did royal grants of newly acquired land to military orders and court favorites become common. As a result throughout Andalusia and Lower Extremadura large sheep-raising estates with absentee landlords and a small number of subordinated Muslim laborers replaced the rich, irrigated Muslim farms. Collective action through the formation of the Mesta, a Castile-wide association of sheepherders, substantially augmented the political influence of these mostly noble landowners. However, having lost the extensive Muslim trade networks, the *reconquista* set back commercial growth for decades. For Castile commerce remained mainly internal. The kingdom became the domain of sheepherders.

In contrast, Aragon with its long Mediterranean coast profited as western Mediterranean trade expanded. The port cities of Barcelona and Valencia in particular prospered, concomitant with enhanced autonomy. By design of necessity, the kings of Aragon presided over an expanding cluster of self-governing polities. The northernmost polity was Catalonia. Only briefly under Muslim rule, the region surrounding Barcelona had been incorporated into the Carolingian Empire as a county within the Spanish March. Following the pattern of other peripheral counties, by the end of the ninth century, Catalonia had become an independent kingdom. A matrimonial alliance resulted in its merger with Aragon, with Catalonia retaining its institutions of governance, including taxation. The Catalan cortes was one of the first representative assemblies in Europe. Military victories in 1148 at Lleida in the interior and Tortosa on the eastern coast had enabled the extension of its southern border to the mouth of the Ebro. Ruled by merchants and professionals, Barcelona had by the middle of the thirteenth century become a banking and commercial center with a significant naval fleet. Also in Catalonia a peasantry with small farms was gradually subordinated with the growth of commercial agriculture.[21]

Matching Catalan autonomy and prosperity was the Kingdom of Valencia. Acquired by conquest in 1238 under James I (1208–1276), Valencia, like Catalonia, was recognized as a separate kingdom within Aragon. As Thomas Glick reminds us, Valencia has three distinct geographical areas: the city, 50 square miles of rich alluvial plains surrounding the city and along the coast, and the dry uplands.[22] The king appropriated much of the Muslim land for himself to become the single largest landholder. Immigration from Catholic Iberia was encouraged by the prospect of land grants as well as commercial opportunities. Valencia

---

[21] *See* Paul H. Freedman, *The Origins of Peasant Servitude in Medieval Catalonia* (Cambridge and New York: Cambridge University Press, 1991).

[22] Thomas F. Glick, *Irrigation and Society in Medieval Valencia* (Cambridge, MA: Harvard University Press, 1970).

also received self-governing privileges. James I's efforts to obtain revenues for his continuing military campaigns, as Robert Burns notes, "were to comprise an important factor in transforming the realms of Aragon from a feudal to a constitutional monarchy."[23] Valencia, unlike Barcelona, was a major Muslim commercial and agricultural center. James had to accommodate both the urban Muslim shopkeepers and the rural Muslim communities in order to preserve its revenue-producing vitality. Despite immigration, for decades after the conquest, the majority of its inhabitants remained Muslim or Muslim converts to Christianity. Not until 1609, over a century after the expulsion from Castile (1492), were all Muslims and Muslim converts expelled. Thus for four centuries productive Muslim peasant farmers dominated the small agricultural communities of the alluvial plain. Growing a mix of cereals, fruits, nuts, vegetables, sugar cane, and rice, with olive oil and wine as staples and saffron and hemp among the most commercially profitable, they had replaced existing irrigation networks with their own. Most required collaborative efforts among several villages or within a village. Only the smallest could be managed by a single family. They had also established a Tribunal of Water, with an arbiter to resolve disputes related to flows and timing. After conquest, this water court was continued as a legally recognized adjudicatory organ, thus incorporating into the formal legal structures of the new kingdom what might otherwise have become a prominent example of private ordering. The parallels with southern China and village Japan are too obvious to ignore. In all three instances, warrior rulers left intact the self-governing structures of productive and highly interdependent communities in order to preserve their economic vitality. In Valencia, however, many of these structures could and would be integrated within a dynamic private law order.

Both Barcelona and Valencia exemplify a reverse trend that was occurring along the coasts throughout Western Europe, concomitant with the advance of centralized territorial rule in England and Castile. Urban centers of commerce were growing in size and autonomy, particularly in the proximity of the largest waterways connecting the sea with productive interior regions. On the Italian peninsula the long history of city and town settlements extending back to the first Etruscan settlements and first Greek colonies ended between the fifth and tenth centuries with the collapse of Roman rule. A few centers—notably Milan and Rome—survived, but most, as Daniel Waley notes, "declined into sordid if

---

[23] Robert Ignatius Burns, *Medieval Colonialism: Postcrusade Exploitation of Islamic Valencia* (Princeton, NJ: Princeton University Press, 1975), p. 17.

picturesque decay."[24] At the turn of the tenth century economic and political developments began to produce an urban revival. The population began to increase, trade began to expand, and, particularly in the north, rudimentary urban communities began to emerge. By the end of the century, as a result of civic actions, revolts, and imperial grants, throughout the region small, autonomous cities reminiscent of the Athenian *polis* and Roman *civitas* had reemerged. Governed initially by landowners, they became increasingly dominated by shopkeepers, artisans, merchants, financiers, notaries, and lawyer-judges. Not perhaps coincidentally, here too arose the first private academies of scholars and students (later, as noted, to become degree-granting universities) in which private law, both classical Roman as well as canon law, became the principal focus of study.

By the middle of the thirteenth century, Castile had become among the most institutionally advanced in Western Europe. Within two generations, it had more than doubled in territorial size and population. In 1252, four years after reclaiming Cordova and Seville, Fernando III (born 1199) died, leaving his newly extended realm to his son, crowned Alfonso X (1221–1284) to become known in history as Alfonso the Wise. The first and foremost task facing the new king was to unify and to govern an effectively integrated kingdom characterized by extremes of religious, linguistic, and economic diversity. Thwarted in his aspirations to establish a new Spanish Empire extending from the Pyrenees through North Africa, he endured continual conflicts with the nobility within Spain, whose control he attempted to wrest, as well as rivals within the Holy Roman Empire; although elected King of the Germans (Romans), he was denied the title of Holy Roman Emperor. Overthrown by his son, Sancho IV (c. 1257–1295), Alfonso died in Seville in 1284. Viewed today as a precursor of the Renaissance, Alfonso was a military leader, poet, promoter of the arts and sciences, and, above all, a law maker.

Law making was his grandest accomplishment. He is credited with having directed, if not personally drafted, the *Espéculo*, the *Fuero Real*, and finally the *Siete Partidas*, Western Europe's first and most enduring law code. Both the *Fuero Real* and related *Espéculo* are believed to have been completed around 1254 or 1255. Their relationship—whether separate or related legislation—remains contested,[25] but most agree that

---

[24] Daniel Waley, *The Italian City-Republics* (London and New York: Longman, 3rd ed., 1988), p. 1.

[25] For this and other issues in dispute related to the *Fuero Real*, the *Espéculo*, and the *Siete Partidas*, *see* Alfonso Garcia Gallo, "Nuevas Observaciones soble la Obra legislativa de Alfonso X," *Amario de Historia del Derecho Español*, vol.

they, like Alfonso X's subsequent legislative effort, the *Siete Partidas*, were designed to provide a uniform set of legal principles, proscriptions, and procedures for the much expanded Kingdom of Castile. Joseph O'Callaghan posits that the *Fuero Real* was not one code but the title of the various codes represented by the *Espéculo*, kept at court as a model, that were granted (or perhaps imposed) by the king as codes of municipal law to supplement prior local laws and create a more uniform system for the cities of Castile.[26] In language, style, form, and substance, they presage the *Siete Partidas*, Alfonso's most ambitious legislative effort, intended, it is generally believed, as law of the realm.

Compiled between 1256 and 1265 and written in Castilian instead of Latin, the *Siete Partidas* is one of the first comprehensive compendia of legal rules and principles to be written in a vernacular European language. The work is remarkably similar to the warrior formularies of thirteenth and fourteenth century Japan in wording, emphasis, and context. Phrased both as admonitions and preferred principles as well as mandatory commands, its provisions, as indicated by the title, are divided by subject-matter into seven parts. The first begins with definitions and general observations but, reflecting an emphatic assertion of royal authority, akin to that of Henry II of England, deals principally with matters of Catholicism and the Church, including the sacraments, qualifications and behavior of bishops, the clergy, and monks, as well as provisions for Church income, heresy, and excommunication, and even the location of cemeteries. The second part deals with the king, the royal household, and the nobles. Its provisions also cover knights, royal officials (including judges), waging war, and schools. The primary theme of the third part is justice: the courts, adjudicatory procedure, and rights *in rem* (property). Part four treats feudal and family relationships. In the fifth are provisions on a common array of economic transactions under Roman law—loans (both *mutuum* and *commodatum*), sales, gifts, deposit, partnership—with mention of merchants and markets, wages and rents, ships and salvage, innominate promises, suretyship, taking care of another's property, pledges, payment, and releases. Provisions on inheritance and succession occupy the sixth part, with the seventh devoted to criminal offenses.

---

46 (1976), pp. 609–670; Aquilino Iglesia Ferreirós, "Alfonso X el Sabio y su Obra legislative: Algunas Reflexiones," *Amario de Historia del Derecho Español*, vol. 50 (1980), pp. 531–561, both cited in Joseph F. O'Callaghan, *Alfonso X, the Cortes, and Government in Medieval Spain* (Farnham: Ashgate, 1998), p. III1.

[26] O'Callaghan, *Alfonso X, the Cortes, and Government in Medieval Spain*, pp. III, 3–4.

Like the Japanese formularies of the same period, adjudication was a principal emphasis. Alfonso, it should be noted, had enabled the effective extension of the Crown's adjudicatory jurisdiction by restructuring the royal courts whose members included the judges that adjudicated ordinary cases (*alcaldes de la corte del rey*); the *justicia mayor*, who maintained order and made arrests on demand by the king; and the *adelantado mayor*, who adjudicated cases involving the nobility, the military orders, and towns.[27] Part Two includes admonitions on the qualification of judges, and Part Three details the procedures and processes to be followed. Judges, the king advises, should be of "good lineage," "good understanding," "orderly and wise," "literate," "impartial." Above all they should be "loyal" and "love the King" (Part Two, Title 9, Law 18). The rationalization of adjudicatory procedures parallels the reforms, noted above, for ecclesiastical courts. Part Three sets out the qualifications, authority, and duties of judges, the parties, attorneys and advocates, the nature and effect of admissions and confessions, definition and requirements of oral and documentary evidence as proof, qualification of witnesses, regulation of arbitration and arbitral awards, and even provision for judge-appointed examiners.

Crime and its prosecution were equally dominant concerns. The legend of Law 4 in Title One, Part One asks the question: "Why the laws [*leyes*] have the name?" In an answer that echoes the Chinese Legalists, the lawgiver writes, because the law (*ley*) "something to be read [*leyenda*], in which instruction is contained, and punishment is set down, to bind and control the life of man, in order that he may not commit wrong, and to demonstrate and point out the good that he should do and practice." The provisions on adjudication and judicial procedure generally apply to all cases without differentiation between criminal and civil actions. Part Three, for example, primarily concerns civil suits; its provisions apply to all cases in which a party seeks compensatory redress for wrongs or prosecutes based accusation. For example, in prosecutions based on accusations Law 12 of Title 14 explicitly disallows proof by presumptions that might otherwise be permitted as proof (see Law 11 on the presumption that an heir may profit by a contract in actions to enforce a debt).

The first title of Part Seven concerns accusations—who can bring an accusation, against whom, and how an accusation can be made. All cases require a complaint, information, or accusation, except for five categories

[27] *See* Joseph F. O'Callaghan, *The Learned King: The Reign of Alfonso X of Castile* (Philadelphia, PA: University of Pennsylvania Press, 1993).

of crimes: forgery, false witness, openly committed or notorious wrongs or wrongs that cannot be concealed, and wrongful use of the office of guardian. Only these offenses may by Law 28 the king or judges initiate prosecution. As expected, treason, the subject of the entire second title, is the principal crime (Part Seven, Title Two, Preamble). Combat and injury to reputation (infamy) are covered in the next two titles. The remaining sections deal with deceit (including counterfeiting), homicide, violence, larceny, theft, robbery, fraud, sexual crimes, and sorcery. Part Seven also includes special provisions on Jews and Muslims. Title 31 sets out the penalties for each offense in a manner that, as noted in an official compilation published in 1807, satisfies Enlightenment notions of appropriate proportionality.[28] The title begins in Law 1 with the two aims of punishment—as "reparation for sin" and deterrence—similarly presaging Enlightenment views.

In all cases where appropriate the principal penalty is compensatory—such as return of stolen goods or their value—however, for more egregious instances Title 31, Law 4 lists seven categories of punishment: death, life imprisonment with labor, banishment with forfeiture of all property, banishment without forfeiture, loss of office or right to practice a profession, and finally corporeal punishment. Imprisonment is also listed but only for slaves. Otherwise, imprisonment is allowed only to secure persons (freemen) awaiting trial.

Whether the *Siete Partidas* were formally promulgated and became effective as law is doubtful. They can be viewed like the Kamakura and Ashikaga shogun formularies as an exercise to buttress the authority of a consolidating but fatally weak monarch. The *Siete Partidas* similarly claimed more than Alfonso X could actually deliver. Opposition by the nobility as well as the Church appears to have prevented their implementation. The *Siete Partidas* did not become effective until 1348, when Alfonso XI (1312–1350) by the *Ordenamiento de Alcalá* commanded that they be "held and received" as law. From that time into the nineteenth century, however, they functioned as the fundament of Spanish law.

Although the influence of scholars on the *Siete Partidas* is sometimes questioned, Alfonso surely sought and received the advice of "wise men" whose "sayings" he credits along with "the words of the saints" as a source of law (Part One, Title One, Law 6). At the time he became king, four universities had been formally constituted on the Iberian

[28] *Las Siete Partidas del Rey Don Alfonso el Sabio*, vol. 1 (Madrid: Law Emprenza Real, 1807), p. ix.

peninsula—in Palencia (1212), Salamanca (1218), Valencia (1245), and Valladolid (1250). The University of Seville was recognized that year (1254) but no other new universities were founded during his reign. A university in Lisbon was established in 1290, but not until 1300 was another Iberian university formed (in Lleida). Even less apparent is any significant debt to the *Corpus Juris Civilis*. To be sure, some sections—particularly the laws on transactions in Part Five and the emphasis on the distinction between ownership and possession in Part One—seem to reflect rediscovered Roman law concepts.[29] The *Siete Partidas* also evidence little influence from budding theological and canon law conceptions of natural law. Natural law is noted but defined in the commonplace terms of Roman antiquity as rules that "naturally" pertain to man and animals. This gives the *Siete Partidas* a misleadingly modern, positivist cast.

The continuing campaign against the remaining Muslim enclaves and the necessity to pacify and govern newly acquired lands led to a variety of accommodative measures. Bargained for charters granting municipal rights in Castile and other Iberian kingdoms as well as tolerance if not encouragement of structures of local governance led to the development of municipal councils, or *ayuntamientos*, in many cities. Self-governing trade guilds also began to flourish. These trends came to an abrupt halt, however, under the *regimiento* of Alfonso XI.

Alfonso XI's pronouncement of the *Siete Partidas* as law nearly a century after their drafting was only part of his effort to consolidate royal authority through tax reform and the reconstruction of local governance under the *regimiento*. During his reign a universal sales tax, the *alcabala*, was imposed on all towns through their royally appointed urban lords (*consejos*). Described by Pablo Sánchez León as "a pioneering example of centralized surplus extraction,"[30] it soon became the principal source of royal revenue. Local assemblies were supplanted by *corregídores*, royal officials with judicial function who were posted to all major urban centers. The often violent reaction to this, as well as opposition by the upper nobility, led to royal allowances (*acostamientos*) as well as exemptions (*situados*) to favored noble houses that reduced revenues while undermining in fact if not in form the centralizing aims of the

[29] Ernst Levy notes that early medieval, "vulgar" Roman law conflated ownership with possession. The emphasis on the distinction could possibly reflect a thirteenth century correction. *See* Ernst Levy, *West Roman Vulgar Law: The Law of Property* (Buffalo, NY: William S. Hein & Co., 2003).

[30] Pablo Sánchez León, "Changing Patterns of Urban Conflict in Late Medieval Castile," *Past & Present*, vol. 195, supplement 2 (2007), p. 223.

reforms. Rebellion and the Black Death—to which Alfonso himself succumbed in 1350—resulted in recurring civil strife, further dilution of royal power, and outright circumvention.

However entrenched the upper nobility became, Castile's centralized adjudicatory structures continued to develop. In 1371 Enrique II re-created the Royal Council, whose members, nearly all lawyers, were responsible for general administrative oversight and functioned as the court of final appeal for criminal cases. During the same year the first *audiencia* was established in Valladolid. Also staffed primarily by law-trained professionals, the *audiencias* were responsible for civil appeals within their districts. At the end of the fourteenth century, all Castilian officials were required to be *letrados*—i.e., to hold a university diploma, nearly always in civil or canon law, or both.[31]

By then most Castilian towns were dominated by nobles. Burgos was the only significant city in the kingdom dominated by merchants. Internal political conflict was taking a severe toll. Despite apparent court opulence, royal finances were insufficient to meet pressing administrative needs. Nor was the economic outlook favorable. The Iberian kingdoms, including Aragon, seemed to be economically also increasingly marginalized. The Black Death had devastated Barcelona and Valencia. Mediterranean trade had also begun to wane even before the fall of Constantinople in 1453 and full Ottoman control over all of the eastern Mediterranean and all trade routes to Asia. Commerce and capital were already shifting to the north. Only with the union of the Spanish kingdoms under the joint reign of Ferdinand and Isabella and their successor, Charles I (1500–1558)—Charles V of the Holy Roman Empire—were the centralizing and imperial aspirations of Alfonso X fully achieved. To that achievement—a narrative of rifles and religion—we now turn.

---

31 *See* Julio Valderón Baruque, *Historia de Castilla y Leon*, vol. 5 (Valladolid: Ambito Editiones, 1985), pp. 83–84.

6. Rifles and religion: the transformation and transplantation of Western law in Hispanic America*

The story of the Castilian conquest of the Americas represents the first chapter in the transplantation and transformation of Western law and its global dominion. It also concludes our narratives with one of rifles and religion and their contributions to law's political foundations.

Two civilizations had emerged in the Americas prior to the Castilian conquests. Both replicated a trajectory noted at least in passing in previous chapters. From sedentary agrarian settlements, chiefdoms had emerged and consolidated governing structures had developed. In Mesoamerica the process culminated with the Aztec Empire. From the highlands of the western Andes of South America, the Inca had just emerged. With the arrival of the Castilians, indigenous processes of political development ended abruptly. The Castilian intrusion at the dawn of the sixteenth century also resulted in the imposition of the first territorial empire by a Western European polity, introducing the full panoply of political and legal structures of a late medieval Castilian kingdom, unconstrained, however, by the fetters of local Iberian law and practice. Hispanic America therefore provides an instructive study in the development of law not only as the first experience of a Western European polity as an advanced territorial empire but also the first major transplantation of Western European law and legal institutions outside of the West. With the introduction of the Western European conception of law as a system of rights in the context of a colonial regime within an otherwise overwhelming emphasis on regulatory administrative controls, the Castilian experience set a pattern that would be followed subsequently by all Western European colonial powers as well as Japan into the twentieth century.

* For an earlier version, see John O. Haley, "Foundations of Governance and Law: An Essay on Law's Evolution Colonial Spanish America," *Díkaion*, no. 18 (2009), pp. 163–203 [University of Sabana, Bogota, Colombia].

MESOAMERICA

By 1200 BCE a significant number of sedentary agricultural communities had formed in Mesoamerica, particularly in the rich alluvial region of the central coastal area along the Gulf of Mexico. At a very early stage among these settlements had also evolved an extensive trading network. During the millennium that followed hundreds of small polities had emerged. Many had separate languages and ethnic identities. Each had its own particular deity. They tended to cluster around urban centers that served as political as well as ceremonial and religious capitals. Several exercised at different intervals a significant degree of control or domination over surrounding communities. Among the earliest were the Olmecs, who established major centers first at San Lorenzo and later at La Venta in the present State of Veracruz during what is referred to as the Formative or Pre-Classical Period of Mesoamerican civilization (2000 BCE to 100 CE). From artifacts found in locations as distant as the Valley of Mexico, Olmec influence may have extended far beyond their Veracruz heartland. They are also credited with having developed what may have been the first writing system in the Western Hemisphere. Olmec domination had waned by 400 BCE. No cultural group regained similar domination of the tropical lowlands until the Mayans of the Classical Period (100–900 CE). Instead, the centers of high culture and power shifted westward to the central highlands and the Oaxaca Valley, where, some argue,[1] also during the Formative Period, the valley's Zapotec chiefdoms had formed a defensive confederation, establishing an administrative center at Monte Albán. From this base the Zapotec engaged in successful conquest of the surrounding communities, establishing a Monte Albán Empire in the Late Formative Period. By the beginning of the Classical Period, however, all agree the central Mexican highlands were dominated by three urban kingdoms at Teotihuacan, Cholula, and Monte Albán. By about 900 CE the Toltecs, a group of northern nomadic warriors, who some believe to have plundered and destroyed Teotihuacan, had, once settled, conquered and consolidated the many small chiefdoms of central Mexico into an empire ruled from their capital, Tula (also known as Tollan or Tolan). Skilled temple builders, their influence spread through much of Mesoamerica, and the Toltec

---

[1] *See* Robert N. Zeitlan, "The Isthmus and the Valley of Oaxaca; Questions about Zapotec Imperialism in Formative Period Mesoamerica," *American Antiquity*, vol. 55(2) (1990), pp. 250–261; Robert N. Zeitlan and Arthur A. Joyce, "The Zapotec-Imperialism Argument: Insights from the Oaxaca Coast," *Current Anthropology*, vol. 40(3) (1999), pp. 383–392.

influence on the Post-Classic Maya of Yucatan is evident.[2] Toltec dominance ended sometime during the mid to late twelfth century with the abandonment of Tula.

The Aztecs were late arrivals to central Mexico. Broadly defined,[3] they comprised nearly two dozen separate ethnic groups—including the Acolhua, Tepaneca, Culhua, Chalca, Xochimilca, and others—united by a common *Nahuatl* language, religious beliefs, and ritual practices, as well as claim to a common ancestral home in the north called Aztlan. Led by priests, each of these groups in turn arrived and settled in the Valley of Mexico and later the surrounding valleys from the beginning of the thirteenth century. The last to arrive were the Mexica, who were left with the least wanted land in an area known as Chapultepec ("grasshopper hill").[4] Each of the three principal Aztec arrivals established cities and polities ruled by their respective warrior chiefs and warrior nobility, gradually assimilating all but a few of the existing tribes, such as the Otomui, who maintained their separate cultural identity within the developing Aztec (Mexica) Empire. The Tepaneca were the first to establish a degree of domination within the Valley of Mexico, aided, it appears, by the Mexica, first as mercenary warriors and later as vassals. The Mexica victory in a Triple Alliance with the city-chiefdoms of the Acolhua (at Texcoco) and dissident Tepaneca (at Tacuba) over the Tepaneca in 1428 ensured Mexica dominance in central Mexico and the preeminence of their capital, Tenochititlán. During the ensuing century until the arrival of the Castilians, the Mexica along with their allies expanded their control, creating one of the two great native consolidated polities of the Western Hemisphere.

The pattern of conquest and rule by the Mexica resembles that of each of the consolidated polities of Mesopotamia and the Mediterranean. As a result of military conquest or acquiescence, one by one an estimated 50 or so city-chiefdoms in the Valley of Mexico and an additional 450 in central Mexico were subordinated to Tenochititlán supremacy. In each instance the subject chiefdoms were forced to relinquish land, pay, and tributes-in-kind, and to provide labor (and human sacrifice) as well as soldiers to their Tenochititlán overlords. In return their hereditary elites

---

[2] For a contrary view, *see* Michael E. Smith, *The Aztecs* (Malden, MA: Blackwell Publishers, 2nd ed., 2003), p. 33.

[3] *See id.*, at 35.

[4] Nigel Davies implicitly equates the Mexica with the Aztecs, treating other presumably *Nahuatl*-speaking groups, such as the Tepaneca and Chalca, as separate, competing tribes. *See* Nigel Davies, *The Aztec Empire* (Norman, OK: University of Oklahoma Press, 1987).

were absorbed into the Aztec administration. Even local deities as idols were physically brought to the Aztec temple in Tenochititlán as subordinate or captive gods. Existing rulers generally retained their positions, but the Aztecs reorganized the local polities into administrative units with distinct offices, thereby initiating a process with the potential to transform personal rule. Those chiefs or high-ranking nobles who pledged loyalty to the Aztecs or Aztec replacements for those who resisted were designated Aztec *tlatoani.* Other higher-ranking nobles were classified as *tecuhtli.* Members of the nobility as a caste, generally *tlatoani* or *tecuhtli* descendants, were referred to as the *pipiltin.* All functioned in effect as collectors of tribute, with each level subject to those above them for the required amounts. The majority of the population—free commoners—were cultivators, referred to as *macehualtin.* They remained organized into kinship-based communities (*calpolli*). Nearly all productive land was communal. The produce from designated fields tilled by commoners was allotted to temples, lineage nobles, or to satisfy community-owed tribute payments. What Frederic Hicks has described as the Aztec middle class[5] comprised lesser officials, usually of collateral noble lineage; non-noble stewards (*calpixqueh*) responsible for the ultimate stages of collection, transportation, and storage of tribute goods; artisans producing luxury and ceremonial goods; merchants traveling long distances (*pocheca*); priests and others responsible for ritual and ideological training and education; and military professionals known for their valor who functioned as "enforcers" (under titles such as *tequihuah*, *cuachic*, *otomitl*, and *achcauhtli*). Subject to forced labor for the nobility were commoners of conquered communities (*mayeques*)—who in combination with slaves constituted an estimated 30 percent of the population.[6] Slavery was generally the result of military conquest or, apparently most often, by ruler or paternal decision to punish wayward subjects or children. All persons, including the offspring of slaves, according to Josef Kohler, were born free.[7]

[5] Frederic Hicks, "The Middle Class in Ancient Central Mexico," *Journal of Anthropological Research*, vol. 55 (1999), pp. 413–419. *See also* Salvador Toscano, *Derecho y Organización Social de los Aztecas* (Mexico, D.F.: Universidad Nacional de Mexico, 1937), p. 17.

[6] Mark A. Burkholder and Lyman L. Johnson, *Colonial Latin America* (Oxford and New York: Oxford University Press, 3rd ed., 2001), p. 8.

[7] Josef Kohler, *Das Recht der Azteken* (Stuttgart: Verlag von Ferdinand Enke, 1892), p. 42; translated by Carlos Rovalo y Fernandez and published in Spanish as *El Derecho de los Aztecas* (Mexico, D.F.: Mexico, 1924), p. 32.

Aztec and other Mesoamerican rulers exercised absolute authority. They were the supreme law givers and functioned as supreme judges. However, as Judith Zeitlan and Lillian Thomas remind us with respect to Zapotec rulers, "traditional expectations" and "ancient ways and rites" on which their political authority was grounded imposed countervailing customary constraints to enhance the well-being of the community.[8]

They were advised by the highest-ranked members of the nobility and, according to Kohler, the Mexica rulers in Tenochititlán had at their side at all times persons with specialized offices—one for military affairs (the *tlacochcálcatl*) and others for law, the cults, and the treasury.[9] In addition, among the most telling aspects of Aztec rule was the embryonic transformation of personal rule, exemplified by the election of Aztec rulers in each of the three domains—Mexica, Texcoco, and Tecuba. In Texcoco and Tecuba, only sons of the prior ruler were eligible. However, for the Mexica, the pool comprising lineage-related candidates, most often the sons of prior monarchs, was somewhat larger. The electors, generally four in number, were in each case members of nobility chosen by the residents of their respective capitals.[10]

Numerous hostile chiefdoms and tribes surrounded the Aztecs north and south. They sought by alliance to fend off the advancing Aztecs. Among the most significant were the autonomous and semi-autonomous communities in the Oaxaca Valley and surrounding areas close to the Pacific Ocean. They included the reemergent Zapotec as well as the Mixteca, who had entered the region as conquering warriors successfully subjugating smaller, less powerful indigenous communities. Although competitors for control of the valley, they shared belief, a common oral language (*nudzahaui*), and a pictographic writing system. Both groups included stratified urban kingdoms with their respective capitals at Tehuantepec and Tapanatepec at opposite ends of the valley. Little is known about their law or modes of enforcement but, as with other early warrior kingdoms, a small group of nobles with lineage ties exercised effective control over the majority of the population and resources.[11]

---

[8] Judith Frances Zeitlan and Lillian Thomas, "Spanish Justice and the Indian Cacique: Disjunctive Political Systems in Sixteenth Century Tehuantepec," *Ethnohistory*, vol. 39 (1992), p. 298.

[9] Kohler, *Das Recht der Azteken*, pp. 14–15.

[10] *Id.*, pp. 23–25; Lucio Mendieta y Nuñez, *El Derecho Precolonial* (Mexico, D.F.: Porrua Hermanos y Cia, 1937), pp. 15–17.

[11] *See* Judith Frances Zeitlan, *Cultural Politics in Colonial Tehuantepec* (Stanford, CA: Stanford University Press, 2005); Kevin Terraciano, *The Mixtecs of Colonial Oaxaca* (Stanford, CA: Stanford University Press, 2001).

Law in the Aztec Empire was administrative and penal. No evidence has yet to be offered, however, of any official forum for impartial resolution of private disputes or rules related to compensation for wrongs. Mechanisms for resolution of private disputes undoubtedly existed, and, as in all known societies, there were what may be classified as private law rules related to inheritance, property, contract, commercial transactions, and private wrongs. However, the rules made and enforced by those who governed the stratified city-chiefdoms of Mesoamerica were designed to maintain political control, access to resources, and order. Infractions had severe penal consequences, most often death or slavery. The tribunals could proceed in some cases, by Kohler's account,[12] simply on the basis of public rumor without accusation, particularly for adultery. Those who governed did establish hierarchies of specialized administrative-judicial tribunals. Local neighborhood (*barrio*) judges elected by residents investigated and determined minor criminal infractions and may perhaps have mediated private disputes. As in the case of the scribes of Deir el-Medina, they reported major infractions to higher authorities.[13] Other tribunals were established with tiers for appeals culminating in multi-member supreme councils. Special tribunals for family, tribute, and trade also existed. Although described as "courts" with "judges" by both Hispanic chroniclers and contemporary writers,[14] they might be more accurately labeled as administrative organs staffed by ruling elites designed to ensure compliance with tribute requirements and ruler-made proscriptions. The jurisdiction of the Texcoco Supreme Council, as described by Offner,[15] for example, included an array of offenses, including treason, homicide, various sexual offenses, theft, and drunkenness, as well as violations of sumptuary regulations and property infractions. The council also had jurisdiction over disputes regarding official status and offices. The Aztec system can thus be reasonably labeled a "legalistic" system with, as Offner himself notes, striking parallels with China.[16]

---

12 Kohler, *Das Recht der Azteken*, p. 108.

13 Mendieta y Nuñez, *El Derecho Precolonial*, p. 20.

14 *See*, e.g., Francisco Avalos, "An Overview of the Legal System of the Aztec Empire," *Law Library Journal*, vol. 86 (1994), pp. 259–276; Jerome A. Offner, *Law and Politics in Aztec Texcoco* (Cambridge: Cambridge University Press, 1983), pp. 55–66.

15 Offner, *Law and Politics*, p. 151.

16 *Id.*, pp. 80–82.

THE INCA

Unlike Mexico the Amerindians of South America had not developed a system of even pictorial writing by the time of the Hispanic arrival in the early 1500s. What we know of the Incas is thus based solely on archeological findings, analytical surmise, and the record of observations by early Hispanic chroniclers. All agree, however, that during the century prior to Pizarro's arrival and conquest in the 1530s, a centralized, administrative empire fundamentally resembling Pharaonic Egypt had emerged to form the largest and most populated polity in the Americas, stretching along the Andes from north of the border separating contemporary Ecuador and Colombia to the Maule River in central Chile.

The evolution of Inca civilization is believed to have followed the familiar trajectory from increasingly stratified agrarian communities bound by kinship and lineage, consolidation into larger political entities, and finally to an advanced centralized order resulting from assimilation, expedient alliance, and conquest. The Incas were also relative newcomers in a region that had been developing for over two millennia. The size, density, and governing structures of the settlements in the central Andes varied. Nearly all were kinship based. Some had well-defined leadership structures. Others were more communal and less stratified. Many were isolated in remote mountain valleys. The Inca political saga begins with domination of the existing communities in the relatively large and well-developed region around the city of Cuzco. Most believe today that they followed in the footsteps of an earlier Wari polity (c. 450–1000 CE) with its capital at Pikillacta in the Lucre Basin southeast of Cuzco, who, with a system of connecting roads, had created a network of semi-autonomous villages. About 1000 CE Wari dominance declined and Pikillacta is thought to have been abandoned. By around 1200 the Incas, by myth a warrior tribe from the south, had begun to fill the vacuum and establish their hegemony in the valley. Archeological evidence of increases in population as well as the settlement of new villages and development of new agricultural lands along the valley slopes suggests expanding Inca dominance through resettlement of communities that sought Inca protection and those they fought and conquered. The appearance of new terraces and irrigation works, Brian Bauer and Alan Covey argue, evidence the capacity of the Inca to mobilize coercively the labor necessary for large construction projects and thereby increase agricultural resources for the Inca elite.[17]

[17] Brian S. Bauer and R. Alan Covey, "Processes of State Formation in the Inca Heartland (Cuzco, Peru)," *American Anthropologist*, vol. 104 (2002), p. 852.

By 1400 the Incas had effectively assimilated the various communities in the Cuzco region by a combination of strategic alliances, often through marriage, military conquest, resettlement, and imposition of a common religious cult and language (*Quechua*). Once Inca domination of the highland heartland was complete, they proceeded to expand into the coastal regions and isolated mountain valleys to the north and south. They followed the familiar combination of alliance and conquest. Those communities who acquiesced to Inca domination or who capitulated were able to retain a degree of autonomy. Those who resisted were subject to annihilation and forced dispersal and resettlement.[18] As did the Aztecs, the Inca transferred to the temple of the Sun god in Cuzco local idols to be incorporated in an expanding pantheon of subordinate deities. Once in control of the outer coastal regions, they, like their Egyptian counterparts, were protected by geography from internal threat and outside invaders—at least until Pizarro.

Within the century before the Hispanic conquest, the Inca had developed an almost fully pyramidal administrative structure. At the apex was the Sapa Inca, notionally the paramount deity as well as temporal ruler. In the words of Nigel Davies, "as the theoretical possessor of all lands, mines and herds, the Inca *was* the state."[19] Below him were the *orejones*, members of the ruling elite, all, presumptively at least, descendants of the present or former Inca. All resided in Cuzco, itself a sacred city. Supported entirely by Inca revenues, the *orejones* were thus deprived of any local base and potential resources that might enable independent or subversive political activity. The Incas divided their domain into four major administrative regions, each of which comprised 80 provinces and over 160 subdistricts. The smallest units were the kinship-based communities referred to as *ayllus*.[20]

Two unique features of Inca rule buttressed their control. The first was a counting system of knotted cords—*quipu*—interpreted by trained specialists, most if not all of whom also resided in Cuzco. The second

---

[18] On Inca subjection of the coastal regions, *see* Geoffrey W. Conrad, "Chiquitoy Viejo: An Inca Administrative Center in the Chicama Valley, Peru," *Journal of Field Archaeology*, vol. 4 (1977), pp. 1–18; Tom D. Dillehay, "Tawantinsuyu Integration of the Chillon Valley, Peru: A Case of Inca Geo-political Mastery," *Journal of Field Archaeology*, vol. 4 (1977), pp. 397–405; Dorothy Menzel, "The Inca Occupation of the South Coast of Peru," *Southwestern Journal of Anthropology*, vol. 15 (1959), pp. 125–142.

[19] Nigel Davies, *The Incas* (Niwot, CO: University Press of Colorado, 1995), p. 114.

[20] Burkholder and Johnson, *Colonial Latin America*, p. 12.

was a technologically advanced and remarkably extensive system of roads that united the Inca domain. The *quipu* enabled the Inca rulers to keep track of people and tribute. The system of roads provided access to the most remote reaches under their control and to regulate all travel. Along the Inca roadways, particularly at vital intersections throughout the empire, Inca officials manned administrative centers to monitor and control all travel and transportation of goods. Their coercive capacity was equally extensive. In response to resistance or rebellion entire communities were uprooted, scattered, and resettled. An echo of Deir el-Medina, they also created communities of specialized laborers—weavers, potters, and producers of other luxury goods.

Although no formal judicial structure as developed under the Aztecs has been identified,[21] the Incas like the Aztecs and other polities in Mesoamerica relied on an essentially penal command-and-control system of subjugation. All subject households and communities paid tribute (*mit'a*) in the form of labor. Apart from *mit'a* labor, the Inca rulers regularly selected young girls for ritual sacrifice (but also marriage or service) from subject communities. For similar purposes they also frequently received offerings of daughters from subject chieftains who, seeking favor or fearing disapproval, thereby, to paraphrase Irene Silverblatt, further corroding community kinship identity and autonomy.[22] Few early consolidated polities had greater capacity to coerce, mobilize, and move people as readily or as effectively as the Inca.

We may assume that some form of dispute resolution within communities and within the Inca elite did exist, but, as noted with respect to other early consolidated polities, they functioned outside of the established political order. Based on Hispanic chronicles, Sally Falk Moore concludes that Inca officials had the authority to investigate and try persons for offenses, and "the higher the official, the more important to the state were the matters he could decide."[23] She lists in an appendix over seven dozen different offenses related by Hispanic chroniclers. The categories include offences related to caste property, breach of rules

---

[21] Sally Falk Moore notes that one Spanish source (*Relación*) mentions a court of a dozen judges from the villages (*ayllus*) in the Cuzco region but dismisses its trustworthiness for lack of collaborating observations. Sally Falk Moore, *Power and Property in Inca Peru* (New York: Columbia University Press, 1958), p. 117.

[22] Irene Silverblatt, "Imperial Dilemmas, the Politics of Kinship, and Inca Reconstructions of History," *Comparative Studies in Society and History*, vol. 30 (1988), pp. 83–102, at p. 92.

[23] Moore, *Power and Property in Inca Peru*, p. 117.

affecting the government, homicide, sexual offenses, theft, and such "miscellaneous" offenses as sleeping in the daytime and burning bridges. Death was the most common penalty. (Those caught sleeping in the daytime were reportedly subject only to a beating.) We may reasonably conclude that the Incas had created an early but paradigmatic regulatory, public law order.

HISPANIC COLONIAL ADMINISTRATION

Within four decades after the first landing by Columbus in the West Indies, the Hispanic (Castilian) Crown had created territorially the largest and most fully structured colonial empire in history. With the Philippines added, it spanned two oceans and three continents. Hispanic America alone encompassed a territory over 30 times the size of the Hispanic kingdoms. No European rulers before or since had as extensive authority over as much territory and as many people. The estimated Amerindian population of central Mexico alone is estimated to have been over three times the total population of the Iberian peninsula, Portugal included.

Within the first century by the most credible calculations between 200,000 and 250,000 Europeans, nearly all from Castile, had emigrated to the new colonies.[24] What began as an enterprise of wealth-seeking adventurers encouraged by a queen and her advisors to establish fortified entrepôts on what were believed to be the fringes of East Asia soon evolved into a territorial domain under expanding royal control. In the process, structures of governance reflecting well-established Iberian institutions and practices were introduced, adapted, and ultimately reconstructed within the distinctive environment of the American lands.

Forming the basic law throughout the colonies was the *Siete Partidas* supplemented by thousands of subsequently enacted Castilian laws—accessible in the four volume *Nueva Recopilaciónde Castilla* of 1567—and by steady flow from Madrid of special royal laws, edicts, decrees, and orders that revised or added to the otherwise applicable private law rules and introduced tens of thousands of new regulatory rules and institutions in response to special needs and Crown concerns in the colonies. They were consolidated and published in 1680 as the *Recopilación de Leyes de las*

---

[24] Nicolás Sánchez-Albornoz, "The Population of Colonial Spanish America," in Leslie Bethell, ed., *The Cambridge History of Latin America*, vol. 2 (Cambridge and New York: Cambridge University Press, 1984), pp. 15–16.

Indias.[25] One consequence was the first significant transplantation outside of Europe of the broad conception of law as a system of rights with corresponding adjudicatory modes of enforcement that, as previously described, had evolved over half a millennium in the West. Within this context, however, now with ample allocable human and material resources, the Castilian rulers had also begun to introduce and develop the institutions of a regulatory, public law system.

Beginning with the *capitulación* for the initial expedition by Columbus, the Castilian Crown followed the practice of the *Reconquista* with grants (*mercedes*) of office, land, and privileges to those who captured new territory and resources on its behalf. As the initial vision of trading enclaves on the Portuguese model gave way to plans for permanently settled territorial colonies, those willing to bear the costs and risks of exploration and conquest received royal orders under seal (*cédula*) confirming grants of land titles, mining rights, and *encomienda*—literally, a charge or commission—over indigenous communities for oversight, conversion, labor, and collection of taxes and church tithes. The allocation (*repartimiento*) of native labor under the *encomienda* system ensured for their holders (*encomenderos*) access to the labor needed for agriculture and mining. For the tributary communities of central Mexico and the Andes the new burdens may not have differed in kind, but unhindered by customary normative or other constraints, they proved to be immensely greater.

The administrative apparatus created for the new territories reflected the two overriding aims of the colonial enterprise from inception. The first was evangelization. As Charles I (Charles V as Holy Roman Emperor)[26] in 1535 instructed his first viceroy for Mexico, Don Antonio de Mendoza, the highest priority was to oversee the "construction of the churches necessary for the Holy Religion and to the conversion and instruction of the native Indians of that land, as well as of other matters

[25] For a detailed overview, *see* Mirow, *Latin American Law*, pp. 19–32, 45–53.

[26] On the death of Ferdinand II in 1516, Charles I succeeded to the throne of Aragon (which included Aragon, Catalonia, Valencia, Naples, Sicily, and Sardinia) and also that of Castile, initially holding the Crown jointly with his mother, Joanna, for whom as a result of her incapacity he was also guardian. His claim to the American colonies rested on his succession to the Castilian throne. Three years later in 1519 as Hapsburg heir, he also became Charles V of the Holy Roman Empire.

pertaining to the service of the Lord Our God."[27] A more secular concern was equally important—to determine whether the native villages could increase their tribute payments in gold or silver or, failing that, goods that could be easily convertible. The first council created for the governance of the new colonies was in fact the House of Trade (*Casa de Contratación*) in 1503, two decades before the Council of the Indies (*Real y Supremo Consejo de las Indias*) in 1524. These two organs under the Crown would remain the principal superintending and law-making bodies of Hispanic colonial rule for over 200 years until the Bourbon reforms of the late eighteenth century. Both were located in Spain and subject only to royal command.

The primary function of the House of Trade was to encourage and regulate trade. Located in Seville until 1717, when moved to Cadiz, the House of Trade operated the merchants' guild (*consulado*), which enjoyed a royal monopoly for all trade with the colonies. Its responsibilities also included licensing and regulating all shipping and emigration, tax and tariff collection, administering royal revenues from the colonies, supervising the convoy system (*flota*) of semi-annual shipments, particularly the shipments of gold from Manila through Mexico to Spain, and adjudicating disputes relating to trade and navigation. Local *consulados* with licensing authority and exclusive jurisdiction to adjudicate commercial disputes were gradually established in the principal cities throughout the colonies. They became the governing organs for local merchants, regulating in minute detail nearly all aspects of local trade and commerce. The *Casa* and *consulado* continued to function until 1790.

The Council of the Indies (*Consejo de las Indias*) was created in 1524 concomitant with the arrival of the first Hispanic administrative officials in Mexico (and 12 years before Pizarro had completed the conquest of Peru). Answerable only to the Crown, for whom it functioned as an advisory body, the Council was in effect the principal governing body for the American colonies as the primary legislative and highest administrative organ of the consolidated polity. In addition to extensive legislative and supervisory functions, which included verification of official accounts, it was responsible for nominating the persons to fill all high colonial posts and confirming officials appointed by those in the colonies. As a final board of appeal, but with original jurisdiction in cases involving large *encomiendas*, it was also the colonies' highest judicial organ. It had a fluctuating membership of six to ten councilors assisted

---

[27] *See* http://faculty.smu.edu/bakewell/BAKEWELL/texts/mendoza-instructions.html. Last visited April 19, 2008.

by numerous minor officials. Most were *letrados*, persons trained in civil law or canon law in the case of ecclesiastics.

As the Crown added new territories to its growing American empire, it imposed local administrative controls based predominantly on existing Castilian administrative and judicial organs and offices. The primary administrative and judicial organ was the *audiencia*, modeled after Castilian medieval courts. In the words of John Lynch, "Combining three classes of functions, judicial, administrative, and consultative, its services to crown and people in keeping watch over the activities of viceroys and governors, and in checking the private conduct of colonists were invaluable at all times and in all parts of Hispanic America."[28] Mark Burkholder aptly likens the resulting administrative structure to two sets of wheels. The hub of the first was the Crown, with spokes of authority and oversight reaching out to the *audiencias*, each of which functioned as the hubs of a second set of separate wheels with their spokes extending to the provinces.[29] The first *audiencia* was founded in Santo Domingo in 1526. In the sixteenth century, nine additional *audiencias* were established in Mexico City (1527), Panama (1535), Lima (1542), Guatemala (1542), Guadalajara (1548), Santa Fé de Bogotá (1548), Charcas (1559), Quito (1563), and Manila (1583). Two others were created in the seventeenth century for Santiago de Chile (1609) and, for a brief time, Buenos Aires (1661). Over a century later the *audiencia* in Buenos Aires was reestablished (1783) and new ones created in Caracas (1786) and Cuzco (1787). Their location, as Burkholder notes to illustrate their enduring influence,[30] can be identified today as (except for Cuzco) capital cities in the states established after independence in the early nineteenth century.[31] Each was also subdivided into local districts—named variously *corregimientos*, *alcaldes mayores*, *gobernaciones*—that, like the *audiencia* to which they reported, exercised both administrative and judicial functions. At the start each *audiencia* generally had three to four legally trained (*letrados*) judges (*oidores*). By the end of the century, the number of ministers in the larger jurisdictions had increased. Lima and Mexico each

---

28 John Lynch, *Spanish Colonial Administration, 1782–1810: The Intendant System in the Viceroyalty of the Rio de la Plata* (London: The Athlone Press, 1958), p. 237.

29 Mark A. Burkholder, "Bureaucrats," in Louisa Schell Hoberman and Susan Migden Socolow, eds., *Cities & Society in Colonial Latin America* (Albuquerque: University of New Mexico Press, 1986), p. 80.

30 *Id.* at pp. 79–80.

31 Charcas, originally Ciudad de la Plata de la Nueva Toledo, was renamed Sucre in 1839 as the capital of Bolivia.

had eight civil judges (*oidores*), four criminal judges (*alcaldes del crimen*), and two Crown attorneys (*fiscales*).[32] The posts were well paid and prestigious. All were salaried and held pursuant to lifetime royal appointments. Most local and lesser royal officials also held lifetime positions but were remunerated largely by fees. Royal administrators at the highest levels—viceroys, captains-general, presidents, and provincial governors—held their posts for stated terms that seldom exceeded six years.[33]

As described by Burkholder, the path to appointment as an *audiencia* minister first required *letrados* qualification with evidence of university education in law—generally a transcript—that with other background and career documentation was reviewed by the Secretariat of the Council's Cabinet (*Cámara*), which issued a resumé (*relación de méritos y servicios*) of the applicant's qualifications. With this resumé in hand, the aspiring office holder (*pretendiente*) could then seek the royal appointment in the form of a formal recommendation (*consulta*) by the Council Cabinet. *Audiencia* ministers and other officials could also receive posts without the review and advice of the Cabinet simply by royal decree or *sobre consulta*, which was also based on royal decree, either to fill a new or vacant post or to replace an official promoted to another position, categorized separately as a *resulta*.[34] Only applicants selected on the basis of a *consulta* had demonstrable merit. Posts filled by decree or *sobre consulta* included offices the Crown sold—a practice that would greatly expand at the end of the sixteenth century as royal finances became increasingly dire.[35] A 1606 *cédula* gave office holders a right that could be "renounced" in favor of another person that in effect gave them a negotiable title to office.[36]

In view of the growing immigrant population and concern for a more coherent administrative structure and oversight, in 1535 Charles I created the Viceroyalty of New Spain (*Virreinato de Nueva España*), the first of what ultimately became four viceroyalties. It initially included all of North and Central America north of the Isthmus of Panama under Hispanic control. The Viceroyalty of Peru (*Virreinato de Peru*) was established in 1542. What are today Colombia, Ecuador, Panama, and

---

32 Mark A. Burkholder and D.S. Chandler, *Biographical Dictionary of Audiencia Ministers in the Americas, 1687–1821* (Westport, CN: Greenwood Press, 1982), p. xii.

33 Burkholder, "Bureaucrats," pp. 80–81.

34 Burkholder and Chandler, *Biographical Dictionary*, pp. xvi–xvii.

35 *Id.*

36 Burkholder, "Bureaucrats," p. 82.

Venezuela were removed from the jurisdiction of the Peruvian Viceroy in 1717 and placed under the new Viceroy of New Granada (*Virreinato de Nueva Granada*) with its capital at Santa Fé de Bogotá. The Viceroy of Rio de la Plata (*Virreinato de Rio de la Plata*) centered in Buenos Aires was not created until 1776. With the establishment of the viceroyalties, the *audiencia* lost some administrative and legislative tasks but remained the primary judicial organ for the colonies, serving principally as courts of civil, criminal, and administrative appeal, and, as noted above, both an agency for review and substitution for absent or vacant viceroyalties. In a structure in which adjudication was a principal mode of law enforcement, the *audiencia* thus continued to play a pivotal role. As the colonies expanded and new officials were needed, their judicial functions became more pronounced. Many new ministers and offices were added to assist the *oidores*. They included *alcaldes*, who, if trained in the law, could serve as adjudicating judges or assist in the proceedings; *fiscales* responsible for royal revenues and other royal interests; and, at the local level, *corregidores*, who commanded district militia in addition to their broad administrative and judicial responsibilities. Each *audiencia* also employed a clerical staff of reporters and scribes. Added as well to the expanding colonial bureaucracy were other royal offices designed to ensure local adherence to Crown policies. They included two with supervisory and investigative authority: the *residencia*, judges responsible for reviewing the conduct of officials upon their retirement or termination, and *visitadores*, who were specially commissioned by the Crown with broad investigatory authority. At the local level by mid century each town established for Hispanic subjects was governed by a *cabildo* with extensive legislative and administrative authority. The *cabildo* selected the local *alcalde* judge as well as administrative officials, such as the *regídor* and *procurador*. The *cabildos* were in turn subject to district officials—the *alcaldes mayores* in New Spain and the *corregidores* in most of the other colonies. Its members were elected. For Amerindians, as described subsequently, colonial policy produced a separate system of governance, restructuring existing native communities and in many instances compelling resettlement in new Amerindian townships.

The Church and principal Catholic orders concomitantly established parallel structures of bishoprics and missions with courts. Unlike the congregational Protestant churches that fostered self-governing communities in the English colonies, the Catholic Church in Hispanic America paralleled the royal colonial regime in its hierarchical distance from those it evangelized and served. Hierarchical but, as noted by John

Schwaller, not monolithic,[37] the Catholic Church divided organizationally into two primary factions. The first comprised parish priests subject to the oversight of bishops or archbishops who served local parishes and thus "living in the world" were referred to as the "secular" clergy. Although under the spiritual authority of the papacy, they were subject to royal nomination or approval. In the American colonies as well as Spain the secular clergy had in effect become officials of the Crown. The second category included those priests, friars, and monks who, as members of one of the mendicant orders—the Franciscans, Dominicans, Augustinians, Mercedarians, and Jesuits—had taken vows to live by rules (*regula*) more stringent and demanding than those of ordinary priests. They are thus commonly referred to as the "regular" clergy.[38] The two groups were separately governed and often competing representatives of the Church in Hispanic America (and the Philippines). Both groups established ecclesiastic courts with clerical judges trained in canon law. As in Spain and other parts of Catholic Europe, they claimed exclusive jurisdiction over disputes related to marriage, espousal, annulment and dissolution of marriage and, until the Crown successfully acquired administrative jurisdiction, succession.

Although not the first to arrive, the regular clergy were the first to establish an institutional presence within the Amerindian communities. The Franciscans arrived in the West Indies with Columbus on his second voyage. In 1505 the first Franciscan Province had been established at Santo Domingo. Franciscans reached Mexico in 1524, followed by the Dominicans in 1526 and the Augustinians in 1533. By 1528 a bishopric of Mexico had been created, which became an archbishopric in 1545 with the creation of additional dioceses in Oaxaca, Michoacán, and Chiapas. Pursuant to the Bull issued by Pope Adrian VI in 1522, known as the *Omnimoda*, as a result of its prefatory words "Exponi nobis Fecisti," granting "*Omnimodam auctoritatem nostrum*," the mendicant orders claimed direct authority from the Pope to perform acts otherwise granted only to bishops. A dearth of secular priests led to the appointment of regular clergy as bishops and priests in dioceses throughout the colonies. The increase in secular clergy by mid century as well as the growing prosperity of mendicant order missions in Amerindian communities led to one of the first major jurisdictional conflicts in the colonies. The conflict formally ended in 1574 with the promulgation by

---

[37] John F. Schwaller, "Introduction," in John F. Schwaller, ed., *The Church in Colonial Latin America* (Wilmington, DE: Scholarly Resources, 2000), p. xi.
[38] *Id.*

Philip II of the *Ordenanza del Patronazgo*, which, in the words of Robert Padden, "subordinated [both the regular and secular clergy] in every respect to the ecclesiastical authority of the Crown."[39]

Ostensible authority did not however negate the reality of independent ecclesiastical influence. Many secular as well as regular clerics held posts as royal officials. Their integration within local native communities also gave them significant influence. By the end of the colonial period, if data on New Granada are representative, priests may have outnumbered officials, regular army officers, and lawyers combined.[40] In view of the repeated complaints from royal officials in the colonies, the influence of the Church in the colonies was often viewed as detrimental to the interests of the Crown.[41] However, supported by compulsory tithes, voluntary contributions, and also individual and mission *encomienda* themselves, both the secular and regular clergy had similar economic interests. Indeed underlying the jurisdictional and other conflicts were the tensions produced by the prosperity of the colonial mendicant orders.

Although any general assessment of the impact of Hispanic rule on the indigenous peoples is well beyond the scope of this study, one aspect, immediate and horrific, had significant consequences for colonial administration and law. Disease arrived with the Castilians. Death followed. The rapidity and the extent of the ensuing depopulation were catastrophic. In the Caribbean islands, entire ethnic communities ceased to exist. The indigenous population in central Mexico is estimated to have declined by at least 25 percent within the first four years after the Castilians arrived, and by the early seventeenth century, only 750,000 of an estimated original population of over 25 million remained.[42] The population decline in the central Andes was less precipitous but hardly less consequential. Within the half century between 1570 and 1620, Sherburne Cook estimates that the population decreased in the highlands from slightly over one million persons to less than 585,000, and along the

---

[39] Robert C. Padden, "The Ordenanza del Patronazgo of 1574: An Interpretative Essay," in Schwaller, ed., *The Church in Colonial Latin America*, p. 62.

[40] *See*, e.g., Victor M. Uribe, "The Lawyers and New Granada's Late Colonial State," *Journal of Latin American Studies*, vol. 27 (1995), p. 122.

[41] *See*, e.g., Charles H. Cunningham, "The Ecclesiastical Influence in the Philippines (1565–1850)," *American Journal of Theology*, vol. 22 (1918), pp. 161–186.

[42] Sánchez-Albornoz, "The Population of Colonial Spanish America," p. 4, citing studies by Sherburne F. Cook and Woodrow Borah (*see* "Bibliographical Essays: The Population in Colonial Spanish America," *id.*, pp. 805–811, at p. 806.

Pacific coast, from 250,000 to 87,000.[43] Disease was not the sole nor, in the first years, the principal cause of death. Virtual enslavement, brutal exploitation, especially in placer mining laborers, and forced resettlement also contributed to the catastrophic loss of life.

The first arrivals took full personal advantage of the privileges of their *capitulaciónes* and status as *encomenderos*. They satisfied their immediate needs for food, construction, and gold with enslavement and coerced labor. Their mistreatment of the native population so appalled newly arrived Dominican friars that they initiated the first efforts to recognize the "natural rights" of all Amerindians. Their campaign had formal success. Isabella had faced an initial test when a number of natives were dispatched by Columbus for sale in Castile. Upon their arrival she is credited for having blocked their intended sale pending an inquiry into the legality of their enslavement under Castilian law. The issue was not resolved, however, before they had been assigned to galleys to await an outcome. Presumably most died in the interim. She did not decide the issue until in a royal *cédula* issued in 1503, she determined that the native peoples under Hispanic dominion were free, but, she added, that, for wages to be assessed as appropriate by local chiefs (*caciques*) in consultation with local officials, they could be forced to build buildings, gather and mine gold, and till the fields to satisfy the needs of settlers and the Crown.[44]

Dominican brothers—Alonso de Espinal, Antonio de Montesinos, and Bartolomé de las Casas in particular—were among the first to protest both in Hispaniola and Spain. Las Casas, a former *encomendero* himself, became the leading publicist for humane (Christian) treatment of Amerindians throughout the colonies. He joined the Dominicans in 1522. Las Casas is well known for his writings following his debate in 1550 with Dominican Juan Ginés de Sepúlveda, the leading apologist for Hispanic rule, at the celebrated assembly (*junta*) of jurists and theologians convened at Valladolid by Charles V. Las Casas, along with like-minded Dominicans, had been very successful in earlier efforts to reform the law. In 1511–1513, after purportedly listening to de Espinal's description of the treatment of natives in Hispaniola, Ferdinand II promulgated the Laws of Burgos, restricting the number of *encomiendas* and the number of natives allotted. In addition the Laws of Burgos attempted to regulate in detail the amount of work, pay, provisioning, living quarters, hygiene,

---

43 *Id.*, p. 6.

44 Lesley Boyd Simpson, *The Encomienda in New Spain: The Beginning of Spanish Mexico* (Berkeley, CA: University of California Press, 1966 ed.), p. 2.

and care required for the subject natives. The Laws also prohibited any punishment by *encomenderos*, reserving such authority to Royal juridical officials.[45] In 1537 Pope Paul III also responded with the Bull entitled *Sublimis Deus*, which prohibited the enslavement of Amerindians and recognized their right to possess property. Largely ignored, the Laws of Burgos failed to bring about the desired changes. In 1542 Charles V issued the New Laws, which recognized Amerindians as free vassals of the Castilian Crown and authorized the *audiencia* to investigate and punish any infractions against them. They terminated all allotments of natives to officials at all levels as well as the clergy and Church institutions. The New Laws also provided for lawsuits among Amerindian subjects to be based on native usages and customs.[46] The remaining question was whether the New Laws would or could be enforced.

By mid century most fundamental issues of legislative authority may have been resolved, but overlapping adjudicatory jurisdiction continued to produce conflicts. The Crown's administration of its American colonies reflected its undisputed authority to legislate an array of regulatory controls not available even in Castile, where, as noted previously, its authority and powers were less fettered than in any of the other Hispanic kingdoms. The Crown did not hesitate to respond legislatively to perceived problems. The Council issued an overwhelming volume of regulatory legislation. Effective enforcement was another matter. The formidable barriers to effective communication across the Atlantic (and the Pacific for the Philippines) in the sixteenth century imposed severe constraints. Many contested claims could only be finally resolved by the Crown and its official agents.[47] Pronouncements made in Madrid were not necessarily heeded by those in the colonies. Simply put, the Crown lacked the capacity to coerce compliance. Those who ruled the Hispanic kingdoms also suffered a conflict in interests reflected in the promulgated rules. Fully protecting the Amerindian from exploitation would, as one official after another reminded the Crown, also reduce the Crown's share of the wealth such exploitation produced. The Crown was as dependent on native labor as the settlers.

---

[45] For fuller treatment and English translation, see Lesley Boyd Simpson, *The Laws of Burgos of 1512–1513: Royal Ordinances for the Good Government and Treatment of the Indians* (San Francisco: J. Howell Books, 1960). See also Simpson, *The Encomienda*, pp. 32–34.

[46] Simpson, *The Encomienda*, pp. 129–132. *See also* http://www.fordham.edu/halsall/mod/1542newlawsindies.html. Last visited April 18, 2008.

[47] *See* Lauren Benton, *Law and Colonial Cultures* (Cambridge and New York: Cambridge University Press, 2002), pp. 80–102.

The *encomienda* system enriched their holders at the expense of the native population and the Crown. From the start the laws related to *encomienda* strictly regulated the terms of labor service that an *encomendero* could legally extract from Amerindians within their charge. Similarly, the commissions never constituted perpetual legal estates or rights *in rem*. Yet, in practice and eventual custom, they became heritable property. As such the *encomienda* threatened to become a competing source for independent authority and power. With dual motives to protect its own as well as native interests, the Crown thus moved to restrict their influence. Attempts to curtail the creation of additional *encomiendas* and to regulate the prerogatives of *encomenderos* were a constant feature of reform legislation issued in Spain. One notable example was a 1536 *cédula* that required the *audiencias* in the colonies to conduct a census of the population, determine how much tribute was being paid previously to the native rulers prior to the Hispanic conquest, and then to determine a just rate that would impose as light and acceptable a burden as possible. The *cédula* also provided that an *encomienda* could pass by inheritance only the term of two natural lives and then only to the children or widow of the holder. Subsequent regulations sought to eliminate the system entirely. When that effort failed, additional instructions further restricted the amount of tribute that could be levied to levels below what had been traditionally due before the conquest. Some reforms were successful. By 1530 in New Spain and 1550 in Peru the collective obligation of native communities to provide services had been replaced by a system of individual payment. With respect to tribute owed the Crown, the amount was usually, according to Mario Góngora, a gold peso plus a bushel and a half (*fanega*) of maize.[48] The New Laws prohibited the establishment of new *encomiendas* and abolished existing ones held by any royal official, clergy, religious orders, or colonists who had abused those natives under their charge. Finally, in 1549 the Crown abolished all tribute in personal services at least in New Spain and Peru.

Power was local. In the face of opposition from all quarters in the colonies—except, of course, the native community—the New Laws of 1542 could not be fully implemented. Lesley Simpson tells of the fate that awaited the four commissioned *visitadores* with plenary authority dispatched by Charles V to oversee their implementation.[49] The Crown's delegate to Peru, Potasco Núñez Vela, arrived in the midst of a rebellion.

---

[48] Mario Góngora, *Studies in the Colonial History of Spanish America* (Cambridge: Cambridge University Press, 1975), p. 138.

[49] Simpson, *The Encomienda*, pp. 133–135.

He was seized and beheaded. Francisco Tello de Sandoval, sent to Mexico, personally fared better, but Viceroy Mendoza promptly suspended the effectiveness of the New Laws with an appeal to the Council of the Indies to have them revoked or amended. Mendoza's action exemplified the legal tactics employed to obstruct enforcement. In addition to direct petitions and appeals to Council and king, at every juncture opponents lodged formal challenges to the legal authority of the officials in charge. With appeals to the Council or petitions to the Crown from any decision by an *audiencia* or other enforcing official taking months if not years, such tactics imposed immense delay to the enforcement of any unwanted measure.

The Crown's own financial interests precluded full termination of forced labor, especially in the mines. The dependency of the Hapsburg monarchs on gold and silver shipments from their American colonies grew steadily after the discovery of major silver deposits at Potosí in Peru in 1545 and Zacatecas in northern Mexico the following year. Differences in demand for silver relative to gold in Ming China and Europe produced during the sixteenth and early seventeenth centuries an arbitrage that by the middle of the seventeenth century had arguably produced a convergence of price.[50] Even after convergence, Chinese demand for silver, continuing unabated, stimulated an extraordinarily profitable trade between Mexico (with intra-colonial silver shipments from Lima) and China via Manila with payments in newly minted silver for China-made luxury goods, particularly silk. Dennis Flynn and Arturo Giraldez surmise that during the seventeenth century the Acapulco–Manila galleons supplied China with as much silver as Portuguese, Dutch, and British traders combined.[51] Gold and silver shipments worldwide from Hispanic America reached their peak between 1575 and 1625, just as the implementation of new restrictions on native service had begun.

Mining depended on native labor. As *encomienda* labor dwindled, other legal means for obligatory labor service prevailed. For Potosí and elsewhere in Peru, the *mit'a* ensured a continuous supply. The system under official oversight required community *kurakas* periodically to draft by lottery a specific number of workers for the mines, who in turn were paid wages but forced to endure up to two to four months of hard labor.

---

[50] *See* Dennis O. Flynn and Arturo Giraldez, "Arbitrage, China, and World Trade in the Early Modern Period," *Journal of the Economic and Social History of the Orient*, vol. 38 (1995), pp. 429–448.

[51] *Id.*, p. 329.

In the meantime Hispanic institutions were further transforming the lives and cultures of the native peoples. The imposition of alien rule, however benign or well intentioned, inexorably produces cultural upheaval and change. The Amerindian conversion to Christianity is exemplary of the process and its effects. What is most notable in the Hispanic colonial experience for our purposes, however, is the role of law. The imposition and use of Western conceptions and varied processes of law had immediate, long-term, and often unintended consequences.

Native rulers in Mesoamerica and the central Andes had imposed tribute, coerced labor, enslaved or resettled those they conquered, and as law givers and judges regulated the lives of their subjects. They did so, however, pursuant to organically evolved sources of authority and customary constraints on their power buttressed by widely shared habits, expectations, and beliefs. The Hispanics may have replicated many of these practices, but without the mediating effects of native cultures. Their extractions were more severe and costly than any experienced before. Introducing new sources of mineral and agricultural wealth, they created unprecedented demands for labor. Legislating new native sumptuary laws, they imposed on their Amerindian subjects not only a variety of demeaning, caste-creating stigmata but also an unfathomed system of regulatory licensing. Equally consequential but, at least occasionally, more liberating were the judicial structures for relief and redress that they introduced.

The Hispanics had initially envisioned a dual structure with separate "republics" or "commonwealths," one of Hispanic settlers, the other of native peoples. Some had argued to the contrary for a single, integrated regime. In the end, a combination of the two prevailed.[52] Existing native communities were administratively incorporated as native townships (*cabeceras*) and subdivided into village subunits (*sujetos*) and neighborhood wards (*barrios*), with existing chiefs, designated as *caciques* or, in Peru, *kurakas*, and ruling nobles, designated *principales*, co-opted as administrative officials but subject to the colonial regime. From the start new native towns were established, often by a mendicant order, as in the case of the Franciscan-sponsored San Francisco Acámbaro in Michoacán. As native depopulation became increasingly severe, resettlement to newly created Hispanic-styled towns accelerated. They tended to be located

[52] *See* Woodrow Borah, *Justice by Insurance: The General Indian Court of Colonial Mexico and the Legal Aides of the Half-Real* (Berkeley, CA: University of California Press, 1983), pp. 29–34.

conveniently in the vicinity of Hispanic towns or *encomendero* holdings for whom their residents supplied labor.

Recognition of the natural rights of the Amerindians was among the most transformational features of colonial policy. As detailed in Chapter 5, law as a system of private rights permeated the law-enforcing processes of the *ius commune* of continental Europe generally and Hispanic law in particular. By the dawn of the sixteenth century, natural law theory had become equally embedded in Western legal culture. Their combination within the political structures of Europe's medieval kingdoms had given rise to the notion of natural rights and a legal order dominated by adjudicatory proceedings and the paramount role of judges in both social and political ordering. Transplanted in the Americas as intrinsic features of governance, the Castilian rulers fused the structures for judicial ordering within an otherwise exemplary public law regime. In so doing they fundamentally transformed patterns of traditional rule.

The preference for *letrados* for appointment to official posts ensured that most administrative as well as nearly all judicial officials were trained in Roman civil or canon law. The pervasive emphasis on judicial processes in colonial administration led to the meticulous provision for both judicial and administrative appeals ultimately to the Crown. These were empowering innovations, however imperfect and limited in actual realization and effect, especially when combined with the recognition that the native inhabitants of the colonial territories enjoyed the legal capacity as claimants with legally enforceable rights to participate in judicial processes, including the right to redress through a colonial version of *amparo*. At no time before had a conquered and subordinated people outside of Western Europe been accorded such extensive participatory and protective voice in governance. Almost immediately individual and collective litigants emerged within Amerindian communities throughout the colonies.

Amerindian lawsuits have been a much studied aspect of Hispanic colonial rule. Susan Kellogg, Judith Zeitlan, and Steve Stern are among the most prominent scholars in the United States to examine and assess their impact in Mexico as well as Peru.[53] They all express agreement that Woodrow Borah's conclusions with respect to New Spain applied throughout the colonies. In Borah's words:

---

[53] *See* Borah, *Justice by Insurance*; Susan Kellogg, *Law and the Transformation of Aztec Culture* (Norman and London: University of Oklahoma Press, 1995); Steve J. Stern, *Peru's Indian People and the Challenge of Spanish Conquest* (Madison, WI: University of Wisconsin Press, 2nd ed., 1993); and Zeitlan, *Cultural Politics in Colonial Tehuantepec*.

> So the Indians of New Spain, after enduring the shocking losses and disruptions of the first years of conquest, found that once a relatively orderly royal administration began ... , they could haul any official into court and challenge his decisions; that any grant of land could be disputed; that boundaries and political arrangements could be challenged; and that any private person or corporate entity could be held for redress for damage done or be forestalled through petition for an order of amparo.[54]

Litigation for Amerindians thus became, again to quote Borah, "the principal means for carrying on the long series of disputes unleashed by the Conquest over land, status, virtually all other relationships" to the amazement of those who ruled "that subjects so meek showed such ferocity and tenacity."[55]

One unintended consequence was to erode the legitimacy of traditional community leaders on whom Hispanic officials relied. Borah quotes the concern expressed by at least one official, Alonso de Zorita, an *audiencia* judge in the mid sixteenth century:

> The suits have brought about great upheavals in the provinces and towns and very great confusion everywhere. Both lords and commoners have been impoverished, brought to ruin, and their substance wasted. They have all suffered great loss, as much spiritual as material. In all New Spain there is no agreement on a single matter between the classes because the commoners have lost respect for their lords and nobles and have risen against them and no longer give them the obedience they once did. Yet such obedience to superiors is very necessary for good government among the Indians.[56]

The saga of Don Juan Cortés, as related by Judith Zeitlan and Lillian Thomas,[57] provides a telling example. Cortés was the native ruler of Thuantepec allied with the Hispanics at the time of the conquest. He was baptized with a Hispanic name and designed *cacique* and governor of the district. Like other native elites being assimilated into Hispanic rule, he was privileged by his position, which included a portion of tribute paid by the district villages, and by special license, entitling him to ride horses and wear Western clothes. As the end of his first two year term of office approached, he became subject to seemingly a routine but secret investigation (*resdencia secreta*) of his performance, on the basis of complaints filed by native residents that he had made excessive tribute demands and

---

54 Borah, *Justice by Insurance*, p. 40.

55 *Id.*, p. 40.

56 Borah, *Justice by Insurance*, p. 41.

57 Zeitlan and Thomas, "Spanish Justice and the Indian Cacique." *See also* Zeitlan, *Cultural Politics in Colonial Tehuantepec*, pp. 52–57.

diverted tribute to his personal use. Accusations of other abuses followed. The *juez de residencia* issued formal criminal charges. Ultimately the complaints were withdrawn "for the sake of peace and harmony," and Don Juan remained in office until just before his death a decade later (1563). He had been subjected to public disgrace and the humiliation of imprisonment during his trial.

Officials were not the only ones who could be held accountable for abuses under Hispanic law. Native litigants also used the Crown's official apparatus for investigatory oversight and adjudication to enforce legal rules regulating *encomendero* extraction of labor services and tributary payments (*mit'a*). Steve Stern relates the reactions of Don Miguel de Bendezú in Huamanga, Peru to a 1622 subpoena to respond to a petition for a formal reinvestigation (*revista*) filed by a local *kuraka* and others to correct the count of the tributary population.[58] Two years earlier, through a similar *revista*, the *kuraka* had successfully lowered the *mit'a* tributes owed under the *encomienda* allotment by 700 pesos on evidence of a significant decrease in the number of persons on which the tributary payments were based.

Both Don Juan and Don Miguel faced what seems best described as judicialized investigatory hearings that could have both penal and administrative consequences. Not only, however, were the investigations initiated by petitioners seeking redress, they proceeded to conclusion so long as those filing the accusation persisted. When the complaints against Don Juan were withdrawn, the proceedings against him were terminated. This was an "accusatory" process little different, as noted previously, from plaintiff-controlled lawsuits in which petitioners as claimants initiated and effectively controlled the proceeding. Both the "right" of the petitioners to be heard and the corresponding obligation of the judges in charge to hear them and adjudicate their claims were taken for granted. Recognition of their lack of prosecutorial discretion was an unstated premise of the many contemporaneous expressions of dismay by officials like Alonso de Zorita over the social consequences of ruinous litigation. Such was the legacy in Hispanic America of the primacy of private law processes as an essential feature of the *ius commune* in sixteenth century Castile.

The official response to increasing litigation by the Crown's Amerindian subjects also reflected the assumption that native complainants had a legal right to redress. During the second half of the century, faced with native depopulation and increasing immigration, and the perceived need

---

[58] Stern, *Peru's Indian People*, pp. 76–77.

to strengthen royal control, viceroys first in Peru and then in Mexico initiated a series of reforms. Among their principal aims was to increase effective Amerindian access to legal redress.

In the wake of a failed neo-Inca millenarian uprising led by the last Inca, Tupac Amaru, the Crown commissioned an extraordinarily able administrator, Francisco de Toledo, as the new Viceroy of Peru. Toledo's twelve year term (1569–1581) was one of the most impressive in colonial history. Pursuant to the findings of a five year (1570–1575) personal *visita* conducted throughout the viceroyalty, Toledo devised and implemented a series of major reforms. He is credited for the revitalization of the Peruvian mines—Potosí in particular—through new amalgamation processes and hydraulic power generation. In order to ensure more responsive and responsible local municipal government, he standardized requirements for *cabildo* membership and election. His administration also advanced the relocation of Amerindians from scattered isolated settlements into new towns (*reducciones*) as well as the related centralization of *mit'a* labor extractions. Most significant for our purposes were the reforms designed primarily to curtail abuses and reduce the costs of adjudication. In so doing, perhaps unintentionally he facilitated even greater native participation as claimants in administrative and judicial processes—civil as well as criminal—at all levels. The reform included jurisdictional clarification to reduce conflicts, procedures for expedited proceedings, elimination or significant reduction of various legal fees, and appointment of salaried judges, counsel, and notaries for cases involving Amerindians paid from a small per capita tax levied on Amerindian communities.[59] Noteworthy among the beneficiaries of these reforms were those who filed complaints against Don Miguel nearly a half century later.

A decade later, New Spain's Viceroy Luis de Vélasco voiced similar concerns for more efficient and effective means to ensure access by Amerindians for judicial redress. To Vélasco, as recounted by Woodrow Borah, the crux of the problem was the exploitation of Amerindian litigants by officials, lawyers, notaries, and scribes alike who lived off of the fees and miscellaneous charges incurred to prosecute or defend an action or to comply with administrative and judicial documentary

---

[59] For biographical data on Francisco de Toledo and details of his tenure as viceroy, *see* Roberto Levillier, *Don Francisco de Toledo: Supremo Organizador del Peru*, 2 vols. (Madrid: Espasa-Calpe, 1935); Arthur F. Zimmermann, *Francisco de Toledo: Fifth Viceroy of Peru, 1569–1581* (Caldwell, ID: Caxton Printers, 1938).

demands.[60] Earlier attempts to simplify proceedings and to reduce the costs borne by naïve litigants had failed. In letters to Philip II in 1590, Vélasco proposed several solutions. First, free legal assistance should be provided to Amerindian litigants through a *defensor de los indios* who would represent Amerindians in all cases regardless of the amount in controversy. His responsibilities would include the preparation of all petitions and complaints. Vélasco also proposed that the viceroy have exclusive adjudicatory jurisdiction for all civil actions involving Amerindians. Such cases, he argued, could also be handled more expeditiously through administrative rather than judicial proceedings.

Philip's reply was prompt. In all cases in addition to the proposed salaried defender, a salaried *letrado* and attorney were to be appointed as the sole legal representatives of any Amerindian party. Their services were to be made available to individual litigants without cost and the towns and *caciques* for half the scheduled fee. The viceroy was to have, as requested, exclusive jurisdiction over all suits between Amerindians or brought by Hispanic claimants against Amerindians. However, presumably to allay European settler concerns, in keeping with established law and practice, cases brought by Amerindians against Europeans were to continue as before to be adjudicated in ordinary local tribunals with appropriate adjudicatory jurisdiction.[61] In response Vélasco protested that Amerindians not Europeans were more often the petitioners in these cases, as they sought access to tribunals capable of redressing wrongs suffered at the hands of Europeans.

Vélasco promptly proceeded with organization of a new central tribunal under the viceroy for Amerindian litigants, to be known as the *Juzgado General de Indios*, the General Indian Court of New Spain. Functioning without interruption from 1592 to 1820, the General Indian Court generally exercised exclusive jurisdiction in all civil and administrative cases brought by a Spaniard (European) against Amerindians in New Spain for an amount in controversy exceeding ten silver pesos, and in cases among Amerindians or brought by Indians against Spaniards or by Spaniards against Amerindians involving an amount of more than 100 silver pesos. Suits with lower amounts in controversy as well as disputes over boundaries, agricultural land, wasteland, and between native townships (*cabeceras*) and their subunits (*sujetos*) were to be adjudicated in ordinary tribunals but subject to special record keeping and procedural requirements designed to avoid delay and to expedite proceedings. Also,

---

60 Borah, *Justice by Insurance*, pp. 84–89.

61 *Id.*, pp. 91–95.

in these cases new royal agents were to be appointed to represent all Amerindian litigants in lieu of all other legal representatives. Individual Amerindian litigants were to be freed from payment of any fees and other charges. *Caciques*, *principales*, and communities could only be charged half the scheduled amount. The regulations notably also prohibited receipt of any gifts.[62]

Woodrow Borah's review of cases decided by the tribunal indicates that disputes over land were the most common.[63] These included boundary disputes, including those between native communities, and disputes over native land grants (*fundo legal*) as well as grants of Crown land to Europeans, native land sales or leases, and land transfers by succession. Complaints against illegal actions by local Hispanic officials constituted the second most frequent category of suits. Many involved forced labor or other allegedly illegal extractions. Others challenged the prices charged under the *repartimiento de mercancia*, the pressured sale of livestock and goods to native households by district governors (*alcalde mayores*, *corregidores*, or *gobernadores*) at prices, usually exorbitant, that they set. Next in frequency were suits related to labor contracts with Spaniards. A typical complaint would allege abuse of a debt-peonage contract to work in payment of a debt. Other cases involved allegation of abusive practices by clergy, *cacique*, and other native officials. Also common were an expected variety of claims ranging from compensation for damage caused by wandering cattle to petitions for exemptions from certain tax levies.

The General Indian Court and related measures represented the progression of paternalistic measures designed to protect Amerindians from exploitation enacted by the Crown throughout the sixteenth century at the instigation and with the support of Dominican friars, royal administrators, and others. They extended, it should be noted, into the hinterland well beyond the urban centers.[64] No complete or accurate evaluation of their effects is possible, however. Nor can they be assessed without also taking into consideration the coercive labor extractions that the Crown continued to impose. Yet, at least judging from the responses, they must have had some influence. The historical record, including the cases brought before the General Indian Court, illustrates the extent to which they were criticized and circumvented or simply ignored. Arguably at

---

[62] *Id.*, pp. 98–99.

[63] *Id.*, pp. 128–222.

[64] *See*, e.g., Charles R. Cutter, "The Administration of Law in Colonial New Mexico," *Journal of the Early Republic*, vol. 18 (1998), pp. 99–115.

least, they also contributed to a gathering process of extralegal subordination of Amerindian and other disadvantaged, mostly urban, groups and the co-option of the imperial administration.

At this point it is worth emphasizing that many groups subject to colonial rule were less benefited or simply excluded from any special legal protection. The members of the growing *mestizo* population were not counted as Amerindians. Nor did they participate fully in the legal, political, economic, or social life of the European community. In addition the number of recently arrived, unskilled Europeans was also increasing, who without office, wealth, or status constituted a growing substratum of the European community at large. A study on race and class by John Chance based on the population of colonial Anteguera (Oaxaca) from census figures for 1792 shows that by the end of the eighteenth century in the city of 4550 non-native household heads, 263 (5 percent) were *peninsulares* (immigrants from Spain but also a few from other parts of Europe); 2417 (53 percent) were creole (*criollos*); 107 (2 percent), were *castizos* (mixed racial ancestry); 1015 (22 percent) were *mestizos* (Amerindian and European ancestry); and 748 (16 percent) were mulattoes (African and European ancestry).[65] Chance finds a significant degree of segregation by both class and race. In other words, the colonial elites were divided by wealth and status, with race (and mixed ancestry) a likely determinant of both.

Increasing numbers of slaves were also being imported into the colonies directly or indirectly from Africa, particularly into Cuba and other Caribbean islands as well as the tropical regions along the eastern coast of Central and South America.[66] In these regions the demand for agricultural labor had begun to grow as colonial settlers began to develop plantations of indigo, cacao, coffee, tobacco, and sugar. Here too the unsatisfied demand for all forms of labor was greater than in New Spain or Peru as a result of a decimated native population. David Eltis estimates that before 1580 roughly 45,000 African slaves had arrived in the Hispanic colonies. The number increased to a peak of 289,000 between 1580 and 1640. Between 1670 and 1700 the number was 1,451,000, and between 1700 and 1760, 271,000. In terms of both number and territorial

---

[65] John K. Chance, "The Ecology of Race and Class in Late Colonial Oaxaca," in David J. Robinson, ed., *Studies in Spanish American Population History* (Boulder, CO: Westview Press, 1981), p. 99.

[66] For an excellent bibliographic review of the literature on slavery in Spanish America through the late 1970s, *see* Magnus Morner, "Recent Research on Negro Slavery and Abolition in Latin America," *Latin American Research Review*, vol. 13 (1978), pp. 265–289.

expanse, the magnitude of African slavery in the British and Portuguese (Brazil) colonies may have dwarfed that of Hispanic America generally but African slavery in the colonies was not insignificant. During this period (1500 to 1700), an estimated total of 746,000 African slaves arrived in the Hispanic colonies in contrast to 1,127,000 in Brazil and 1,252,000 in the British colonies.[67] Nearly half, by some estimates, were destined for Cuba.[68]

Hispanic law extended to slaves many of the protections as well as regulatory restrictions applied to Amerindians. Addressing slavery in medieval Spain, the *Siete Partidas* and other Castilian laws contained both. Among the former were rules to facilitate manumission and to prevent mistreatment. Notions of royal justice that underlay the Crown's obligation to provide special protection to the poor and other *miserables* extended to slaves. Thus locally appointed Defenders of the Poor (*Defendores de los Pobres*), who represented disadvantaged persons as guardians and legal counsel, were also required to provide legal assistance to slaves.[69] Such ostensible access to legal protection serves also, however, to underscore their lack of legal rights and capacity. Slaves in the colonies were also subject to special regulations, such as the Black Codes (*Códigos de Negros*), which restricted their movement and proscribed a variety of potentially threatening and unwanted activities. In all events far more important was access to freedom.

Special edict had negated the Castilian legal rule that the children of slaves were born free, but the rules on manumission laid out in the *Siete Partidas* and subsequent legislation allowed slaves to purchase their freedom and gave them priority to purchase their offspring.[70] Since slaves in urban settings frequently worked for wages, keeping a portion of what they earned, and could in mining communities work for themselves on free days, some were able to accumulate sufficient capital to purchase their freedom.[71] However enabled, large numbers of slaves did in fact buy themselves and their families out of slavery. Free manumission by owners was also relatively common, particularly in areas that were economically stagnant, such as Costa Rica where, by one estimate,

[67] David Eltis, *The Rise of African Slavery in the Americas* (Cambridge: Cambridge University Press, 2000), Table I-I, p. 9.

[68] *See*, e.g., *id*., p. 24.

[69] David L. Chandler, "Family Bonds and the Bondsman: The Slave Family in Colonial Colombia," *Latin American Research Review*, vol. 16 (1981), p. 119.

[70] Mirow, *Latin American Law*, p. 81.

[71] *See*, e.g., Chandler, "Family Bonds and the Bondsman," pp. 119–120.

two-thirds of all manumissions were voluntary.[72] Thus, largely as a result of manumission, with each generation the number of free Africans in Hispanic America increased significantly. And, as indicated in Chance's study of Oaxaca, so did the number of persons with partial African ancestry (mulattoes and *castizos*). They joined the predominantly urban, racially and occupationally segregated underclass.

As colonial legal institutions matured from the late sixteenth through the seventeenth centuries, three interrelated trends contributed to a political and social structure characterized by stratification, private subordination, and weakening Crown control. First and foremost, as production and trade in agriculture and minerals expanded, wealth, particularly in New Spain, tended to concentrate increasingly in city-dwelling, rural landowners with large and productive estates (*haciendas granaderas*).[73] As described by Susan Ramírez, these "grand" *hacendero* families dominated not only livestock and agricultural production but also all facets of domestic, intra-colony, and export commerce in the commodities and related goods produced on their estates.[74] Although some may have had early *encomendero* origins, many were wealthy investors using the gains of their success and connections as well-established merchants, high-ranking officials, or new peninsular arrivals with the benefit of official patronage. Combining wealth with influence they constituted an elite caste that increasingly dominated colonial society and the instruments of governance.

The Crown adhered to two fundamental policies in the initial appointments to colonial office. Those nominated for royal appointment should be persons with demonstrable merit and should be Hispanic born. As noted, university training in law was required as a mandated qualification for all judicial posts. Unless a *letrado*, even the viceroys who presided over the *audiencias* in their respective capitals could not by law participate as an adjudicating judge. Although from the start the Crown did sell

---

[72] Lowell W. Gudmundson, *Mechanisms of Social Mobility for the Population of African Descent in Colonial Costa Rica: Manumission and Miscegenation* (Costa Rica: IDELA, Facultad de Filosofía y Letras, Universida Nacional, Heredia), cited in Morner, "Recent Research," pp. 269, 284.

[73] For a survey of the literature through the early 1970s on the origins and significance of the *hacienda*, *see* Magnus Morner, "The Spanish American Hacienda: A Survey of Recent Literature and Debate," *Spanish America Historical Review*, vol. 53 (1973), pp. 183–216.

[74] Susan E. Ramírez, "Large Landowners," in Hoberman and Socolow, eds., *Cities & Society in Colonial Latin America*, p. 19.

some posts and most appointments could be renounced in favor of a named successor and thus became negotiable, the Crown generally adhered to both principles until 1558 when a bankrupt Philip II introduced the notion of an office as a source of revenue and began to sell the relatively low-ranking posts of notary or scribe (*escribano*) and municipal standard bearer and *cabildo* member (*alférez*). With the issuance of a *cédula* in 1606 listing a full range of salable district and municipal offices, the sale of local posts escalated. As a result, by the early seventeenth century most local offices were held by creoles, sufficiently wealthy to afford their purchase. In 1633 even administrative posts with responsibility for Crown revenues became salable. By 1677 even the offices of *alcalde mayor* and *corregidor* could be purchased.[75] For the highest judicial offices the *letrado* requirement remained a barrier to appointment of creoles unless sufficiently wealthy to afford a university education in Spain. However, by 1600 universities had been established either by royal grant or papal Bull in nearly all of the *audiencia* cities. (Both the University of Mexico and the University of San Marcos in Lima claim to have been the first.) The principal faculties were theology and law, the graduates of which would have had the opportunity to study either canon or civil law, thereby acquiring *letrado* status. The consequence was a dramatic increase in the number of creole appointments to high judicial office as an *audiencia* minister. Burkholder documents the numbers. Creoles constituted at least a quarter of all appointments to the colonial *audiencias* between 1610 and 1687. The percentage increased to 45 percent of the appointments made between 1687 and 1750.[76]

Forms of subordination of Amerindians living outside of native communities had long existed. In Peru *yanacona* natives who without allegiance to a chief were tied to settlers for personal service, are exemplary of long-standing practices. While wealthy ruling elites developed, several other subordinated groups that included non-Amerindians also began to emerge. The first, at least in central Mexico, were the free agricultural workers tied effectively to the *haciendas granaderas* that buttressed the elite status of the large landowners. Debt-peonage is a much studied and contested feature of Hispanic America. It is sufficient for our purposes to note its legal foundations and its social and political consequences. Debt-peonage originates in a credit transaction that requires the borrower to work for the lender to pay off the incurred debt.

75 Burkholder, "Bureaucrats," pp. 84–87.
76 *Id.*, p. 90.

Like crop-sharing agreements, such transactions may be beneficial to both debtors and creditors by enabling access of the debtor to otherwise unavailable sources for gain, such as land or seed, and to the latter in the form of a dependable supply of labor without payments in cash for wages. Issues of fairness and manifest abuse arise in relation to the context and terms of the arrangements. Used as a means for long-term indebtedness that legally binds workers for what may become lifetime employment, it prevents labor mobility and impedes agricultural wage competition to the benefit of the landholder. Throughout history it also tends to create communities of subordinated workers dependent on their patron landholders. The legalistic character of Hispanic colonial rule arguably gave such arrangements additional validity and justification. With elite control over the judicial organs in the colonies, challenges to their legality would presumably have become even less likely to succeed.

Elite control over the principal sources of commercial wealth also had predictable consequences. As merchants they could more readily dominate the *consulados* and thereby the rules regulating commercial entry and practice. They were also in the most favorable position to channel goods into distant markets or, more ominously, to the Amerindian communities through *repartimientos de mercancia*. Other less wealthy creoles were similarly privileged in contrast to the growing number of free Africans and the racially mixed in colonial cities. Whatever legal rights and protections the subordinated and less privileged members of colonial society had enjoyed in theory were again increasingly subject to enforcement by creole officials. The number of judges and other officials who were apt to share the paternalistic values and concerns of the Crown dwindled with creole replacement of *peninsulares*. The economically less advantaged of all non-Amerindian descent were also left unprotected by the prohibitions against fees, charges and "gifts" officials and the legal professions could charge. With limited prospects of effective recourse to law, their best bet as a strategy of survival was to ally themselves to those with position and power. Under such circumstances the growth of urban as well as rural clientage was a predictable outcome.

By mid century these trends had become an acute concern in metropolitan Spain. As the Hapsburg wars in Europe continued to draw on the royal treasury and revenues from the Americas stagnated and American silver shipments declined, the Crown and its advisors searched for ways to expand sources for revenue in the colonies with new tax levies. In response "[n]ative sons and peninsular-born Spaniards with strong local connections (*radicados*)," to quote Kenneth Adrien, "used their political power to delay, obstruct, and ignore" the Crown's new demands.[77] The century proceeded with an advancing decline in the Crown's capacity to enforce effectively the regulations most central to its primary interests and thus to reverse its loosening hold on governance in its overseas consolidated polity.

In 1700 Philip V, the first of five Bourbon kings, ascended to the Hispanic thrones, ending Hapsburg rule. The toll of the Hapsburg wars and the resulting military conflict over the Hispanic succession prompted reexamination of existing structures of governance within Spain and its American (and East Asian) consolidated polity. Under Philip fundamental governing institutions were reorganized on French patterns. His first order of business was fully to unite the Hispanic kingdoms by abolishing the *fueros* of Aragon and Valencia and dissolving the Council of Aragon and transferring its authority to the Council of Castile (1707). He had the Cortes of Castile similarly absorb the procurators of both Aragon and Valencia. With similar measures a decade later he effectively incorporated Catalonia within the Castilian governing structure. He then abolished the Council of Castile along with the other state councils—including the Council of the Indies—with their mixed administrative and judicial functions, substituting in their stead specialized secretaries (ministries) under the Crown for foreign affairs, finance, justice and ecclesiastical matters, war, navy, and the Indies, sheared of any general adjudicatory responsibilities. In 1711 Philip appointed several men as intendants (*intendentes de ejército*) to oversee army finances. Their success apparently prompted the king to extend the system nationwide, and by 1718 intendants had been appointed to administer each of the Hispanic provinces. The extension of these metropolitan reforms to the colonies awaited Charles III, his son by a second wife, who was crowned in 1759 after the relatively short reign (1746–1759) of Philip's first son, Ferdinand VI. Under Charles the intendant system was introduced in the colonies. The resulting revitalization of Crown controls exercised by officials directly responsible to the Crown produced predictable antipathy and reaction in the colonies and is credited as a significant stimulus for independence and creole supremacy.[78]

By the end of the century the governing structures of Hispanic America like Spain reflected the allocations of functions and governmental powers that characterized the most advanced European states and

---

77 Kenneth J. Adrien, "Corruption, Inefficiency, and Imperial Decline in the Seventeenth-Century Viceroy of Peru," *The Americas*, vol. 41 (1984), p. 4.

78 *Id.*

the newly emerged republic to the north. The preexisting mix of judicial and regulatory controls along deeply embedded patterns of hierarchy, executive dominance, social and economic privilege, extensive subordination, and patrimonialism differentiated the reformed colonial regimes of Hispanic America from its northern neighbor. Many of these patterns were to be replicated, however, in the European colonies of the next century and the independent states they were to spawn thereafter.

CONVERGENCE OF EMPIRES

In 1519 Ferdinand Magellan, the Portuguese navigator in the service of the Hispanic Crown, set sail from Seville on a voyage with historic consequences. His was the first known circumnavigation of the globe. He crossed the Atlantic from Sierra Leone to Argentina, then through the straits that today bear his name, across the Pacific. In April 1521 he landed at the island of Cebu in what are today the Philippines. A few weeks later he was killed nearby. Four decades later in 1565, the Hispanic Crown added the Philippine islands to its American consolidated polity. The new colony was incorporated into the Viceroyalty of New Spain and governed from Mexico City. Manila, established as the capital city, soon became one of the world's great entrepôts. The ensuing commercial relationship between Ming China and the Hapsburg consolidated polity in Europe via the Castilian Crown's American colonies had profound global consequences.

The Manila galleons and Spain's semi-annual flotillas or convoys have become legendary. American silver, principally from the Potosí mines in Peru (now Bolivia), exchanged for Chinese gold at rates relative to those prevailing in Europe, made profitable the transport of silver first from Peru to Mexico then across the Pacific to Manila, and the return shipment of gold back across the Pacific again to Mexico, to be unloaded: on the Pacific coast, transported overland to Veracruz, reloaded on ships bound for Seville or Cadiz, and then on to Spain across the pirate-infested waters of the Caribbean and the Atlantic. The volume of these shipments was so great that within a generation the rates of exchange of gold and silver between China and Europe had largely equalized.[79] Gold was not the only commodity traded. Chinese merchants bartered or sold all manner of goods for Hispanic American silver. As exchange rates equalized, Chinese goods replaced gold. As described by Antonio de

79 Flynn and Giraldez, "Arbitrage, China, and World Trade," p. 412.

Morga, the President of the *audiencia* of Manila, by the mid seventeenth century Chinese merchants were trading a wide variety of products—ivory, musk, crystal, sapphires and rubies, copper and iron pots, nails, sheet iron, tin, lead, saltpeter, and gunpowder, not to mention porcelain and textiles—cotton cloth, linen made from grass, Damask, satins, taffeta, and all manner of silk and silk products.[80] The volume of the trade in silk alone grew to become so great that silk producers in Andalucia in Spain complained to the Crown that Chinese silk was flooding the Mexican market at their expense in what was perhaps the earliest East–West textile dispute.[81]

Hispanic trade with China juxtaposed two of the world's great legal traditions: the legal order of Imperial China and the European civil law tradition. In terms of political and legal institutions, the former was the world's oldest and most highly developed public law regime; the latter, arguably (with apologies to English legal historians), Western Europe's most advanced private law system. The convergence of the two in Manila presaged not only the future of globalized trade but also the coming dawn of an era of legal transplants and transformations grounded in trajectories nurtured by rivers, rifles, rice, and religion.

---

80 *See* William Lytle Schurz, *The Manila Galleon* (New York: E.P. Dutton, 1959); Brook, *Confusions of Pleasure*, pp. 205–206; Timothy Brook, "Communication and Commerce," in Twitchett and Loewe, eds., *The Cambridge History of China*, pp. 579–707.

81 Flynn and Giraldez, p. 434.

Epilogue: beyond Magellan's world

A half a millennium after Magellan's voyage both the Chinese and Hispanic empires had met their mutual final demise. Both had been dominant since the dawn of the sixteenth century, but at the turn of the twentieth century two states—Japan and the United States—had replaced both by victories in war to become the prevailing economic and military forces in the Pacific, thereby joining a theretofore exclusively European club of imperial powers. Almost simultaneously a newly unified Western European nation-state, Germany, had established its accession as Western Europe's preeminent continental state. Thereafter well into the twenty-first century these three states—Japan, the United States, and Germany—would be the world's dominant military and economic powers. Despite the mid century wartime devastation of both Japan and Germany, in per capita terms the three had emerged as the most economically successful industrial democracies by the turn of the twenty-first century. China, however, has regained its prominence. After a hiatus of two centuries, almost equaling the total gross domestic production of the entire European Union, China has today regained its status as the world's largest national economy—dominated by private ordering.

For those concerned with law's development, the rise of Japan, the United States, and Germany is equally notable. Each represents the twentieth century's most influential legal regimes within their separate spheres of regional influence. Japan, through colonial imposition in Taiwan and Korea but also emulation by the Kingdom of Siam (Thailand after 1938) and Republican China, became the primary East Asian intermediary for transplantation of Western law. It remains today a model for developing non-Western states. Upon independence all of the newly formed states of Latin America looked to their northern neighbor for an appropriate constitutional model. All today have presidential systems based on the United States example. German legal influence has long surpassed both. For over a century German legal science was the world's preeminent source of legal transplants as German codes, legal theory, and fundamental private law conceptions spread worldwide.

Simultaneously another transformation occurred. Just as Western private law seemingly triumphed as a universal model via colonial imposition and emulation, law in the West underwent an equally profound change. Warfare remained a catalytic force but it no longer limited governments' capacity to rule. The Industrial Revolution, relative political stability, economic growth, and technological advances in the nineteenth century, combined to enable governments in the West to acquire and to devote economic resources to both regulatory and military purposes. In the process by the middle of the twentieth century the regulatory state had replaced the "civil law" tradition as Western law's dominant paradigm.

Administrative regulation and criminal law today prevail over private law in almost all industrial democracies. The United States is exemplary. Who can even count the number of federal and state administrative regulatory rules? Moreover, by one relatively conservative estimate, there are today well over 4500 federal regulatory crimes, with new ones being added almost daily.[1] In most jurisdictions, criminal prosecutions outnumber civil cases by a wide margin. In California, for example, of a total of almost 8,500,000 cases filed state wide in the Superior Courts in the decade between 2002 and 2012, nearly 7,000,000 were criminal cases.[2] The real triumph may thus belong to the Chinese public law order and private ordering. No longer do rivers, religion, and even rifles play decisive roles in law's trajectory. Only legacies of rice remain.

---

1 See John S. Baker Jr., "Revisiting the Explosive Growth of Federal Crimes," Legal Memorandum No. 26, June 16, 2008 (Heritage Foundation). http://www.heritage.org/research/reports/2008/06/revisiting-the-explosive-growth-of-federal-crimes. Last visited February 8, 2016.

2 Judicial Council of California, 2013 Court Statistics Report: Statewide Caseload Trends 2002–2003 Through 2011–2012, xvii. http://www.courts.ca.gov/documents/2013-Court-Statistics-Report.pdf. Last visited February 8, 2016.

References

Adolphson, Mikael and J. Mark Ramseyer, "The Competitive Enforcement of Property Rights in Medieval Japan: The Role of Temples and Monasteries," *Journal of Economic Behavior and Organization*, vol. 71 (2009), pp. 660–668.

Adrien, Kenneth J., "Corruption, Inefficiency, and Imperial Decline in the Seventeenth-Century Viceroy of Peru," *The Americas*, vol. 41 (1984), pp. 1–20.

Alford, William P., "On the Limits of 'Grand Theory' in Comparative Law," *Washington Law Review*, vol. 61 (1986), pp. 945–956.

Allam, S., "Egyptian Law Courts in Pharaonic and Hellenistic Times," *Journal of Egyptian Archaeology*, vol. 77 (1991), pp. 109–127.

Asakawa, Kan'ichi, *The Documents of Iriki* (Westport, CN: Greenwood Press, 1925).

Avalos, Francisco, "An Overview of the Legal System of the Aztec Empire," *Law Library Journal*, vol. 86 (1994), pp. 259–276.

Baines, John, "Literacy and Ancient Egyptian Society," *Man* (New series), vol. 18 (1983), pp. 572–599.

Baker, John S. Jr., "Revisiting the Explosive Growth of Federal Crimes," Legal Memorandum No. 26, June 16, 2008 (Heritage Foundation). http://www.heritage.org/research/reports/2008/06/revisiting-the-explosive-growth-of-federal-crimes. Last visited February 8, 2016.

Barker, Rodney, *Political Legitimacy and the State* (Oxford: Clarendon Press, 1990).

Barnes, Gina L., *State Formation in Japan: Emergence of a 4th Century Ruling Elite* (Abingdon, Oxon and New York: Routledge, 2007).

Bauer, Brian S. and R. Alan Covey, "Processes of State Formation in the Inca Heartland (Cuzco, Peru)," *American Anthropologist*, vol. 104 (2002), pp. 846–864.

Beardsley, Richard K., John W. Hall and Robert E. Ward, *Village Japan* (Chicago and London: University of Chicago Press, 1959).

Bellah, Robert N., *Tokugawa Religion: The Values of Pre-Industrial Japan* (Boston: Beacon Press, 1970), p. 13.

Bellomo, Manlio, *The Common Legal Past of Europe, 1000–1800* [Lydia G. Cochrane trans.] (Washington, DC: The Catholic University of America Press, 1995).

Benton, Lauren, *Law and Colonial Cultures* (Cambridge and New York: Cambridge University Press, 2002).

Berman, Harold J., *Law and Revolution: The Formation of the Western Legal Tradition* (Cambridge, MA: Harvard University Press, 1983).

Berry, Mary Elizabeth, *Hideyoshi* (Cambridge, MA: Harvard University Press, 1989).

Bethell, Leslie, ed., *The Cambridge History of Latin America*, vol. 2 (Cambridge and New York: Cambridge University Press, 1984).

Bisson, Thomas N., "The Military Origins of Medieval Representation," *American Historical Review*, vol. 71 (1966), pp. 1199–1216.

Blair, Peter Hunter, *An Introduction to Anglo-Saxon England* (Cambridge: Cambridge University Press, 2nd ed., 1977).

Bloch, Marc, *Feudal Society*, 2 vols. (Chicago: University of Chicago Press, 7th ed., 1968).

Borah, Woodrow, *Justice by Insurance: The General Indian Court of Colonial Mexico and the Legal Aides of the Half-Real* (Berkeley, CA: University of California Press, 1983).

Braithwaite, John, *Crime, Shame and Reintegration* (Cambridge and New York: Cambridge University Press, 1989).

Bray, Francesca, *Agriculture* [Joseph Needham, *Science and Civilization in China*, vol.6, Biology and Biological Technology, Part II] (Cambridge: Cambridge University Press, 1984).

Bray, Francesca, *The Rice Economies: Technology and Development in Asian Societies* (Oxford: Basil Blackwell, 1986).

Brook, Timothy, *The Confusions of Pleasure: Commerce and Culture in Ming China* (Berkeley, Los Angeles, and London: University of California Press, 1998).

Brown, Delmer M., ed., *The Cambridge History of Japan*, vol. 1, *Ancient Japan* (Cambridge: Cambridge University Press, 1988).

Brown, Delmer M., "The Impact of Firearms on Japanese Warfare, 1543–98," *Far Eastern Quarterly*, vol. 7 (1948), pp. 238–253.

Burg, David F., *A World History of Tax Rebellions* (New York: Routledge, 2004).

Burkholder, Mark A. and D.S. Chandler, *Biographical Dictionary of Audiencia Ministers in the Americas, 1687–1821* (Westport, CN: Greenwood Press, 1982).

Burkholder, Mark A., D.S. Chandler , and Lyman L. Johnson, *Colonial Latin America* (Oxford and New York: Oxford University Press, 3rd ed., 2001).

Burns, Robert Ignatius, *Medieval Colonialism: Postcrusade Exploitation of Islamic Valencia* (Princeton: Princeton University Press, 1975).

Butzer, Karl W., Juan F. Mateu, Elizabeth K. Butzer, and Pavel Kraus, "Irrigation Agrosystems in Eastern Spain: Roman or Islamic Origins?" *Annals of the Association of American Geographers*, vol. 75 (1985), pp. 502–503.

Carneiro, Robert L., "A Theory of the Origin of the State," *Science*, vol. 169(3947) (1970), pp. 733–738.

Chaffee, John W., *The Thorny Gates of Learning in Sung China* (Cambridge: Cambridge University Press, 1985).

Chandler, David L., "Family Bonds and the Bondsman: The Slave Family in Colonial Colombia," *Latin American Research Review*, vol. 16 (1981), pp. 107–131.

Chandler, Tertius, *Four Thousand Years of Urban Growth: An Historical Census* (Lewiston, NY: The Edwin Mellen Press, 1987).

Chang, Kwang-Chih, *Shang Civilization* (New Haven, CT: Yale University Press, 1980).

Chen, Weitsheng, "Arbitrage for Property Rights: How Do Foreign Investors Create Substitutes for Property Institutions in the Developing World?" (unpublished paper, 2014).

Christ, Matthew R., "Liturgy Avoidance and *Antidosis* in Classical Athens," *Transactions of the American Philological Association*, vol. 120 (1990), pp. 147–169.

Cioffi-Revilla, Claudio and David Lai, "War and Politics in Ancient China, 2700 B.C. to 722 B.C.," *Journal of Conflict Resolution*, vol. 39 (1995), pp. 467–494.

Cohen, Jerome Alan, R. Randle Edwards, and Fu-mei Chang Chen, eds., *Essays on China's Legal Tradition* (Princeton, NJ: Princeton University Press, 1980).

Conrad, Geoffrey W., "Chiquitoy Viejo: An Inca Administrative Center in the Chicama Valley, Peru," *Journal of Field Archaeology*, vol. 4 (1977), pp. 1–18.

Cook, Constance and John S. Major, eds., *Defining Chu: Image and Reality in Ancient China* (Honolulu: University of Hawai'i Press, 1999).

Creel, Herrlee G., *The Origins of Statecraft in China, Vol. One, The Western Chou Empire* (Chicago: University of Chicago Press, 1970).

Cunningham, Charles H., "The Ecclesiastical Influence in the Philippines (1565–1850)," *American Journal of Theology*, vol. 22 (1918), pp. 161–186.

Cutter, Charles R., "The Administration of Law in Colonial New Mexico," *Journal of the Early Republic*, vol. 18 (1998), pp. 99–115.

Damaška, Mirjan, "A Continental Lawyer in an American Law School: Trials and Tribulations of Adjustment," *University of Pennsylvania Law Review*, vol. 116 (1968), pp. 1363–1378.

Davies, Nigel, *The Aztec Empire* (Norman, OK: University of Oklahoma Press, 1987).
Davies, Nigel, *The Incas* (Niwot, CO: University Press of Colorado, 1995).
de Longrais, Joüon, *L'Est et L'Ouest* (Tokyo and Paris: Maison Franco-Japonais, Institut de Recherches Histoire, 1958).
Dillehay, Tom D., "Tawantinsuyu Integration of the Chillon Valley, Peru: A Case of Inca Geo-political Mastery," *Journal of Field Archaeology*, vol. 4 (1977), pp. 397–405.
Dowling, Brian M., "Medieval Origins of Constitutional Governance in the West," *Theory and Society*, vol. 18 (1989), pp. 213–247.
Durand, John D., "The Population Statistics of China, A.D. 2–1953," *Population Studies* (1960), pp. 209–256.
Ebrey, Patricia Buckley, Anne Walthall, and James B. Palais, *Pre-Modern East Asia: A Cultural, Social, and Political History* (Boston, MA: Houghton-Mifflin Company, 2006).
Ebrey, Patricia Buckley, Anne Walthall, and James B. Palais, "Review Article: The Dynamics of Elite Domination in Sung China," *Harvard Journal of Asiatic Studies*, vol. 48 (1988), pp. 493–519.
Edgerton, William F., "The Government and the Governed in the Egyptian Empire," *Journal of Near Eastern Studies*, vol. 6(3) (1947), pp. 152–160.
Edwards, Lindy, *Consensus in Conflict: Competing Conceptual Structures and the Changing Nature of Japanese Politics in the Postwar Era* (Canberra, ACT: Australia Japan Research Centre, 1997).
Eisenstadt, S.N., *The Political Systems of Empires* (London and New York: Free Press of Glencoe, 1963).
Eisenstadt, S.N., *Japanese Civilization: A Comparative View* (Chicago: University of Chicago Press, 1996),
Eltis, David, ed., *The Origins & Diversity of Axial Age Civilizations* (Albany, NY: State University of New York Press, 1986).
Eltis, David, *The Rise of African Slavery in the Americas* (Cambridge: Cambridge University Press, 2000).
Fairbank, John King and Merle Goldman, *China: A New History* (Cambridge, MA: Harvard University Press, 2006).
Fairgrieve, Duncan, *State Liability in Tort: A Comparative Study* (London and New York: Oxford University Press, 2003).
Fang, Qiang and Roger Des Forges, "Were Chinese Rulers above the Law? Toward a Theory of the Rule of Law in China from Early Times to 1949 CE," *Stanford Journal of International Law*, vol. 44 (2008), pp. 101–146.
Farenga, Vincent, *Citizen and Self in Ancient Greece* (Cambridge and New York: Cambridge University Press, 2006).

Feldman, Eric, "The Tuna Court: Law and Norms in the World's Premier Fish Market," *California Law Review*, vol. 94 (2006), pp. 313–369.

Finer, Samuel E., *The History of Government from the Earliest Times*, 3 vols. (Oxford and London: Oxford University Press, 1999).

Flynn, Dennis O. and Arturo Giraldez, "Arbitrage, China, and World Trade in the Early Modern Period," *Journal of the Economic and Social History of the Orient*, vol. 38 (1995), pp. 429–448.

Fogel, Joshua A., ed., *The Teleology of the Modern Nation-State: Japan and China* (Philadelphia, PA: University of Pennsylvania Press, 2005).

Foucault, Michel, *The History of Sexuality: Volume 1: An Introduction* (New York: Vantage Books, 1990).

Franke, Herbert and Denis Twitchett, *The Cambridge History of China*, vol. 6, *Alien Regimes and Border States* (Cambridge and New York: Cambridge University Press, 1994).

Freedman, Paul H., *The Origins of Peasant Servitude in Medieval Catalonia* (Cambridge and New York: Cambridge University Press, 1991).

French, Rebecca R. and Mark Nathan, eds., *Buddhism and Law: An Introduction* (Cambridge and New York: Cambridge University Press, 2014).

Frőhlich, Judith, "Land Administration in Medieval Japan: Ito no shō in Chikuzen Province, 1131–1336," *The Historical Association* (Oxford: Blackwell Publishing Ltd., 2003).

Gillin, J.P., "Crime and Punishment Among the Barama River Carib," *American Anthropologist*, vol. 36 (1934), pp. 331–344.

Glick, Thomas F., *Irrigation and Society in Medieval Valencia* (Cambridge, MA: Harvard University Press, 1970).

Góngora, Mario, *Studies in the Colonial History of Spanish America* (Cambridge: Cambridge University Press, 1975).

Grossberg, Kenneth A., *The Laws of the Muromachi Bakufu* (Tokyo: Monumenta Nipponica, 1981).

Guy, R. Kent, *The Emperor's Four Treasuries: Scholars and the State in the Late Ch'ien-lung Era* (Cambridge, MA: Harvard University Press, 1987).

Haley, John Owen, *Authority without Power: Law and the Japanese Paradox* (Oxford and New York: Oxford University Press, 1991).

Haley, John Owen, *The Spirit of Japanese Law* (Athens, GA: University of Georgia Press, 1998).

Haley, John O., "Rivers and Rice: What Lawyers and Legal Historians Should Know about Medieval Japan," *Journal of Japanese Studies*, vol. 36(2) (2010), pp. 313–349.

Haley, John O. and Toshiko Takenaka, eds., *Legal Innovations in Asia: Judicial Law-Making and Influence of Comparative Law* (Cheltenham, UK and Northampton, MA: Edward Elgar Publishing, 2014).
Hall, John Whitney, *Government and Local Power in Japan: 500–1700* (Princeton, NJ: Princeton University Press, 1966).
Hall, John Whitney and James L. McClain, eds., *The Cambridge History of Japan: Early Modern Japan*, vol. 4 (Cambridge and New York: Cambridge University Press, 1991).
Hall, John Whitney, Marius B. Jansen, Madoka Kanai, and Denis Twitchett, eds., *The Cambridge History of Japan: Medieval Japan*, vol. 3 (Cambridge and New York: Cambridge University Press, 1990).
Hamilton, Gary G., ed., *Business Networks and Economic Development in East and Southeast Asia* (Hong Kong: Centre for Asian Studies, University of Hong Kong, 1991).
Hamilton, Gary G., *Commerce and Capitalism in Chinese Societies* (Abingdon, Oxon and New York: Routledge, 2006).
Hamilton, Gary G. and Robert C. Feenstra, *Emergent Economies, Divergent Paths: Economic Organization and International Trade in South Korea and Taiwan* (Cambridge and New York: Cambridge University Press, 2006).
Hansen, Valerie, *The Open Empire: A History of China to 1600* (New York and London: W.W. Norton Co., 2000).
Hardy, Grant and Anne Behnke Kinney, *The Establishment of the Han Empire and Imperial China* (Westport, CN: Greenwood Press, 2005).
Hart, H.L.A., *The Concept of Law* (Oxford: Clarendon Press, 1961).
Hawley, Samuel, *The Imjin War: Japan's Sixteenth Century Invasion of Korea and Attempt to Conquer China* (2nd ed., n.p.: Conquistador Press, 2014).
Heather, Peter, *The Goths* (London and Malden, MA: Blackwell Publishers, 1998).
Hegel, Robert, *True Crimes in Eighteenth-Century China: Twenty Case Histories* (Seattle: University of Washington Press, 2009).
Henderson, Dan Fenno, *Conciliation and Japanese Law: Tokugawa and Modern*, 2 vols. (Seattle: University of Washington Press, 1965).
Henderson, Dan Fenno, *Village "Contracts" in Tokugawa Japan* (Seattle: University of Washington Press, 1975).
Hicks, Frederic, "The Middle Class in Ancient Central Mexico," *Journal of Anthropological Research*, vol. 55 (1999), pp. 413–419.
Hiramatsu, Yoshirō, "Tokugawa Law," *Law in Japan: An Annual*, vol. 14 (1981), pp. 1–48.
Hoberman, Louisa Schell and Susan Migden Socolow, eds., *Cities & Society in Colonial Latin America* (Albuquerque: University of New Mexico Press, 1986).

Hoebel, E. Adamson, *The Law of Primitive Man* (Cambridge, MA: Harvard University Press, 1954).

Hohfeld, Wesley Newcomb, *Fundamental Legal Conceptions as Applied in Judicial Reasoning and Other Legal Essays* (New Haven, CT: Yale University Press, 1919).

Hsu, Cho-Yun and Katheryn M. Linduff, *Western Chou Civilization* (New Haven, CT: Yale University Press, 1988).

Hsu Dau-Lin, "Separation between Fact-Finding (Trial) and Law-Finding (Sentencing) in Sung Criminal Proceedings," *Sung Studies Newsletter*, vol. 6 (1972), pp. 3–18.

Huang, Philip C.C., *Civil Justice in China: Representation and Practice in the Qing* (Stanford, CA: Stanford University Press, 1996).

Hulsewé, A.F.P., "The Legalists and the Laws of China," in W.L. Idema, ed., *Leyden Studies in Sinology* (Leiden: E.J. Brill, 1981), pp. 1–22.

Hymes, Robert P., *Statesmen and Gentlemen: The Elite of Fu-Chou, Chiang-His, in Northern and Southern Sung* (Cambridge and New York: Cambridge University Press, 1986).

Hymes, R.P. and C. Schirolauer, eds., *Ordering the World: Approaches to State and Society in Sung Dynasty China* (Berkeley, Los Angeles, and London: University of California Press, 1993).

Jaspers, Karl, *Ursprung under Zeil der Geschichte* (Munich: Piper Verlag, 1949).

Jiang Yonglin, *The Mandate of Heaven and the Great Ming Code* (Seattle: University of Washington Press, 2011).

Jimbo Fumio, "Edo Bakufu Deirisuji no Saiban ni Okeru Honkuji-Kanekuji no Bunka ni Tsuite," [Differentiation between main suits and money suits in adjudication of adversarial suits under the Edo bakufu] *Hōseishi kenkyū*, vol. 45 (1995), pp. 1–38.

Judicial Council of California, 2013 Court Statistics Report: Statewide Caseload Trends 2002–2003 Through 2011–2012, xvii. http://www.courts.ca.gov/documents/2013-Court-Statistics-Report.pdf. Last visited February 8, 2016.

Katary, Sally L.D., *Land Tenure in the Ramesside Period* (London: Kegan Paul International, 1989).

Keightley, David N., *Working for His Majesty: Research Notes on Labor Mobilization in Late Shang China (ca. 1200–1045BC), as Seen in the Oracle-Bone Inscriptions, with Particular Attention to Handicraft Industries, Warfare, Hunting, Construction, and the Shang's Legacies.* China Research Monograph 67. Berkeley: Institute of East Asian Studies, University of California, Center for Chinese Studies, 2012.

Kellogg, Susan, *Law and the Transformation of Aztec Culture* (Norman and London: University of Oklahoma Press, 1995).

King, P.D., *Law and Society in the Visigothic Kingdom* (Cambridge: Cambridge University Press, 1972).

Kiser, Edgar and April Linton, "Determinants of the Growth of the State: War and Taxation in Early Modern France and England," *Social Forces*, vol. 80 (2001), pp. 411–448.

Kiser, Edgar, April Linton, and Yong Cai, "War and Bureaucratization in Qin China," *American Sociological Review*, vol. 68 (2003), pp. 511–539.

Knoblock, John, *Xunzi: A Translation and Study of His Complete Works*, vol. 3 (Stanford, CA: Stanford University Press, 1988).

Kohler, Josef, *Das Recht der Azteken* (Stuttgart: Verlag von Ferdinand Enke, 1892). Translated by Carlos Rovalo y Fernandez and published in Spanish as *El Derecho de los Aztecas* (Mexico, D.F.: Mexico, 1924).

Las Siete Partidas del Rey Don Alfonso el Sabio, vol. 1 (Madrid: Law Emprenza Real, 1807).

Laws of Manu, Chapter VIII, Sections 3–7 (trans. Buhler), *Indian History Sourcebook*, www.fordham.edu/halsall/india/manu-full.html. Last visited January 26, 2016.

Ledyard, Gari, "Galloping Along with the Horseriders: Looking for the Founders of Japan," *Journal of Japanese Studies*, vol. 1 (1975), pp. 217–254.

Levillier, Roberto, *Don Francisco de Toledo: Supremo Organizador del Peru*, 2 vols. (Madrid: Espasa-Calpe, 1935).

Levy, Ernst, *West Roman Vulgar Law: The Law of Property* (Buffalo, NY: William S. Hein & Co., 2003).

Lewis, Mark Edward, *China Between Empires: The Northern and Southern Dynasties* (Cambridge, MA: Harvard University Press, 2009).

Li Feng, *Bureaucracy and the State in Early China: Governing the Western Zhou* (Cambridge: Cambridge University Press, 2008).

Li Feng, *Early China: A Social and Cultural History* (Cambridge and New York: Cambridge University Press, 2013).

Li Feng, *Landscape and Power in Early China* (Cambridge: Cambridge University Press, 2006).

Li Yu-Ning, *Shang Yang's Reforms and State Control in China* (White Plains, NY: M.E. Sharpe, 1977).

Lidin, Olof G., *Tanegashima: The Arrival of Europe in Japan* (Copenhagen: Nordic Institute of Asian Studies, 2002).

Littlefield, Daniel C., "The Varieties of Slave Labor." Freedom's Story, TeacherServe©. National Humanities Center, 20 August 2014. http://nationalhumanitiescenter.org/tserve/freedom/1609-1865/essays/slavelabor.htm. Last visited January 29, 2016.

Loewe, Michael and Edward L. Shaughnessy, eds., *The Cambridge History of Ancient China: From the Origins of Civilization to 221 B.C.*, vol. 8, 2 pts. (Cambridge and New York: Cambridge University Press, 1999).

Lorton, David, "The Treatment of Criminals in Ancient Egypt: Through the New Kingdom," *Journal of the Economic and Social History of the Orient*, vol. 20 (1977), pp. 2–64.

Lowie, Robert H., *The Origin of the State* (New York: Harcourt, Brace & Company, 1927).

Lynch, John, *Spanish Colonial Administration, 1782–1810: The Intendant System in the Viceroyalty of the Rio de la Plata* (London: The Athlone Press, 1958).

Lyttkens, Carl Hampus, "Institutions, Taxation, and Market Relationships in Ancient Athens," Working Paper, Department of Economics, Lund University, Sweden. http://ideas.repec.org/p/hhs/lunewp/2008_009.html. Last visited January 26, 2016.

Lyttkens, Carl Hampus, "Reflections on the Origins of the *Polis*: An Economic Perspective on Institutional Change in Ancient Greece," *Constitutional Political Economy*, vol. 17 (2006), pp. 31–48.

MacCormack, Geoffrey, *The Spirit of Traditional Chinese Law* (Athens, GA: University of Georgia Press, 1996).

MacIntyre, Alasdair, *After Virtue* (Notre Dame, IN: University of Notre Dame Press, 2nd ed., 1984).

Malinowski, Bronislaw, *Crime and Custom in Savage Society* (New York: The Humanities Press; London: Routledge & Kegan Paul, 1951).

Mass, Jeffrey P., *The Development of Kamakura Rule, 1180–1250* (Stanford, CA: Stanford University Press, 1979).

Mattha, Girgis, *The Demotic Code of Hermopolis West* (Paris: Bibliothèque d' Étude [Institut Français d'Archéologie Orientale du Caire], George R. Hughes, trans., 1975).

Max Weber Gesamt Ausgabe, vol. 1/17 (W.J. Mommsen and W. Schluchter, eds., Tubingen: J.C.B. Mohr [Paul Siebeck], 1992).

McDowell, A.G., *Jurisdiction in the Workmen's Community of Deir el-Medina* (Leiden: Nederlands Institut voor het Nabia Oosten, 1990).

McDowell, A.G., *Village Life in Ancient Egypt: Laundry Lists and Love Songs* (Oxford and New York: Oxford University Press, 1999).

McKnight, Brian E., *Village and Bureaucracy in Southern Sung China* (Chicago: University of Chicago Press, 1971).

Mendieta y Nuñez, Lucio, *El Derecho Precolonial* (Mexico, D.F.: Porrua Hermanos y Cia, 1937).

Menzel, Dorothy, "The Inca Occupation of the South Coast of Peru," *Southwestern Journal of Anthropology*, vol. 15 (1959), pp. 125–142.

Middleton, John and David Trait, eds., *Tribes Without Rulers* (London: Routledge & Kegan Paul, 1958).
Mirow, M.C., *Latin American Law: A History of Private Law and Institutions in Spanish America* (Austin, TX: University of Texas Press, 2004).
Moll-Murata, Christine, "Chinese Guilds from the Seventeenth to the Twentieth Centuries: An Overview," *International Review of Social History*, vol. 53(16) (2008), pp. 213–247.
Moore, Sally Falk, *Power and Property in Inca Peru* (New York: Columbia University Press, 1958).
Morner, Magnus, "Recent Research on Negro Slavery and Abolition in Latin America," *Latin American Research Review*, vol. 13 (1978), pp. 265–289.
Morner, Magnus, "The Spanish American Hacienda: A Survey of Recent Literature and Debate," *Spanish America Historical Review*, vol. 53 (1973), pp. 183–216.
Morris, Ian, *Burial and Ancient Society: The Rise of the Greek City* (Cambridge and New York: Cambridge University Press, 1987).
Mote, F.W., *Imperial China, 900–1800* (Cambridge, MA: Harvard University Press, 1999).
Nakada Kokichi. "Gōrisei no shikō to sonraku," *Rekishigaku kenkyū* [Journal of Historical Studies], no. 550 (1986), pp. 30–38.
Needham, Joseph, *Science and Civilization in China*, vol. II (Cambridge and New York: Cambridge University Press, 1985).
North, Douglass C., "Institutions," *Journal of Economic Perspectives*, vol. 5 (1991), pp. 97–112.
O'Callaghan, Joseph F., *Alfonso X, the Cortes, and Government in Medieval Spain* (Farnham: Ashgate, 1998).
O'Callaghan, Joseph F., *The Learned King: The Reign of Alfonso X of Castile* (Philadelphia, PA: University of Pennsylvania Press, 1993).
O'Connor, Richard A., "Agricultural Change and Ethnic Succession in Southeast Asian States: A Case for Regional Anthropology," *Journal of Asian Studies*, vol.54 (1995), pp. 968–996.
Offner, Jerome A., *Law and Politics in Aztec Texcoco* (Cambridge: Cambridge University Press, 1983).
Oka, Masao, Yawata Ichirō, and Egami Namio, "Nihon minzoku bunka no genryū to Nihon kokka no keisei," *Minzokugaku*, vol. 13 (1949), pp. 207–277.
Ōshima Takehiko, et al., eds., *Nihon o shiru jiten* (Tokyo: Shakai Shisōsha, 1971), pp. 68–101.
Ostrom, Elinor, *Governing the Commons: The Development of Institutions for Collective Action* (Cambridge and New York: Cambridge University Press, 1990).

Palais, James B., "A Search for Korean Uniqueness," *Harvard Journal of Asiatic Studies*, vol. 55(2) (1995), pp. 409–425.
Perrin, Noel, *Giving Up the Gun: Japan's Reversion to the Sword, 1543–1879* (Jaffrey, NH: David R. Godine, 1988).
Piggott, Joan R., *The Emergence of Japanese Kingship* (Stanford, CA: Stanford University Press, 1997).
Putnam, Robert D., *Making Democracy Work: Civic Traditions in Modern Italy* (Princeton, NJ: Princeton University Press, 1993).
Reiji, Harashima, *Nihon kodai shakai no kiso kōzō* (Tokyo: Miraisha, 1968).
Richter, Michael, *The Formation of the Medieval West* (New York: St. Martin's Press, 1994).
Robinson, David J., ed., *Studies in Spanish American Population History* (Boulder, CO: Westview Press, 1981).
Robinson, O.F., T.D. Fergus, and W.M. Gordon, *An Introduction to European Legal History* (Abingdon, Oxon: Professional Books, 1985).
Sánchez León, Pablo, "Changing Patterns of Urban Conflict in Late Medieval Castile," *Past & Present*, vol. 195, supplement 2 (2007), pp. 217–232.
Scheidel, Walter, *Population and Demography*, Princeton/Stanford Working Papers in Classics, Version 1.0, April 2006.
Schram, S.R., ed., *Foundations and Limits of State Power in China* (Hong Kong: Chinese University Press, 1987).
Schubert, Werner and Jürgen Regge, eds., *Preussische Gesetzrevision*, 1825–1848 [Prussian legislative reforms, 1825–1848), vol. 11 (Vaduz, Liechtenstein: Topos, 1981).
Schurz, William Lytle, *The Manila Galleon* (New York: E.P. Dutton, 1959).
Schwaller, John F., ed., *The Church in Colonial Latin America* (Wilmington, DE: Scholarly Resources, 2000).
Scott, James C., *The Art of Not Being Governed: An Anarchist History of Upland Southeast Asia* (New Haven, CT: Yale University Press, 2009).
Seidlmayer, Stephan, "The First Intermediate Period," in Ian Shaw, ed., *The Oxford History of Ancient Egypt* (Oxford and New York: Oxford University Press, 2000), pp. 108–136.
Service, Elman R., *Origins of the State and Civilization: The Process of Cultural Evolution* (New York: W.W. Norton & Co., 1975).
Shively, Donald and William H. McCullough, eds., *The Cambridge History of Japan: Heian Japan* (Cambridge and New York: Cambridge University Press, 1999).
Silverblatt, Irene, "Imperial Dilemmas, the Politics of Kinship, and Inca Reconstructions of History," *Comparative Studies in Society and History*, vol. 30 (1988), pp. 83–102.

Simpson, Lesley Boyd, *The Encomienda in New Spain: The Beginning of Spanish Mexico* (Berkeley, CA: University of California Press, 1966 ed.).

Simpson, Lesley Boyd, *The Laws of Burgos of 1512–1513: Royal Ordinances for the Good Government and Treatment of the Indians* (San Francisco: J. Howell Books, 1960).

Smith, Julia M.H., *Europe after Rome: A New Cultural History, 500–1000* (Oxford: Oxford University Press, 2005).

Smith, Michael E., *The Aztecs* (Malden, MA: Blackwell Publishers, 2nd ed., 2003).

So, Sufumi and Billy K.L. So, "Population Growth and Maritime Prosperity: The Case of Ch'uan-Chou in Comparative Perspective, 946–1368," *Journal of the Economic and Social History of the Orient*, vol. 45 (2002), pp. 96–127.

David Stasavage, "War, Geographic Scale, and Constitutional Control," unpublished manuscript, January 2009. http://politics.as.nyu.edu/docs/IO/5395/geographic_scale.pdf. Last visited February 5, 2016.

Steenstrup, Carl, *A History of Law in Japan until 1868* (Leiden, New York, Copenhagen, and Cologne: E.J. Brill, 1991).

Stern, Steve J., *Peru's Indian People and the Challenge of Spanish Conquest* (Madison, WI: University of Wisconsin Press, 2nd ed., 1993).

Stoutenborough, James W., Donald P. Haider-Markel, and Mahalley D. Allen, "Reassessing the Impact of Supreme Court Decisions on Public Opinion: Gay Civil Rights Cases," *Political Research Quarterly*, vol. 59(3) (September 2006), pp. 419–433.

Swope, Kenneth, "Crouching Tigers, Secret Weapons: Military Technology Employed During the Sino-Japanese–Korean War, 1592–1598," *Journal of Military History*, vol. 69 (2005), pp. 11–41.

Talhelm, Thomas, et al., "Large-Scale Psychological Differences Within China Explained by Rice Versus Wheat Agriculture," *Science*, vol. 344(6184) (2014), pp. 603–608.

Taryo, Obayashi, "Uji Society and Ie Society from Prehistory to Medieval Times," *Journal of Japanese Studies*, vol. 11 (1985), pp. 3–27.

Terraciano, Kevin, *The Mixtecs of Colonial Oaxaca* (Stanford, CA: Stanford University Press, 2001).

Tetsuji Okazaki, "The Role of the Merchant Coalition in Pre-modern Japanese Economic Development: An Historical Institutional Analysis," (unpublished paper, 1999). http://www.computer-services.e.u-tokyo.ac.jp/p/cemano/research/DP/documents/coe-f-33.pdf. Last visited February 3, 2016.

Todd, S.C., *The Shape of Athenian Law* (London and New York: Oxford University Press, 1995).

Toscano, Salvador, *Derecho y Organización Social de los Aztecas* (Mexico, D.F.: Universidad Nacional de Mexico, 1937).

Turner, Karen G., James V. Feinerman, and R. Kent Guy, eds., *The Limits of the Rule of Law in China* (Seattle: University of Washington Press, 2000).

Twitchett, Denis, ed., *The Cambridge History of China: Sui and T'ang China, 589–906*, vol. 3, part 1 (Cambridge and New York: Cambridge University Press, 1979).

Twitchett, Denis and Michael Loewe, eds., *The Cambridge History of China: The Ch'in and Han Empires*, vol. 1 (Cambridge: Cambridge University Press, 1986).

Twitchett, Denis and Frederick W. Mote, eds., *The Cambridge History of China: The Ming Dynasty, 1368–1644*, vol. 8, part 2 (Cambridge and New York: Cambridge University Press, 1998).

Tyler, Tom R., "Legitimacy and Legitimation," *Annual Review of Psychology*, vol. 57 (2006), pp. 375–400.

Unger, Roberto, *Law in Modern Society* (New York: The Free Press, 1976).

Uribe, Victor M., "The Lawyers and New Granada's Late Colonial State," *Journal of Latin American Studies*, vol. 27 (1995), pp. 517–548.

Valderón Baruque, Julio, *Historia de Castilla y Leon*, vol. 5 (Valladolid: Ambito Editiones, 1985).

van Kleffens, E.N., *Spanish Law until the End of the Middle Ages* (Edinburgh: Edinburgh University Press, 1968).

VerSteeg, Russ, *Law in Ancient Egypt* (Durham, NC: Carolina Academic Press, 2002).

Vinogradoff, Paul, *Historical Jurisprudence*, vol. 1 (London: Oxford University Press, 1920).

Waley, Daniel, *The Italian City-Republics* (London and New York: Longman, 3rd ed., 1988).

Warren, W.L., *Henry II* (Berkeley and Los Angeles: University of California Press, 2nd ed., 1983).

Weber, Max, *Politik als Beruf* (Munich and Leipzig: Duncker & Humblot, 1919).

Weber, Max, *Economy and Society: An Outline of Interpretive Sociology* (G. Roth & C. Wittich, eds., Berkeley, CA: University of California Press, 1978).

Webster, David, "Warfare and the Evolution of the State: A Reconsideration," *American Antiquity*, vol. 40(4) (1975), pp. 464–470.

Whitelock, Dorothy, ed., *English Historical Documents*, vol. 1, *c. 500–1042* (New York: Oxford University Press, 1955).

Whitelock, Dorothy, *The Beginnings of English Society* (Baltimore, MD: Penguin Books, 1952).

Wigmore, John Henry, *Panorama of the World's Legal Systems* (St. Paul, MN: West Publishing Co., 1928).
Williams, E.T., "Taxation in China," *Quarterly Journal of Economics*, vol. 26 (1912), pp. 482–510.
Wittfogel, Karl, *Oriental Despotism: A Comparative Study of Total Power* (New York: Random House, 1957).
Yamamura, Kozo, "The Decline of the Ritsuryō System: Hypotheses on Economic and Institutional Change," *Journal of Japanese Studies*, vol. 1 (1974), pp. 3–37.
Yasusuke, Murakami, "Ie Society as a Pattern of Civilization," *Journal of Japanese Studies*, vol. 10 (1984), pp. 281–363.
Yates, Robin D.S., "Social Status in the Ch'in: Evidence from the Yün-meng Legal Documents. Part One: Commoners," *Harvard Journal of Asiatic Studies*, vol. 47(1) (June 1987), pp. 219–231.
Young, Suzanne M.M., et al., eds., *Metals in Antiquity* (Oxford: Archaeopress, 1999).
Zeitlan, Judith Frances, *Cultural Politics in Colonial Tehuantepec* (Stanford, CA: Stanford University Press, 2005).
Zeitlan, Judith Frances and Lillian Thomas, "Spanish Justice and the Indian Cacique: Disjunctive Political Systems in Sixteenth Century Tehuantepec," *Ethnohistory*, vol. 39 (1992), pp. 285–315.
Zeitlan, Robert N., "The Isthmus and the Valley of Oaxaca: Questions about Zapotec Imperialism in Formative Period Mesoamerica," *American Antiquity*, vol. 55(2) (1990), pp. 250–261.
Zeitlan, Robert N. and Arthur A. Joyce, "The Zapotec-Imperialism Argument: Insights from the Oaxaca Coast," *Current Anthropology*, vol. 40(3) (1999), pp. 383–392.
Zhao, Dingxin, "Comment: Spurious Causation in a Historical Process: War and Bureaucratization in Early China," *American Sociological Review*, vol. 69 (2004), pp. 603–607.
Zimmermann, Arthur F., *Francisco de Toledo: Fifth Viceroy of Peru, 1569–1581* (Caldwell, ID: Caxton Printers, 1938).

Index

adjudication
in Athenian law 52–53, 54
in Castile 159, 162, 163
in Catholic Church 60, 137–138
in Deir el-Medina (Egypt) 47–48
as hallmark of Western European legal structures 151–153
in Hispanic colonial administration 182, 189, 190–191
in Japan 40, 55–56, 99–100, 110, 120–127
in medieval Europe 129–130, 139, 141–142, 143, 149–150
as mode of law making and enforcement 33–34, 55
of private and public law rules 18
Adrian VI (pope) 179
Adrien, Kenneth 196–197
Africans in Hispanic America 192–194, 196
agriculture
crops grown by Muslims in Iberia 148, 157
cultivator status groups in Japan 110
dry-field vs. wet-paddy cultivation 42, 56–58
millet 42, 62–64
sedentary communities defined by 38, 40, 42–43, 62–63, 98, 101, 130, 136, 144, 165
see also rice
Alamanic Laws (*Lex Alamannorum*) 142
Alaric (Visigoth leader) 135
Alaric II (Visigoth leader) 140
Alfonso X (king of Castile) 158–161, 163
Alfonso XI (king of Castile) 161–163
Alford, William 94
Alfred the Great (king of Wessex) 145–146
Allam, S. 47
Americas *see* Hispanic America
Amerindians
recognition of natural rights 181, 182–183, 186–192
separate system of governance and 178, 185
Anglo-Saxon kings
territorial division of England 145
Aquinas, Thomas
Summa Theologica 154–155
Aragon 31, 128, 130, 133, 148, 155, 156–157, 163, 174, 197
see also Valencia
arbitration, binding private (Athenian law) 53
Asakura, Kan'ichi 110
Ashikaga period 114, 123, 161
Asia, East
authority in sedentary communities 38, 56–58
China's contributions to neighboring states 61
influence of Tang and Ming Codes 85
regional influence of Japan's legal regime 200
variations in rice cultures 57–58
see also individual countries
Asia, Southeast
maritime polities subjected to Chinese tributary status 89
assizes, as alternative to manorial courts 147
Asturias 148
Athens
ostrakophoria (exile) 26
private law regime 48–55

taxes 14, 28–29, 51
Attila's Hunnic domination 134–135
audiencias 163, 176–178, 182–184, 194–195
Augstinians 179
authority
of Church 137–138, 139
distance from custom and political 31–32
extension of law's domain and 43, 59, 139
Henry II's augmentation of sheriff's 147
legal rules require recognition by political 9
to legislate 115
in pre-Hispanic America 168–169, 185
royal vs. ecclesiastical 180
in sedentary communities 38, 56–58
sources and boundaries defined by law 131
see also legitimacy; power
Aztec Empire 166–169

Babylonia 41
bafuku see Kamakura *bafuku* (tent government)
Barcelona/Catalonia 148, 156
Barker, Rodney 9
Barnes, Gina 103
Bauer, Brian 170
Bavarian laws (*Lex Baiuvaiorum*) 142
Becket, Thomas 147
Bellah, Robert 124–125
Bellomo, Manlio 153
Bendezú, Don Miguel de 188, 189
Berman, Harold 131
Black Death, devastation of Barcelona and Valencia 163
Blakeley, Barry B. 81
Bloch, Marc 130
Borah, Woodrow 186–187, 189–190, 191
Braithwaite, John 24
Bray, Francisco 78
bronze *see* copper and bronze
Bronze Age 65–66
Brook, Timothy 88
Buddhism 75, 103, 104, 107, 111, 118, 124
bureaucracy *see* centralization and bureaucracy; officials
Burg, David 42
burghal system 145
Burgos, Laws of 181–182
Burkholder, Mark 176–177, 195
Burns, Robert 156
bushi see warrior elites

canon law 131, 138, 152, 154, 158, 163, 176, 179, 186
Canute *see* Cnut (king of Denmark, Norway, and England)
capital cities
of China 77
of Japan 105
capital punishment, upon emperor's approval 92–93
Carneiro, Robert 35
Carolingian Empire 142, 144–145, 148, 156
Castile
adjudication in 159, 162, 163
as institutionally advanced country 80, 128, 157–163
reconquista (recovery) 147–148, 155–156, 174
see also Hispanic America; Spain
Catalonia *see* Barcelona/Catalonia
Catholicism *see* Roman Catholic Church
centralization and bureaucracy
Castile 157–163
China 61, 63, 66–67, 70–77, 84–86
Japan 102–109, 111, 113–114, 116–120, 121–124, 126
law as means of unification 145–146
Spanish Crown reforms 189–192
Visigoth unification 147
Chaffee, John 76
Chance, John 192, 194
Charlemagne 142, 144
Charles I (king of Spain, Charles V, Holy Roman Emperor)
convened Valladolid assembly 181

creation of viceroyalties 177–178
New Laws 182–184
union of Spanish kingdoms 163
Charles III (king of Spain) 197
China
age of gunpowder 56, 70
capital cities usually in north 77
coercive power in revenue collection 18
continuity of Chinese rule after Mongol invasion 83–89
customary commercial order 25
dominance of private ordering 200
hydraulic society as basis for authoritarianism 64
law and the Legalist tradition 70–71, 72, 89–97, 169
law of empire 71–77
local control and ordering 81–83
political/legal influence on Japan 99–100, 103–106, 108–109, 114, 120–121, 125–126
as public law regime viii, 15, 39, 199, 201
rivers 62–65, 66, 69, 74, 85–86, 88, 133
self-governing structures intact 157
separation of law and morality 5, 90–91
trade with Europe 7–8, 149, 175, 184, 198–199
warfare under Shang and Zhou Dynasties 65–69
wet-paddy rice impact on political development 56–57, 77–81
see also individual dynasties; *individual rivers*
Chu polity of China 69, 81
Cioffi-Revilla, Claudio 67
civil officials *see* officials
clergy, regular vs. secular 179–180
Clovis 135, 141
Cnut (king of Denmark, Norway, and England) 143, 145
Codex Euricianus 140
coercion
Chinese and Roman revenue collection 18
compelling compliance by use of force 11–12, 33–34
element missing from *Kenmu* formulary 124
Incan capacity for 172, 173
see also power; warfare
colonization and transplantation of Western law 128–129, 173–174
commerce
adjudication as means of ordering 99
in Castile set back by *reconquista* 156
commercial private ordering 7–8, 24–25, 29–32, 81–82, 96, 120
elite control in Hispanic America 196
European city-states and merchant oligarchies 143–144
foreign trade limits in Japan 117
Mediterranean trade expanded in Aragon 156
Ming surplus grain sales 88
as mobile means of wealth creation 42
Ottoman control over 163
practices as judicially enforceable 40
Spain's House of Trade 175
trade throughout Islamic world 148–149
see also gold; silver
Common Law *see* England; *ius commune* (common law)
comparative law 2–4, 20, 37–40
compliance *see* enforcement
confession, in Chinese law 92, 93
Confucian/Neo-Confucian ideology 10, 60, 70–71, 72, 80, 90, 94, 95, 117, 124
consensus
capacity of legal rules to create 11
community acceptance of legitimacy 12, 32
development of representative assemblies and 136
in Japanese judicial law making 58, 124, 126–127
supported by legalization 13
constitutions as frameworks for political orders 22
contracts 20, 30, 40, 95

control *see* authority; power
Cook, Sherburne 180–181
copper and bronze 65–66, 69
Corpus Juris Civilis 128–131, 153–154, 162
Cortés, Don Juan 187–188
Council of the Indies (*Real y Supremo Consejo de las Indias*) 175–176
Covey, Alan 170
Creel, Herrlee Glessner 67
criminal law
  dependence on complaints/accusations 142, 151
  enforcement of 48, 121
  legislation required to apply 71
  offenses vary with social values 23, 30
  penal command-and-control system in pre-Hispanic America 169, 172–173
  in *Siete Partidas* 160–161
  see also Ten Abominations
customary ordering
  in Athens 52
  within China's public law system 82–83
  in earliest societies 37–38
  in international law 20–21
  in law's development 23–30, 96–97, 139, 143–144
  see also private ordering

daimyo see warrior elites
Damaška, Mirjan 1
Danube River 131, 132, 134
Davies, Nigel 171
debt-peonage 195–196
Decretum (Gratian) 154
Deemings (Book of Dooms) 145
Defenders of the Poor (*Defendores de los Pobres*) 193
Deir el-Medina (Egypt) 45–48, 169
derivative legitimacy 10, 12, 13, 131
Des Forges, Roger 90, 92
dikai actions (Athenian law) 52–54
Dominicans 154, 179, 181, 191
dōri (reason) 122, 123, 125
due process vs. natural justice 2
duties *see* private law regimes; rights

Ebro River 133–134
Egypt
  Inca empire's resemblance to 170, 171
  Pharaonic regime 43–48
  as public law regime 41, 43–48, 169
Eisenstadt, S.N. 125
Eltis, David 192–193
encomienda system 174, 175, 180–186, 188
enforcement
  by community disapproval or shaming 24
  distinction between authority and power 10–13
  of law required by Zhou 68
  in Legalist tradition 89
  modes of 32–34, 55
  of norms and sanctions 6–10, 19, 26–28, 30
  public vs. private law regimes ix, 13–21
  of Spanish law in colonies 182–184
  status of local officials responsible for 80
  see also adjudication; coercion
England
  Common Law 129, 154
  legal and administrative development 145–147
  rivers 42, 133
Enrique II (king of Castile) 163
Espéculo 158–159
Espinal, Alonso de 181
Ethelbert (king of Kent) 141
Euric (Visigoth king) 140

Fairbank, John 77
Fang, Qiang 90, 92
Feldman, Eric 31
Ferdinand II (king of Aragon, king of Spain) 155, 163, 174, 181–182
Fernando III (king of Castile) 158
feudalism 143–144
fiscal systems *see* revenue; taxation

Five Dynasties and Ten Kingdoms, period of 76, 80
Flynn, Dennis 184
France
Abbey of Cluny canon law reforms 151
ascent of Bourbon kings to Hispanic thrones 197–198
Frankish duchies unified by Louis XIV 144–145
rivers 42, 133
Franciscans 179
Franks, Kingdom of the 135, 141, 144–145
Fuero Juzgo (*Liber Judiciorum*) 129, 140–141, 150
Fuero Real 158–159

General Indian Court of New Spain (*Juzgado General de Indios*) 190–191
geography
ancient Greece 49–50
Japan 100–101
protection for Inca 171
see also rivers
German legal science 14, 200
Gesetz, use of term 3
Giraldez, Arturo 184
Glanvill, Ronulf 147
Glick, Thomas 156
Go-Daigo, *Kenmu* Restoration 114
gold
deposits in Japan 117
measurement of tribute 183
trade between China and Europe 149, 175, 184, 198–199
Goldman, Merle 77
Góngora, Mario 183
Goths 134–135, 140–141
see also Ostrogoths; Visigoths
governance
appropriation of Roman models 140
legal institutions as product of systems of ix
local participation in 81, 162
patterns in China 61, 63, 94, 95–96
of politically advanced societies 38
privatization and militarization 112
separate system envisioned for Amerindians 178, 185–186
see also adjudication; centralization and bureaucracy; Confucian/Neo-Confucian ideology; officials
Grand Canal of China 62, 72, 74, 79, 88
graphai actions (Athenian law) 52–53, 54
Gratian, customary rules as law 154–155
Great Ming Code 85
Great Wall of China 72, 74
Greece 49–50, 51, 52
see also Athens
Gregory I (pope) 139
Gregory VII (pope) 151
guilds 88–89, 96, 120, 162, 175
gunpowder age, in China 56, 70

habitual legitimacy 9
Hall, John Whitney 110–111
Hamilton, Gary 58
Han Dynasty 73–74, 77
Han Wudi 73
Hansen, Valarie 75
Hart, H.L.A., rules of recognition 2–3, 8
Hawai'i, penalty for shirking 26, 27, 28
Hegel, Robert 93
Heijdra, Martin 64
Henry II of Anjou (king of England) 146–147, 159
hereditary succession *see* kinship
Hicks, Frederic 167
Hideyoshi, Tototomi 116–117, 118
Hildebrand *see* Gregory VII (pope)
Himiko (Kofun queen) 102
Hispanic America
convergence of empires (China and Spain) 198–199
the Inca 167, 170–173, 189
Mesoamerica 165–169
transplantation of Western law 128, 164, 173–174, 186
Hispanic colonial administration
encomienda system 174, 175, 180–186, 188

judicial and administrative organs 175–178, 182–184, 194–195
largest fully structured colonial empire in history 173–174
private rights of Amerindians 186–192
race and class 185, 192–197
religion 174–175, 178–180
reorganization of institutions on French patterns 197–198
rights in regulatory colonial regime 164
Hoebel, Adamson 27
Holy Roman Empire 142, 144–145
Hongwu 84–89
House of Trade (*Casa de Contratación*) 175
hōritsu, use of term 3
Hsu, Cho-Yun 67
Hsün Tzu *see* Xun Zi (Hsün Tzu)
Huai River 62
Huang, Philip 95
Hulsewé, A.L.P. 72
Huns 134–135
hunting and gathering societies 25–26
Hymes, Robert 81–82

Iberian Peninsula *see* Muslims; Portugal; Spain; Visigoths
Inca 167, 170–173, 189
Indus-Ganges river valleys, no lasting polities 41
institutional ordering, private and public (legal) 30–36
international law 2, 20–21, 59–60
iron weapons and tools 69, 102
Isabella (queen of Castile) 155, 163, 181
Italy
commerce 82, 130
control of medieval 135, 140, 143, 144
surviving settlements 157–158
universities 152–153
see also Rome/Roman Empire
ius civilis (Roman private law) 15
ius commune (common law) 30–31, 129, 138, 153, 186, 188
James I (king of Aragon) 156–157
Japan
adjudication 120–127
community ordering 58, 119–120
comparison with Western Europe 129–131
development of private law system viii, 109
geography 100–101
influences from Asian mainland 103–109
land use and proprietorship 105–112
money suits 40
murahachibu (ostracism) 26
post Paleolithic periods 101–103
private law and private ordering 29, 98–100
rise of warrior ruler houses 111–116
ritsuryō period 103–109, 111, 113, 121
sato (village) 108
self-governing structures left intact 157
shōen (tax-exempt estates) system 107, 108, 109–111, 113, 114
shiki (entitlements of office) 39, 107, 108–111
Siete Partidas remarkably similar to formularies of 159–160
sō (agricultural communities) 108, 115, 119
transplantation of Western law viii, 200
Tuna Court for Tokyo fish market 31
unification under Tokugawa shogunate 116–120
wet-paddy rice impact on political development 56–57
Jōei formulary (*Goseibai Shikimoku)* 123, 161
Jin Dynasty 79
justice
as legal and moral norms 60
righteousness vs. 5, 90–91
universal and morally binding applicability 131

kabu nakama, counterpart of guilds 120
Kamakura *bafuku* (tent government) 113–114, 121–124, 161
Kellogg, Susan 186
Kenmu formulary (*Kenmu Shikimoku*) 123, 161
Kenmu Restoration 114
Khitans, Song Dynasty and 76
kinship
  familial and clan influences under Song Dynasty 81–83
  family hierarchy as source of legitimacy 104
  political orders based on 12, 35–36, 38
  sedentary communities defined by 101–102
  Shang Dynasty 65–66
  warriors' local ties 112
Kiyomihara Code 103
Kleisthenes 51
knbt (municipal council in Deir el-Medina) 46–48
Kofun Period (Japan) 101–103
Kohler, Josef 167–168, 169
Korea
  Hideyoshi's invasion of 116
  influence of Chinese models of governance 61
  rice culture 57–58
  South Korean criminal offense based on Imperial Chinese law 23
Kumon Shumpei 107, 112

labor
  China 66, 72, 74, 86
  corvée 18, 42, 145
  Hispanic America 174, 180–186, 191
  Japan 106–107, 108
  see also encomienda system; slaves; tribute
Lai, David 67
land
  landholders in Egypt 44
  lineage property 68
  ownership in Athens 50, 51
  regional and local variations in productivity 86–87
  rents based on control of 39, 141–142, 146–147
  Tang equal-field system 75
  tenure in Japan 105–112
  tenure in northern vs. southern China 77–79
language, law as 1–6
Las Casas, Bartolomé de 181
Latin
  maxims on criminal penalties 71
  origins of legal language in Roman law 2–4, 137, 149
law
  adjudication *see* adjudication
  aims 22–23, 90
  canon law *see* canon law
  criminal law *see* criminal law
  development of x, 23–36
  elements of 6–10
  enforcement of *see* enforcement
  function of 4–6
  making of 19–20
  as matter of words 1–6
  private law regimes *see* private law regimes
  private ordering *see* private ordering
  public law regimes *see* public law regimes
  Tang, Ming, and Qing codes and European codes 93–94
  see also individual countries; *individual laws and codes*
lawsuits, Amerindian 186–192
Legalist tradition
  Aztec system as legalistic 169
  Castilian echoes of Chinese Legalists 160
  Chinese law and 70–71, 72, 89–97, 169
legality, principles of 71
legitimacy
  of Amerindian leaders eroded by litigation 187
  consent of governed as basis for legal 60
  derivative 10, 12, 13, 131
  as essential for authority to rule 29, 33, 59

of legal norms 9–10
Mandate of Heaven 67, 68, 91
religion as source of 51, 59, 60, 138, 139, 149–150
sources for Japanese rulers 104, 109–110, 112–113, 117–118, 122–125
Léon 148
letrados (university graduates) 80, 163, 176–177, 186
Levy, Ernst 140
lex mercatoria (merchant law) 7–8
Lex Romana Visigothorum (*Brevarium Alarici)* 140
Li Feng 67, 68
Li Yuan (Gaozu), promulgation of Tang Code 75
Linduff, Katheryn M. 67
Liu Pang 74
loans 51, 106, 107, 114, 125–126
Lowie, Robert 26
Lynch, John 176

MacCormack, Geoffrey 90
Magellan, Ferdinand 198
Mahayana Buddhism *see* Buddhism
Mair, Victor 63
Malinowski, Bronislaw 25–26
Mandate of Heaven 67, 68, 91
Maya 165, 166
McDowell, Andrea, on Deir el-Medina 46
McKnight, Brian 80
mediation
in early Japan 105
as mode of law making and enforcement 27, 32–33
Mediterranean Sea, as natural highway 132–133
mendicant orders 179–180, 185–186
Mendoza, Don Antonio de 174, 184
merchants *see* commerce
Mesoamerica, succession of polities 165–169
Mesopotamia, no lasting polities 41
Mexica/Tenochititlán, dominance in Central Mexico 166, 168
Mexico *see* Hispanic America
military *see* warfare; warrior elites
millet 42, 62–64
mines and mining
China 60, 65
Greece 51, 52
Hispanic America 181, 184, 189, 193, 198
see also copper and bronze; gold; silver
Ming Dynasty 82, 84–85, 126
Mixteca 168
money suits 40
Mongols *see* Yuan Dynasty (Mongols)
Montesinos, Antonio de 181
Moore, Sally Falk 172
morality
joining of law and 10, 29, 59–60
separation from law in China 5, 90–91
see also Confucian/Neo-Confucian ideology
Morga, Antonio de 198–199
Mote, Frederick 76
Murakami Yasusuke 107, 112
Muromachi period *see* Ashikaga period
Muslims
expulsion from Spain 157
reconquista (recovery from) 147–148, 155–156
rising threat 144
rule of Iberia 147–149
self-governance in Valencia 57

natural justice vs. due process 2
natural law
Chinese notions of law and nature vs. 90
theory of natural rights 131, 138, 154, 162, 186
Navarre 148
Needham, Joseph 91
New Laws issued by Charles V 182–184
Nile River *see* Egypt
Nobunaga, Oda 116
Norman kings 145–146
norms
changing 28
as core element of law 6–10

enforcement of 6–10, 19, 26–28, 30
no Japanese notion of universally applicable 124
see also Confucian/Neo-Confucian ideology
North, Douglass 96–97
North and South dynasties 77–78
Nueva Recopilación de Castilla 173
Núñez Vela, Potasco 183–184

Obayashi, Taryo 112
O'Callaghan, Joseph 159
O'Connor, Richard 56
officials
elites under Tang Dynasty 75
examinations vs. appointments 72–73, 76, 80
in Hispanic colonial administration 175–178, 179–180, 184, 189–191, 194–195, 196
in Japan 39, 106, 107, 108–111, 113–114
merit-based bureaucracy 61, 79–80, 85, 96, 177, 194
in pre-Hispanic America 167–169, 171
see also letrados (university graduates); *shiki* (entitlements of office)
Offner, Jerome A. 169
Olmec 165
Ōmi Code 103
Omnimoda 179
Ōnin wars 114
Ordenanza del Patronazgo 180
Osborne, R.G. 53
ostracism/out-casting 26
Ostrogoths 134–135, 140
Ottoman Empire 129, 163

Pactus Legis Salicae 141
Padden, Robert 180
path dependency, in development of legal systems x
Paul III (pope), *Sublimis Deus* 182
Peisistratos 51
Peru
beheading of Crown's delegate 183–184
case of Don Miguel de Bendezú 188
establishment of viceroyalty 177
labor services replaced by individual payment system 183
silver mines 184, 189, 198
subordination of Amerindians 195
see also Inca
Philip II (king of Spain) 180, 190, 194–195, 197
Philip V (king of France) 197
Philippines
addition to Spain's colonies 173, 198–199
audiencia established in Manila 176
Ifugao *monkalun* (mediator) 27
Manila and Chinese-Spanish trade 7–8, 175, 184
Piggott, Joan 104, 106
political development
as factor in formation of legal traditions 1
legal institutions rest on political institutions 37–40
legal systems and maintenance of political order 22–23
role of rivers in 40–43, 45
see also individual countries
poor in Hispanic America 193
see also debt-peonage
population
determination of tribute via census 183, 188
diversity in Western Europe 134
growth in southern China 79
Hispanic colonial empire's depopulation 173, 180–181, 185–186, 188–189, 192
hundreds and tithings 85, 145
Portugal
introduction of musket 116
under Léon and Castile rule 148
rivers 42, 133
power
authority *see* authority
capacity to enforce compliance 10–13, 36, 136

Church and law as source of authority and 139
coercion *see* coercion
Confucianism and Legalist emphasis on prosperity and 71
constraints on native rulers 185
enforcement of *see* enforcement
independent bases of 121
local opposition to New Laws 182–184
need for resources and control ix, x, 1, 18, 23, 33–35, 41–42, 57, 63–64
political regimes require authority and 22, 27, 32–36, 39
warfare *see* warfare
see also individual countries

private law regimes
adjudication *see* adjudication
Chinese lack of rules regarding private relationships 94–95
convergence with public law system 199
Deir el-Medina (Egypt) 46–48, 169
Enforcement of *see* enforcement
extension of law's domain within 39–40
parallels between Valencia, southern China, and village Japan 157
primacy and global reach 129–131
primacy as essential to *ius commune* 188
public law regimes vs. 13–21
rights and *see* rights
rights and duties requirement 14–15, 17–18
rights applicable to public law regimes 4, 94, 164
Roman private law in twelfth century Europe 151–155
see also Athens; Japan; Western Europe

private ordering
China now dominated by 200
institutional ordering 30–36
Japan 98–103, 105–112, 119–120, 126–127
local control and 81–83
for matters not of state concern 94–95
substitute for both public and private law regimes ix–x
see also customary ordering; social ordering

Protestantism's self-governing congregations 60

public (legal) ordering and private ordering 30–36

public law regimes
convergence with private law system 199
depend on control over resources ix, 35
enforcement of *see* enforcement
extension of law's domain within 39
within Hispanic colonial regime 164
Inca 171–173
judicial ordering in 186
private law regimes vs. 13–21
private law rights applicability 4
see also China; Egypt

Putnam, Robert 82

Qin Dynasty 71, 72–73, 77
Qing Dynasty 88, 93
quipu (counting system) 171–172

race and class *see* Hispanic colonial administration; social ordering
Ramírez, Susan 194
reconciliation for violation of norms 27
reconquista (recovery) 147–148, 155–156, 174
Recopilación de Leyes de las Indias 173–174

regulation
as mode of law making and enforcement 33–34
replacement of civil law by regulatory state 201

regulatory regimes *see* public law regimes

religion
local deities subordinated by Aztec and Inca 167, 171
morality *see* morality
no deistic claims for Chinese law 90, 92

no deistic claims to legitimacy in Athens 51, 54
political/legal development and 59–60
priestly governing elite in Egypt 43–44
Protestantism 60
tax exemptions for Japan's temples and shrines 106
see also Buddhism; Confucian/Neo-Confucian ideology; Mandate of Heaven; Roman Catholic Church

revenue
accommodation of Muslims to preserve Valencia's production of 157
appropriation of wealth from producers 18–19
based on proprietary lands in early Europe 141–142, 145, 146–147
Ming system as ineffective 86–88
need for access to wealth 22–23, 136
principal sources of wealth for Athens 51
regulatory rules foremost for all regimes 38–39
shiki (entitlements of office) 108–109
Zhou sources of 68
see also taxation; wealth

Rhine River 132, 134

Rhône River 131, 132

rice
as basis of private ordering in China 78–79, 81–83, 96–97
as basis of private ordering in Japan 98–103, 105–112, 119
legal legacy of 201
wet-paddy cultivation 38, 42, 56–58, 77–81, 98, 108

rifles *see* warfare; warrior elites

righteousness vs. justice 5, 90–91

rights
of Amerindians 181, 182–183, 186–192
as basic feature of private law regimes 4, 14–15, 17, 129, 131, 164, 174
evangelization and Western European understanding of law 154–155
see also natural law

ritsuryō period *see* Japan

rivers
Japan's lack of sizable 98
role in political development 40–43, 45
Western Europe 42, 131–135
see also individual countries; *individual rivers*

roads, Inca system of 172

Roman Catholic Church
canon law reforms 151–152
competition with state 138
evangelization as overriding aim of Hispanic colonial enterprise 174–175
God's law as supreme 154–155
hierarchical structures in colonies 178–180
monastic orders as self-contained communities 143
role in European political and legal development 60, 137–138, 139

Rome/Roman Empire
coercive power in revenue collection 18
Latin as origin of legal language 2–4, 137, 149
law as basis for claims by rulers 143
rediscovery of classical Roman private law 152–153
rivers as northern boundaries 132–133
withdrawal from the northwest 134–135

Rule of Law vs. Rule by Law 90, 92, 96

sacrifice, human 166, 172

Saline, Martin 64

Sánchez León, Pablo 162

sanctions
Athenian law 53–54
by community disapproval 26–28, 30, 95
as core element of law 6–10

non-compensatory 151
punishment should fit crime 71, 89–90
ruler-imposed 33
see also enforcement
Sandoval, Francisco Tello de 184
sato (village) 108
Satō Seisaburō 107, 112
Savigny, Friedrich Carl von 14
Schwaller, John 178–179
scutage (monetary payment in lieu of military service) 147
Sepúlveda, Juan Ginés de 181
Service, Elman 32, 34, 64
shaming 24
Shang Dynasty 65–66
Shang Yang 71
shōen (tax-exempt estates) system *see* Japan
Shi Huangdi 71–73
shiki (entitlements of office) *see* Japan
shire administration and courts 145–146
shirking, as unacceptable 26–27, 28
Shotoku (Japanese prince) 104
Siete Partidas 128–129, 151, 158–162, 192–194
silk 88, 105, 184
silver
Chinese goods exchanged for Spanish 7, 149, 184, 198–199
decline of shipments and new tax levies 196
mines of Laurion (Greece) 51, 52
Peruvian mines 184, 189, 198
surplus grain sold for 88
tax payable in 87
tribute payments in gold or 175
Silverblatt, Irene 172
Simpson, Lesley 183–184
Single Whip Reform 87
slaves
Aztec forced labor and 167
citizens of Athens vs. subordinates and 49, 52, 55
in Hispanic America 181–184, 192–194
in Korea 57
not major source of labor in Japan 105
Smith, Julia 139–140
sō (agricultural communities) *see* Japan
social ordering 23–26, 35, 61, 71, 95, 99, 110, 119
see also private ordering
social status and castes, in Tokugawa Japan 118
Solon, and Athenian reforms 50–51
Song/Southern Song Dynasties 76, 79–84, 85, 92–93
Spain
advanced legal order in Castile and Aragon 128–129
control of Ebro and Tagus headwaters 133
independent kingdoms beyond Muslim control 148
political consolidation and law (1200-1492 CE) 155–163
political restructuring under Bourbon rule 197–198
trade with China 7–8, 149, 175, 184, 198–199
union of Ferdinand of Aragon and Isabella of Castile 163
see also Barcelona/Catalonia; Castile; Hispanic America; Valencia
Steenstrup, Carl 102
Stern, Steve 186, 188
stratification 33–34, 119, 127
Sublimis Deus 182
succession, problem assuring orderly 35–36, 136
Sui Dynasty 74–75
Sumer 41
Summa Theologica 154–155
surveys
China 87
Japan 105, 115, 116, 119
suzerain system 67

taboo *see* sanctions
Tagus River 133
Taihō *ritsuryō* 104
Taika reforms 103, 115

Taira, defeat by Yoritomo 113
Taiwan
investors in China 96–97
reciprocity based on shared ties 58
Tang Code (*Tang-lü shu' yi*) 75, 85, 104
Tang Dynasty 75–76, 79
taxation
alcabala sales tax as centralized surplus extraction 162
Athens 14, 28–29, 51
colonial obstruction of Crown's levies 196–197
corvée labor as earliest form of 42
law not needed to justify 18–19
may be customary 28–29
non-resident citizen income 20–21
under Qin Dynasty 72
taxes paid in commodities 81, 86, 105
see also revenue
technology
capacity of rulers to control new x
development through warfare 55–56, 116
Ten Abominations 18, 22, 23, 94
tent government *see* Kamakura *bafuku* (tent government)
Tepaneca 166
Tetsuji Okazaki 120
Theodoric (Ostrogoth) 135, 140
Thomas, Lillian 168, 187
three son approach, in Song Dynasty 82–83
Todd, S.C. 53
Tokitaka, Tanegashima 116
Tokugawa Ieyasu/Tokugawa regime 100, 116–120, 125–127
Toledo, Francisco de 189
Toltec 165–166
tribute
Castilian desire for gold or silver 175
census to determine what native rulers were paid 183
diverted to personal use 187–188
as form of labor (*mit'a*) 172, 184, 188–189
see also revenue; taxation
trust
as basis for commercial ordering 24–25
as basis of private ordering in China 96
Twitchett, Denis 74

uji (clan-based chiefdoms) 101–102
Unger, Roberto 29
unification *see* centralization and bureaucracy
United States
as constitutional model for Latin America 200
replacement of civil law by regulatory state 201
taxation of non-resident citizen income 20–21
universal human rights 59
universities
in Hispanic America 195
on Iberian peninsula 161–162
law as primary discipline taught 152–154, 158
law library rules at public vs. private 7

Valencia
absorbed by Castile 197
Black Death 163
Ebro's wetland delta 133
as prosperous port city 156–157
rice cultivation 42, 57
Tribunal of Water of Valencia 31
see also Spain
Vandals 135
Vélasco, Luis de 189–191
viability 12–13, 19–20, 24
viceroyalties 177–178
Vietnam
city of Annam recaptured by Ming China 89
influence of Chinese models of governance 61
new rice strains introduced to China 79
Vinogradoff, Paul 27, 31
violence, Weber on legitimate use of 34–35

Visigoths
conquered by Islamic Berbers 143
control of southern Gaul and Iberia 135
first lawmakers of Western Europe 129, 140–141, 150
written laws as means of national unification 147

Waley, Daniel 157–158
warfare
age of gunpowder 56, 70
bronze weapons 65–66
capacity to enforce rules and maintain organized armies 33
civil war in England 146
governments' capacity to rule and 201
Greek phalanx a formidable advantage 50
Inca conquests 170–171
invasions on all sides of Europe 142–144
iron weapons 69
matchlock rifle and Japanese victory 116
pivotal in defining politics 55–56
political development of China and 65–73, 76, 84–85, 89
political development of Western Europe and 128, 136
as prime mover in process of change 35
rivers enabled military conquest 40–42, 55
scutage (monetary payment in lieu of military service) 147
tribal conquests in Mesoamerica 165–168
see also warrior elites
Wari polity of South America 170
warrior elites
dominance of Chinese governance under Han Dynasty 73–74
of Japan 19, 98–100, 107, 111–118, 121–124, 126, 129–130
Tang emperors as pawns of 76
warrior retainers in Western Europe 19
wealth
concentration in Hispanic America 193–197
of Nile Valley, Egypt 45
in return for loyal service 113
sources and uses determine political institutions 37–43, 129–130
stratification and diffusion in Tokugawa Japan 119, 127
see also revenue; rice
weapons *see* warfare
Weber, Max 34–35
Wei-Jin Dynasty 77–78
wergeld (restitution) 142, 146
Western Europe
commercial rules 30–31
law and the early kingdoms (c. 450-650 CE) 139–142
law's eleventh century foundations and adjudication 149–150, 151–155
political consolidation, fragmentation, and reconsolidation (700-1200 CE) 142–149
primacy of private law in Western Europe 128–131
religion 137–138
rifles and warfare 128, 136, 142–144
rivers 42, 131–135
transplantation of Western law viii, 100, 128, 164, 174, 186, 199, 200
see also Spain; *individual countries*
wet-paddy cultivation *see* rice
Wigmore, John H. 126
Wittfogel, Karl 64
Wu polity of China 69

Xun Zi (Hsün Tzu) 89–90

Yamato kings 103
Yangzi River 62, 64, 69, 74, 85–86, 88
Yayoi Period (Japan) 101
Yellow River (*Huáng Hé*) 62, 65, 66, 69, 74

yi settlements 67
Yoritomo Minamoto 113
Yōrō Code 104
Yuan Dynasty (Mongols) 83–84, 85
Yue polity of China 69

Zapotec 165, 168
Zeitlan, Judith 168, 186, 187
Zhao Dingzin 70
Zhao Kuangyin 76
Zhao Zheng *see* Shi Huangdi
Zhou Dynasty 66–68, 70–71, 81
Zhu Yuanzhang (Taizu) *see* Hongwu
Zorita, Alonso de 187, 188